DATE DUE

AP 29 '98			
DE 13 '02			
OC 24 '03			

DEMCO 38-296

THE
STAGE CLOWN
IN SHAKESPEARE'S
THEATRE

Recent Titles in
Contributions in Drama and Theatre Studies

THE
STAGE CLOWN
IN SHAKESPEARE'S
THEATRE

Bente A. Videbæk

Contributions in Drama and Theatre Studies,
Number 69

GREENWOOD PRESS
Westport, Connecticut • London

Library of Congress Cataloging-in-Publication Data

Videbæk, Bente A.
    The stage clown in Shakespeare's theatre / Bente A. Videbæk.
        p.   cm.—(Contributions in drama and theatre studies, ISSN
    0163–3821 ; no. 69)
    Includes bibliographical references and index.
    ISBN 0–313–29872–6 (alk. paper)
    1. Shakespeare, William, 1564–1616—Characters—Clowns.
    2. Shakespeare, William, 1564–1616—Stage history—To 1625.
    3. Clowns—England—History—16th century.   4. Clowns—England—
    History—17th century.   5. Rogues and vagabonds in literature.
    6. Fools and jesters in literature.   7. Comic, The, in literature.
    8. Theater—England—History.   9. Clowns in literature.   I. Title.
    II. Series.
    PR2992.C6V53   1996
    822.2′3—dc20   95–20556

British Library Cataloguing in Publication Data is available.

Library of Congress Catalog Card Number: 95–20556
ISBN: 0–313–29872–6
ISSN: 0163–3821

First published in 1996

Greenwood Press, 88 Post Road West, Westport, CT 06881
An imprint of Greenwood Publishing Group, Inc.

Printed in the United States of America

For John Styan, Flemming, and the kids.

Contents

Introduction

William Shakespeare wrote a surprisingly large number of plays using the speech heading "clown," as can be seen from a reading of the First Folio. In fact, almost every play has a clown character making an appearance. These characters range from rogues, speaking only a line or two, to important, full-fledged parts.

Shakespeare is the only playwright of his time who explores the possibilities of the clown's part, and uses it to the fullest. We may often find clowns or clownlike characters in Elizabethan plays, but Shakespeare alone has deliberately used the clown's part as a major contribution to the understanding of the play. His London audience derived great pleasure from the fact that the company clown was a well-known actor, whose antics were predictable; but a modern-day audience may have benefits of equal importance once we realize the degree to which the stage clown aids us on our path to an interpretation of the play in hand.

The size and composition of a company of Elizabethan actors might vary with the circumstances, expanding with commercial success or shrinking during a plague, but we know that each company would always have two or three clowns in it. Of these, one would be the "star performer," while the others would take on the parts of minor clowns or comic characters, or they would double in other small parts. A well-known clown such as Will Kemp or Robert Armin, however, would not be doubling, as his appearance would carry the wrong connotations for the audience in nonclown parts and raise expectations the part could not honor.

Though the clown may appear in one scene or a few scenes only and have very little actual dialogue written down for him to speak, even small parts prove to be placed at significant turning points in the action. Unfortunately, in modern times, the part of the clown has often seemed irrelevant to both critics and directors. Critics may say that the part has been written in by somebody other than Shakespeare because the style seems inconsistent with the rest of the play, or the clown's presence is seen as a mere filler. Often a character as lowly as the clown has been considered a contaminant because his language is less than lofty; and when the play is read like any other text and not considered in the living element of performance, it is easy to lose track of the clown's importance. Directors, working within the limitations given by the budget for the performance, may get rid of a problem easily enough by cutting the tiny part altogether. The stage clown, delicately poised as he is between actual involvement in the proceedings and calculated distance, can become a prime target for elimination, especially in plays where the part has not had a chance to establish a niche for itself in modern performance practice.

Neither of these attitudes takes into consideration the significance of the clown, even in his smallest parts, and the impact his appearance may have on the audience's perception of the scene or, in some instances, the whole play. Shakespeare always times his clown's appearance perfectly to fit the audience's need, sometimes for relief from tension, but most often to serve as a guide through the maze of the play. Cutting the clown's part can deprive the spectators of the useful tool they need to keep a sound perspective on the play as a whole.

Another issue which tends to be forgotten or overlooked in modern productions is the Elizabethan theatre's room for improvisation. Though a clown in an Elizabethan play has a very small written part, he may well have made much of it. There was always the possibility for the jig or a similar exhibition at the end, which would show the clown's dancing or tumbling ability to advantage. What looks like an insignificant part on the pages of a book could easily expand into a significant, lively contribution on the boards.

The Elizabethan stage clown is a conglomerate of a large number of different ancestors, all of whom have contributed to the formation of the clown's characteristics. Some of these diverse elements belong in quite a distant past, others are still part of the theatrical culture, while some are contemporaries of the clown's. The comic servant in Greek and Roman plays, the Vice of the mediaeval morality plays, and the *Commedia dell'Arte* tradition contributed to the clown's skillful repartee and the tradition for his acrobatic tumbling. The idea of "the village idiot" and "the country clod" gave him his straightforwardness and naivete, which often serves him well when he delivers home truths to unwilling ears. Finally, the historical court fool or jester added to the clown's part his free license of speech, his professionalism, and many articles of dress. And even the figure of "the malcontent" may find his place among the stage clown's effects. Shakespeare's clowns do not employ all these characteristics simultaneously; rather, Shakespeare carefully selects the mixture of clown traits that will best serve the audience and the interests of the play in hand. I shall use the word "clown" as a term that touches phenomena as diverse as Desdemona's clown in *Othello*, and the aspect of Falstaff which could be called "The Lord of Misrule."

Historically the clown is an artificial creation who will never be seen outside of some form of roleplaying, but not necessarily connected with the theatre. We find him in a variety of roles, spanning from the folk tradition of England in the Middle Ages over famous modern-day circus performers to film and television stars such as Charlie Chaplin. Film and television, however, are media with hardly any feed-back from the audience, and this takes away a most important aspect from the function of the clown in his original form, that of his role as mediator. Always, a clown performer simultaneously participates in the proceedings and stands apart from them in a position not unlike that of the audience. He has a mark to distinguish him so he is easily recognized; the mummer is grotesquely dressed, the circus clown exaggerates one or more features of head or dress, and Chaplin wears his trademark "uniform" with the too-big shoes. Shakespeare's stage clowns sometimes wear rags, sometimes motley. Still, whatever their cultural or historical circumstances, clowns are in direct contact with the audience, address the spectators, and often comment on the proceedings they take part in even as they occur. Their goal is laughter, though they do not always aim for the guffaw, and very often the laughter may leave the spectators wiser.

Shakespeare offers us a rich variety of these figures. They all share an inherent artificiality, which allows them to move freely up and down the social scale, using their clown language wherever they may find themselves, and always firmly in contact with the audience. Because of their lack of realistic personality traits, the clowns may appear and disappear without any introduction or excuse, and the audience will not miss them when they are not seen, for they are indeed more function than character.

Most often the clown's appearance in Shakespeare's plays is timed to comment pertinently on what action has just been seen. He gives to the events on stage a certain coloring, which will linger with the audience even after the clown has disappeared. He shares traits with the Chorus of Greek plays, but demonstrates much more than he explains, and be the play a comedy or a tragedy, he still angles for our laughter. The group of Shakespearean clowns span a wide variety of subcategories, and the sizes of their parts vary widely from play to play. The subcategory that most easily comes to mind is "court fools" or "jesters" such as Feste, Touchstone, and Lear's Fool, probably because this group are almost like real characters who almost have believable personalities, and who are often present throughout the length of the play. Other subcategories we may find in Shakespeare are "the rustic," "the constable," "the bawd," and "the servant." There is also the unruly category of clowns of various occupations, including the Gravedigger in *Hamlet* and the *Macbeth* Porter, who appear once only at a crucial moment, deepening or lightening the atmosphere, but always signaling a turning point of the action.

Clown figures share a number of traits in common, most notably a love of creature comforts. Food, money, and leisure are much coveted, but not always forthcoming. Sexual pleasures the clown usually foregoes, though a large portion of his joking is based on the tricks sexuality plays on hapless humans, and the ridiculous and inexplicable behavior it prompts. His language when discussing sexual matters is most spicy, and his jokes may span from the most delicate similes to the basest puns imaginable. His freedom of speech and social mobility leave him free of deep involvement in the proceedings of the play, and enable him to comment on the actions and feelings of his fellow characters with some distance. He is not fully integrated, yet not apart either. His contemporary audience would certainly have missed him if they saw him cut for this reason, and not only because he could be a vehicle for low comedy and a pleasure for the groundlings, though he certainly was all of that. The clown, even in a tiny part, and especially when he is handled with Shakespeare's skill, can influence the audience's perception of crucial moments of the play, just because he is a figment of a theatrical imagination and in no way realistic. Even when the clown's part is as major as that of Sir John Falstaff, the function of the clown as mediator between stage and audience takes precedence over his place in the plot. Keeping these characteristics firmly in mind and conforming to them, Shakespeare experimented with the clown's part throughout his writing career.

It is interesting to see how the clown's role and inherent characteristics can be tailored to conform to two such different actors as Will Kemp and Robert Armin, both star clowns in Shakespeare's company. During Kemp's residency, the clown parts were created to allow for much improvisation; with his talents for jig dancing and quick repartee, Kemp could be trusted to make the most of any opportunity given him. For him were created the down-to-earth, bawdy clowns, those with much wit and great hearts, if not always great intelligence: busy Dogberry, bumbling Bottom, and that mountain of flesh, Sir John Falstaff. Armin brought to the company a talent for subtle acting and a flair for music. For him were written clown parts with lyrics to sing, and he was given openings for elegant tumbling. He inspired the beloved court jesters, Touchstone, Feste, and Lear's Fool. Still, however different the abilities and acting styles of these two performers were, and no matter how diversely they inspired Shakespeare's imagination, the basic clown functions still furnish the solid foundation of this multitude of different characters.

But Shakespeare expands the use of clown traits to serve a larger purpose. He is unique in using the clown's freedom of speech and mobility, paired with his intimate connection with the audience, to serve the need of protagonists. Richard of Gloucester makes use of the clown's distancing to endear himself to the audience, and the Bastard in *King John* plays the spectators much like a clown would. In a very significant way, the Prince of Denmark also makes use of clown traits in *Hamlet*, where his "antic disposition" gives him the freedom of the mentally weak, and his behavior during the play-within-the-play reflects that of the licensed jester.

The stage clown shares traits with other groups of characters, but he is set apart from them all by being the audience's guide and teacher, someone who breaks down barriers of various kinds, notably between stage and audience, and someone who opens eyes and minds to the deeper reaches of the play. Even very small clown parts have a unique contribution to make.

Part I

Minor Roles: Cameo Appearance, Great Effect

1

Rustic Clowns in *Titus Andronicus*, *The Taming of the Shrew*, *Antony and Cleopatra*

Though a small number of Shakespeare's plays have no part for a clown, the vast majority have at least one clown making at least one appearance. Plays in which we see the clown only once or rarely can be found throughout Shakespeare's writing career. The plays with clowns are not of one genre; we find minor clown parts in tragedies and romances as well as in comedy. Taken together, these clowns represent a broad spectrum of the lower levels of society; we find fishermen and bawds, pedlars and servants, porters, gravediggers, and rogues, and even a court jester.

Every clown part, no matter how minor it may be, is important for the audience's understanding of the play, or the point of view on which we base our final interpretation. Even a clown in a minor role can be a teacher and guide for the audience, open hitherto unexplored approaches, and lend depth or dimension to the character with whom the clown interacts. This effect can be accomplished with great economy, because the clown usually appears at a turning point in the action, and so his very presence comes to signal change and opportunity for greater insight.

The clown in *Titus Andronicus* is not as well developed as the minor clown figure will be in some of Shakespeare's later plays, but already here we see an example of Shakespeare's use of a minor clown to trigger the audience's perception of contrasts, and to create links and comparisons from one plot section to another. The *Titus Andronicus* clown is not an integrated part of the plot, and his clowning is therefore not confined to the situation in which it takes place, but his effect on the audience is large and much needed.

Titus Andronicus, teeming with wanton cruelty and severed body parts, rape, adultery, and betrayal, nevertheless introduces a character, who in both the First Folio and the Quarto is announced by the stage direction "Enter the Clowne with a basket and two pi(d)geons in it"; "Clowne" here clearly means a rustic fellow. The clown makes his appearance very late in the play, and stays for only a short time, IV.iii and iv. Titus, who has been driven to madness by the unjust persecution of himself and his whole family, is trying desperately to get justice and help for his cause from the gods. He is in the act of sending letters to Jupiter, Apollo, Mars, every god but Saturn, having tied them to arrows which are shot into the skies (IV.iii.49–75).[1] Just then the clown arrives, carrying two pigeons, the symbols of peace and hope since the days of the Flood, and he is indeed going to use them as a peace offering at court. The clown has a bribe ready for the oppressors; Titus never thought of that possibility. Titus's preoccupation with his letters to the gods makes him take the clown for a messenger from Jupiter. The clown, who of course knows nothing of Jupiter or of Titus and his situation, takes the whole thing in his stride, first mistaking— or pretending to mistake—Jupiter for the gibbet maker, then for a boon companion. This provides more than release of tension for the audience, who are shown two people whose situation in life could hardly be more diverse. They are both trying to right injustice from the same source, but going about the problem each in his own way, one loftily absurd, one extremely practical. The Clown is indeed a messenger, but from his uncle, not from heaven, and his malapropisms and misunderstandings are probably spoken as much to the pit as to Titus, for though the Clown is seemingly polite to him, Titus is clearly a madman, and the Clown will make as much of that as possible, gesturing to the audience, winking, and making signs behind Titus's back. Titus's madness and his ways of going about solving his conflicts are put in dire relief, and even Titus himself comes to realize that.

He buys the Clown's services as a messenger to get a letter to the court, a much more direct and realistic way than writing the gods. The encounter with the Clown partially opens Titus's eyes and snaps him out of his madness. His directions to him on how to deliver the supplication are indeed sane enough (IV.iii.107–110), and when the Clown is sent off, Titus clearly expects to see him again with an answer.

This, however, is not to be. The emperor has received Titus's letters by arrow, and Saturninus is enraged when the Clown arrives at court (IV.iv.39). The clown has apparently forgotten Titus's instructions, and treats the emperor in his rage as if he were an ordinary fellow rustic at the tavern. There is not time for much clowning here, but the impression made by the Clown in his previous scene is carried directly over into this one, as there is hardly any time lapse between his two appearances. The audience remembers his handling of Titus the madman, and we are delighted by the way in which the Clown takes the enraged Saturninus in his stride. When he is told that he is to be hanged for bringing Titus's supplication, his first reaction is, "How much money must I have?" (46). When Tamora repeats the sentence, he accepts it unruffled, and even makes a joke of it (48–49). Both Quarto and Folio give the stage direction "Exit" for the Clown. He is not escorted out or molested in any way as far as can be seen from the texts; there are no threatening guards present.

Apparently the Clown disappears as suddenly as he arrives, and the audience does not miss him or think about him further. The threatened execution does not bother us either, as he himself takes it lightly and exits unmolested. We have never experienced him as a person, only as a device of Shakespeare's, who serves as a link between Titus and the court, and who provides amusement for us by opening our eyes to the grotesqueness of both Titus's and Saturninus's actions.

Our pity for Titus is not lessened, but our perception of him is changed by the encounter with the clown. The wanton cruelty of Saturninus and Tamora is shown to stretch further than to Titus and his clan, but cruelty like this is made almost ridiculous when used on a character who does not take it seriously. The encounter with the Clown is our last glimpse of a Titus still capable of sanely employing ordinary and acceptable means in his quest for justice, and it is Saturninus's last extravagance before Titus's revenge descends upon him.

Shakespeare uses the rustic clown repeatedly throughout his work. In *The Taming of the Shrew* there is a rustic clown audience, Christopher Sly, the tinker. He is presented at the opening of the play as a drinking man in deep trouble with the female sex; both the Hostess and Sly's wife are shrews. His "transformation" into a wealthy Lord not only gives him the opportunity to meet with a gentle representative of the female sex, impersonated by one of the Lord's pages, but also offers him an opportunity to be an audience to a "how to" play, which ought to hold his interest as he has every reason for wishful identification with Petruchio's success as a woman tamer. Shakespeare deliberately has the Lord set up Sly with a boy page in disguise, providing an added joke in this play where so much depends on the accepted male and female behavior patterns, and where both gentle Bianca and impish Kate originally were created by boy actors. Sly's part is not taken up again after the "Induction" to the play is over, but that is no reason to take him and his small court off the stage for the rest of the play. His role presents admirable opportunities for rustic clowning of every variety, and enough hints have been given in the "Induction" to carry him for the rest of the play; after all,*The Taming of the Shrew* is played for his benefit. He would provide added enjoyment for the audience as he works at the hopeless task of being a lord: eats and drinks, sleeps and snores, is prodded awake, and calls to the players and the audience at appropriate and inappropriate moments, trying unsuccessfully to practice on his "madam wife" what Petruchio preaches.[2] And the end would gain added momentum if Sly were thrown out by the Lord's men after the final bows of the "actors." Inside *The Taming of the Shrew* proper, there is a servant clown, Grumio, who is a true*Commedia dell'Arte Zanni*, but if Christopher Sly is not taken off stage, it becomes debatable indeed who is the star clown of the play.

Shakespeare's last minor rustic clown is found in *Antony and Cleopatra*. His is another late appearance at a crucial moment (V.ii.240–278), but he has been introduced by the guard earlier (232–234). Antony is dead, Cleopatra is caught in her monument unable to escape Augustus, and her spirits are at their lowest point ever when she thinks about both her future and the image of her which now is likely to be left for the future,

> Thou [i.e. Iras], an Egyptian puppet shall be shown
> In Rome as well as I: mechanic slaves
> With greasy aprons, rules, and hammers shall
> Uplift us to the view . . .
> . . . saucy lictors
> Will catch at us like strumpets, and scald rhymers
> Ballad us out o' tune. The quick comedians
> Extemporally will stage us . . .

> ... and I shall see
> Some squeaking Cleopatra boy my greatness
> I' the posture of a whore.
>
> (V.ii.207–220)

Horrible prospects indeed for the Queen the audience has come to care about deeply for her power, her pride, her spirits, and her sexuality. Like Antony, she seems to us too large for this world. How does Shakespeare solve her dilemma and create her opportunity to die suitably and at the right moment, saving herself and the future's view of her? "Enter Guardsman, and Clowne." Cleopatra clearly expects him; before he is announced she has suicide in mind, and is asking her maids to dress her in her best attires; after, she will be dismissed "till doomsday" (V.ii.231). The arrival of the Clown fixes her resolution: "he brings me liberty; /My resolution's placed, and I have nothing/Of woman in me" (236–238).

The moment the unlikely pair begin their forty-odd lines of conversation, the level of style drops suddenly from the most lofty to the most rural and down-to-earth; it is more than a shift from verse to prose, it is a shift in vocabulary, attitude, and mindset, in which Cleopatra takes part. The actual effect of the shift on the audience is a heightening of awareness of Cleopatra's personal, human tragedy.

The Clown has no awe of the Queen; he talks to her as if she were on his own level, and, gregarious and talkative as he is, he has trouble understanding that she wants to be rid of him. In view of Cleopatra's "immortal longings" (280) later, the Clown's malapropism is a revealing one. The snake's bite is "immortal: those that do die of it, do seldom or never recover" (246–247). Cleopatra's feigned death that brings about Antony's suicide is also subject to comment, as the Clown knows of a "very honest woman" who gave "a very good report" of the snake after her death from its bite, though this woman was "something given to lie" (250–254). There is also a harking back to Act I, scene v, where Cleopatra longs to be reunited with Antony, and remembers him calling her "my serpent of old Nile" (I.v.25). Like a serpent, she has indeed caused his death, though Antony had much "joy of the worm" (V.ii.259, 278). The Clown also reminds the audience that the snake does only what it has to do according to its nature, but that it cannot be trusted. This seems to express his attitude to women in general as well. They may be divine creatures, but half of them are marred by the devil. The remarks on women echo back in the play also, to the split between Octavia and Cleopatra. Not everybody in the audience will catch all these allusions, but in a play as well structured as this, with word images emphatically stressed and repetitions so ingeniously made, it should be surprising if some of it would not be at least passively caught and understood, especially if the Clown addresses his speeches partly to the audience. Though these few lines of the Clown's are amusing and draw laughter from the audience on more than one occasion, they also serve to place Cleopatra in a more understandable context. The discrepancy between the Queen and the Clown serves the purpose of strengthening and augmenting the audience's perception of the fundamental humanity of Cleopatra's character.

During their short conversation, the Clown provides a running commentary on Cleopatra, her relationship with Antony, her longing for everlasting fame, and the mortality and fear of pain her body shares with any other. Coming from the lips of a rustic Clown, this exposure of the great Queen provides some much-needed comedy for the audience, but more importantly it also serves to place the great Cleopatra within our ordinary experience; it humanizes her and brings her feelings and longings into a perspective everybody can understand and sympathize with, just as the echoes of Cleopatra's and Antony's love, and of Cleopatra's dual nature, increase our awareness of her essential humanity. The Clown and his "pretty worm of Nilus" serves the same purpose as the crown later (V.ii.317–318). After Cleopatra has died but still looks alive, Cæsar's messenger indeed speaks to her. Her greatness and beauty are unblemished, her attire perfect, she is larger than life again, except for the crown, slipped slightly to one side, which the audience sees the maid put right before anybody sees her mistress.

NOTES

1. Unless otherwise specified, all references to scenes and lines refer to the Arden Edition of Shakespeare's plays.

2. See 115–117 of the Induction.

2

Servant Clowns in *Romeo and Juliet*, *Othello*, *Macbeth*, *Timon of Athens*, *The Tempest*

The servant clown in a minor role is another richly represented category among Shakespeare's minor clowns. The earliest example can be found in *Romeo and Juliet*.

Giorgio Melchiori has made a good case for much doubling by the main company clown in *Romeo and Juliet*, "Peter, the Nurse's man," when named.[1] Melchiori is most convincing in his arguments for doubling, and though many of the appearances he gives the clown are mere glimpses, a gifted performer may still make something of them. Moreover, the very appearance of a well-known company clown would trigger laughter from the audience though very little actually is said or done. The question of changing dress in a very short time is solved by having the clown wear one Capulet livery, only changing his sword— long, short, none—as his class of servant changes, a very attractive solution to the, admittedly, large number of servant roles to fill. This multipurpose servant clown has three major appearances, I.ii, II.iv, and IV.v.

The Clown as servant first appears with Old Capulet as Count Paris seeks Juliet's hand in marriage. Capulet has planned the feast at which the two lovers will meet, and he has the list of the prospective guests with him. The Clown is given the task of inviting them all, a task indeed, for the Clown cannot read. Though the stage directions in the Quartos and Folio disagree about "Exit" and "Exeunt" for Capulet and Paris, it seems best for the Clown to be left alone for a moment with the audience. His speech (I.ii.38–44) has the character of a short comic monologue, and as this is the Clown's first appearance he needs to establish himself with the audience. We also need the illusion of passing through some space, as the Clown's scene will involve the Montague side of the feud.

The Clown establishes himself as illiterate and endearingly confused. He mixes up shoemakers and tailors, fishermen and painters, and the implements of their trades, not leaving out the occasional bawdy quibble, and probably pointing

at individuals in the audience as he mentions the trades. He resolves to seek the
help of "the learned" to read his list, and ironically enough this means Romeo,
sunk deep in puppy love and not exactly what "the learned" usually look like.
Romeo and Benvolio converse for a while, and the Clown tries to attract their
attention, probably waving his piece of paper and circling them while he signals
exasperation to the audience. Romeo does break off one of his stilted speeches on
love when he notices him, but it takes a while to snap him out of his lover's
sadness,

> *Servant.* . . . I pray, sir, can you read?
> *Romeo.* Ay, mine own fortune in my misery.
> *Servant.* Perhaps you have learned it without book. But I pray
>   can you read anything you see?
> *Romeo.* Ay, if I know the letters and the language.
> *Servant.* Ye say honestly; rest you merry.
>
> (I.ii.57–62)

This interchange, almost like a tug-of-war, is very amusing. The Clown has
finally attracted Romeo's attention and made him curious, but because he himself
cannot read he is perfectly understanding when he thinks Romeo cannot read
either, so he pockets his paper and is about to leave; the greeting "rest you
merry" is delightfully out of place when addressed to the moping Romeo.

Finally Romeo reads the list aloud, and on the spur of the moment decides to
go to the feast himself, as his lady love's name is on the list. But it proves
difficult to get the Clown to disclose the place where the feast is to be held. The
Clown pays Romeo back for not reading his list to him immediately, and at the
same time shows great pride in belonging to the household of "the great rich
Capulet," whose livery he is probably wearing, while signaling his amused
incredulity to the audience—this young puppy does not even *know* who *we* are.

This short scene provides great possibilities for the Clown to endear himself
to the audience, and gives him good opportunity to play both Romeo and the
house for all both are worth. Shakespeare lets him show a mixture of ignorance
and mock learning in the monologue, and disdain for Romeo in the role of lover
of the medieval convention. There is also considerable wit, and somewhat ill-
placed pride during his conversation with Romeo. If the doubling theory is
accepted, he must impress himself on the audience so they will recognize him
readily and delightedly on each of his other appearances, and this he has every
chance to do. He is independent of the plot, even as the Nurse's man. We notice
him and are amused by him, but he is not missed when he leaves, because he has
no integrated function. Romeo and Juliet could easily have been brought together
by some other plot device.

On his next major appearance as Peter, the Nurse's man (II.iv.101–212), the
Clown may not have much to say, but his surroundings give him rich
opportunities. Mercutio informs us that now Romeo is truly himself (II.iv.89),
his wit sparkles, and the young men establish an atmosphere of happy, easy,
male togetherness. Mercutio especially continues the banter when the Nurse
enters with Peter to seek out Romeo for Juliet. The Nurse, hiding behind her
fan, deeply resents Mercutio's sexual wordplay, because his wit bounces off her

advanced age. When the young men leave Romeo with her, she attacks Peter for not defending her honor, and is equally disappointed in him; the Clown continues in Mercutio's innuendo, and has seen nothing that the Nurse needs saving from.

The Clown probably takes his cues from the Nurse. She is herself a Capulet servant, and revels in the importance of having someone assigned to her, and so orders Peter about whenever there is occasion. Because Mercutio teases her mercilessly, the Clown has every chance to further emphasize the effect by gestures behind her broad back to the audience, narrowly escaping detection. His behavior towards the Nurse herself could be excessively deferential with that one little bawdy slip that makes her ire descend upon him. In this scene, the Clown and Mercutio are used both to poke fun at the Nurse and to lend a sexual aura to the relationship between the two lovers. There is something deeper and more real going on than an exchange in a sonnet and conventional sighing beneath a balcony. This effect is augmented by having Peter appear with the Nurse in II.v. for the intimate interview with Juliet. Peter is sent to "stay at the gate" (II.v.20), but the gate could well be on stage still, and from the background Peter could be an amused audience to the Nurse's teasing of Juliet.

The stage directions for the Clown's last major scene vary, but there is no doubt that the person intended is the Clown.[2] Juliet's body is still on stage, and if hidden at all it will be in the discovery space. The mourning relatives and servants have just left; the musicians, who now find themselves without a job, have remained behind. It is all very solemn, but the audience knows the truth about Juliet's "death" and can therefore react freely to the Clown's scene with the musicians. This scene reveals the depth of an outsider's grief. At the outset, Peter claims to be heartbroken, but the moment something takes his mind off his sorrow, we see how superficial it is. He does not need much provocation to fling himself into a battle of wit and puns with the musicians, who are genuinely out of sorts as they have been done out of a profitable engagement. Peter pokes fun at their profession, their performance, and their low pay. The musicians lose the battle, but decide to stay for dinner to get something out of this day.

The transformation of the Clown from the depths of grief and, in mockery of his betters, the conventional need of soothing music, into a firecracker of offended wit is very amusing in itself and reveals much about human nature and social conventions. The audience does not truly need the release of comedy at this point, and therefore they are free to enjoy both the clowning and the superficiality of the Clown's grief, as well as the musicians' professional lack of involvement.

As long as amusement is possible in *Romeo and Juliet*, and the tragedy has not swallowed up the audience's attention and feelings, the clown is there to remind us of the common human condition, of food, drink, and sex, and the futility of thinking that anything more lofty can have any permanence. That we probably do not leave the theatre with this thought foremost in our minds, and that we are not supposed to, is another matter; but in each of his appearances the clown has served to deflate human pretensions.

The clown in *Romeo and Juliet* and the one in *Othello* have very little in common apart from being servants, and sharing the traits needed to define them as stage clowns, though they are both elements in tragedies. Just as endearing as is the *Romeo* Clown, just as distasteful may the *Othello* Clown seem to be, and largely because both clowns make use of the same means to their comic end: human sexuality. Exposing Juliet to the audience as a sexual being only enhances our delight in her sweetness and cleverness, and our sorrow at her needless death. Desdemona, on the other hand, could be seen as a Juliet taken one step further. She has married the man forbidden to her, and from the first moment Iago attempts to malign her by references to her sexual relationship with Othello and the sexual *mores* of both in general. Any sex-related comment of the Clown's will be colored by the seeds Iago has already sown in the audience's consciousness, and so the Clown becomes linked with the darker forces of this play, where he provides the light element in *Romeo and Juliet* .

Though the Clown in *Othello* is a servant in Othello's household, he is linked up with Iago's Cassio plot in both his scenes (III.i.1–30, III.iv.1–18). Iago has begun to spin his web around Cassio, Othello, and Desdemona, telling Cassio that "[o]ur general's wife is now the general" (II.iii.305–306). In III.i, Cassio brings musicians to mollify Othello after the degrading fight the night before. The Clown apparently hears the music and is displeased with it, for he uses it to set off a string of jokes of the sex and excrement variety, and he probably uses the space the music gives him to mime to the audience just how infernal this noise is. He degrades Cassio's attempt at reconciliation in front of Cassio himself, and as he buys off the musicians and sends them packing, he builds on the image of the Moor-as-stereotype, which Iago has launched. "[T]o hear music, the general does not greatly care" (III.i.16–17) implies that Othello is not civilized enough to appreciate it. When he accepts money from Cassio to fetch Emilia, who is to be his go-between, the audience is reminded forcibly of the scene just before this. There Iago both worked on his Rodrigo-plot and planned to prepare Emilia for just this event, so she could be used in his web against Othello and Desdemona. Now the Clown is used as a representative of one or more of Iago's tentacles, reaching into Cassio's innocent efforts to get back into Othello's good graces—a sinister use of an amusing figure indeed.

Much the same structuring device is used for the opening of III.iv. Iago and Othello have closed the preceding scene. Othello has made Iago his lieutenant (III.iii.485) after the latter has convinced him that Desdemona and Cassio must both be killed, thus preparing for the ultimate success of his plan. When the next scene opens, Desdemona, who is deeply worried about the missing handkerchief, sends the Clown to seek Cassio. The Clown's punning succeeds in combining the actual errand with the question of lying or speaking the truth, a sexual level, "I dare not say he [i.e., Cassio] lies anywhere" (III.iv.2), and a reference to coming death, "to say a soldier lies, is stabbing" (4–5). Again, some of Iago's tentacles reach out for him through the Clown, references back are made, and events are foreshadowed. This scene too has a dark and sinister quality, and the humor is black indeed. The compassion we feel for Desdemona's plight is augmented by this scene, for the Clown's remarks may be delivered for laughter, but it is an uneasy laughter at best.

When the Clown is viewed as an extension of Iago's plotting against Othello and Desdemona, it becomes possible to imagine him on stage as early as II.i. He is never shown with Othello, so he could have come to Cyprus with Desdemona and be present in the background. His clowning would then be inspired by the general dialogue, while the unprotected Desdemona is exposed to Cassio's gallantry and Iago's taunt of women. Granville-Barker views Desdemona's altered behavior during this part of the scene (96–166) as an expression of her extreme anxiety about Othello's safety set onto a comic background.[3] Having the Clown appear as early as this scene, already Iago's echo, would both enhance the comedy and connect him with Iago's plotting. This use of the clown figure would be unorthodox indeed, but could be very effectual.

On the other hand, it is possible to see the *Othello* Clown as a monstrosity of his kind, a comic element that does not work. Because of the use Shakespeare makes of him within the structure of the play, it may well be claimed that he was put there merely because, by popular demand, he had to be there. It would be extremely difficult for any playwright to create a space for this kind of comedy within the world of Othello's happiness, suffering, and final obliteration of basic character elements. Though the Clown appears more than once, and thus could seem to be intended as more integrated than some, he strikes me as a creature arising more from the theatrical culture of Shakespeare's time and place than from the world of the play *Othello*. Cutting him from performance could remove a distraction from the audience's experience of the play itself, where one of the stage clown's main effects should be to enhance perception. In contrast, the Porter in *Macbeth* does exactly what he has to do despite his isolated and seemingly superfluous appearance. The Porter is rarely cut from modern performance; the *Othello* Clown almost always is. Staging tradition may dictate this, but when the two are compared the Porter stands out as a valuable tool for the audience to use in the unlocking of Macbeth's character.

In *The Masks of Macbeth*, Marvin Rosenberg includes in his treatment of the Porter's scene (II.iii) an appealing stage interpretation of him with one foot in the real world and one foot in the hell he has created on stage and in the audience.[4] The Porter, in spite of all his jokes and clowning, should indeed envelop the audience in yet another hell. Glynne Wickham also takes this view of the Porter's scene, likening it to "The Harrowing of Hell."[5]

The murder of Duncan is Macbeth's entry into a living hell, which will only be left behind definitively with his death. In the preceding scene, Macbeth is still capable of horror at his deed and unable to implicate others as the murderers calmly and coldly. For the audience, there is still the possibility of pity for Macbeth, and a spark of hope. The Porter's scene marks the turningpoint, after which there is no going back for Macbeth. As Macduff and Lennox knock at the gate on the realistic level, Macbeth, as it were, knocks at Hell Gate on another. For Shakespeare's audience, the Mystery Play Hell Mouth, into which Macbeth is slowly dragged during the remainder of the play, was not a piece of distant theatre history; many might have seen or heard of this and knew that such a "gate" had its porter or janitor, who would often use language as spicy as our Porter's. For them, the association would not have been difficult. For our modern-day audience something more has to be done, but the same effect can be created.

The servants have probably used the evening of Duncan's stay at the castle to good advantage. The reason why the Porter is so slow at getting to the gate and opening it could hardly be anything but a combination of old age and copious drinking, the latter of which he readily admits to (II.iii.24). There is excellent possibility for clowning on the way across the stage to the gate in the dark. The Porter is getting dressed, having trouble with buttons, and generally stumbling around, possibly missing his direction and being set to rights again by the knocking. "The drunkard" and his meandering way of getting at both physical places and insights into the truth are an ever-flowing source of laughter. To the audience, a main source of comedy is the ability to identify with the Porter's situation, familiar as it is to most adults, but the comic ingredients are used for a dark purpose. The many twisted allusions, sexual and otherwise, in the Porter's Hell Porter speech have been explained and enlarged on often enough, but how his monologue comments on events and foreshadows things to come has been left relatively unnoticed.

His words to the farmer, who hangs himself "on the expectation of plenty," reminds the audience of others who have great expectations and have taken the first steps into building the remainder of their life on this. Later we see what happens to Macbeth, who builds his entire future on the expectations created in him by his wife. The equivocator, who swears false oaths, commits treason, and ends in hell, again reminds us of Macbeth and the horrible way be broke his oath to his liege lord; he is a traitor to kin and country, as well as friendship. Finally, the tailor goes to hell for stealing; Macbeth has stolen Duncan's life, and is on his way to steal his crown as well.

The Porter has plans for many more sinners, but he is relatively decently dressed by now, and beginning to feel the cold of night, so he finally opens the gate saying, "I pray you, remember the Porter." This remark should certainly be directed at the audience as well as Lennox and Macduff, a feat the Porter may accomplish by winking at us over his shoulder or talking past the visitors. The audience will have good reason to remember the Porter. In his twenty-one lines of monologue he has been more than the amusing clown, he has been a messenger from hell, possibly Macbeth's own private hell. He has shown the unerring certainty with which deeds catch up with their perpetrators, and shown the audience the only possible way Macbeth can go after he made the fatal choice of murdering Duncan.

The remainder of the Porter's lines are lighter in mood, and the sinister cloud lifts as he embarks on the traditional staples of the stage clown's act. His "remember the Porter" begins this transition as he holds out his palm for a gratuity, and his punning speech on the incompatibility of drink and lechery, accompanied by appropriate gestures, completes it. Those critics who attribute comic relief to the Porter must be referring to this part of the scene, for the Porter, stumbling and fumbling in the dark, reminds us far too much of the sinners' stumbling towards Hell Gate and Macbeth's first steps on the road there. A fine effect could be achieved if the Porter were left on stage, lurking in the background during the rest of scene iii. When Macbeth comes back on stage, his insecurity has been conquered to some extent, and he is able to react with feigned shock to the news of Duncan's murder. The presence of the Porter might be a reminder of the Hell Porter's sinners and their way down the "primrose path," on which Macbeth has now firmly embarked. This parallel is taken up again at the very end of the play, where Scotland is purged of its "Lucifer," and the rightful heir is reinstated.

The Porter is a jewel among Shakespeare's clowns, and rarely does any clown accomplish as much with such economy. In *Timon of Athens*, Shakespeare has to employ both a philosopher and a clown, and still the effect is much less impressive, but then Timon's fate is much less impressive than Macbeth's.

The *Timon* clown is Fool in the stage directions, and he is called "fool" by the other characters in the play, but there is clearly no reference to a professional jester, rather to "the natural fool" or idiot. He appears early in the play (II.ii.51–127), at the point where Timon has used up all his wealth on nothing, and where the tables are about to turn on him. The Fool is in the company of Apemantus the Philosopher, who has tried in vain to open Timon's eyes to the foolishness of his behavior and the naivety of his trust in his "friends," whose servants are now on stage, waiting to pounce on Timon. Where Apemantus's replies are scathing and intelligent, the Fool's are seemingly naive, but both hit home. The Fool puns on the parallels between serving a prostitute and serving a usurer, likening the usurers' servants to himself, and exposing the general corruption of the Athenian society, in which Timon has been too trusting.

It can seem strange that Shakespeare did not incorporate the Fool in Apemantus's character. A few years before, he had given Thersites of *Troilus and Cressida* a role not unlike Apemantus's, and it does seem a logical thing to do, because the scathing impact of such a character would be much more effective. The Fool does not represent Timon, he exposes him, but so does Apemantus; the Fool's remarks are amusing, but so are Apemantus's, and little is gained by this one instance of the learned and the natural philosopher complementing each other. The time lapse needed for Timon and his steward to discuss financial matters could easily have been created using Apemantus alone. Moreover, this clown character does not have much possibility for clowning besides punning, and he leaves nothing substantial behind for the audience to remember him by. He may be a loose end; if so, he is not the only one in this play. Possibly Shakespeare was experimenting with the effect of a pair of amusing characters; if so the success of the team is much greater in *The Tempest*, where Trinculo and Stephano work together for effect instead of working as each other's parallels; the contrast is provided by the nonclown Caliban.

Trinculo, the jester of *The Tempest*, seems to have a greater part than, in reality, he does, because he is part of a team of three, completed by the drunken butler and fellow clown Stephano, and Caliban, Prospero's "salvage and deformed slave." The trio has a total of four appearances, one in each of the last four acts. Indeed, the structure of *The Tempest* depends on the manipulation of separated groups and individuals, and the formation of individuals into groups, often intermingling the unreality of Prospero's island with the realistic world of rivalries and political manipulations. The groups and individuals are structured and arranged to mirror one or more other individuals or groups; Caliban and Miranda form one such mirroring pair, as do Caliban and Ferdinand. The clowns' group is a mixture of the outside world from which Stephano and Trinculo are brought, and the island where Caliban was born and has lived all his life. All are servants, and for Stephano and Trinculo this may be the first time they are in a position not defined by masters, while for Caliban it is a chance to exchange one kind of servitude for another, immediately more appealing one. In II.ii, the group is formed.

There is vast potential for comedy and clowning in first Trinculo's, then Stephano's, encounter with Caliban. They cannot see him, but have to go by smell, feel, and intuition in the best *Commedia dell'Arte* tradition. Trinculo finds Caliban huddled under his cloak, hiding from another of Prospero's monsters out to plague him; Caliban's best defense is keeping quiet, and this gives Trinculo ample opportunity to set to work on the bundle. He is wet through and frightened after the storm and the shipwreck and pounces on Caliban as a distraction and possible object to be exploited. There is the audience to communicate with, and Trinculo certainly does as he feels the bundle and shares with the house the sensation of powerful stink surrounding Caliban. He also manages to ridicule them when he talks about their hankering for anything exotic; in England, "any strange beast makes a man," they will all "lay out ten to see a dead Indian" (II.ii.31–34). As the storm returns, Trinculo with much show of reluctance creeps in along with Caliban; this leaves room for Stephano to pick up the thread where Trinculo left off. Stephano's mood is markedly different from Trinculo's, thanks to the wine he has saved and the bottle he has fashioned and brings on stage with him. His singing is too much for Caliban, who fancies that his punishment has begun and starts moaning and pleading. Upon investigation, Stephano finds a four-legged creature and decides to tame it with alcohol and exhibit it. Again we have a chance for much fingering and lifting up of Caliban's cloak, seeing four legs at one end and one head at the other; the whole process is shared with the audience, and Stephano clearly finds the "monster" confusing.

Finally, after much fear and talk of devils, Caliban's would-be exploiters are united, but Caliban begins to institute hierarchy in the group. Stephano is "a brave god and bears celestial liquor" (118), Trinculo he does not deign to notice. But soon all are made subject to the bottle, offering another rich opportunity for clowning as they push and shove to get at it. Where Trinculo recognizes and comments on the comic aspects of their situation only, Stephano immediately understands its possibilities and begins to take advantage of it. Caliban happily subjects himself to another slavery, less burdensome maybe, but also less in every other way.

The first scene of Act II has shown a picture of the ideal state. The second scene mocks and mirrors the first, the bottle rather than the sword being the conquering weapon. Act III, scene ii continues in the same vein, now with the addition of a love/sex interest. Caliban deepens the split between Trinculo and Stephano to the point of violence, well aided by Ariel's tricks and well knowing that he himself will soon oust Trinculo, who has nothing to offer in the world of the island. Caliban himself has plenty. He offers to help kill Prospero and give Miranda to Stephano. For Trinculo, the whole thing is still a joke, for Stephano a good prospect, a kingdom with even the music free (III.ii.142–143), but for Caliban the business is becoming urgent. Now the clowns are more deeply immersed in the plot than they were at their first appearance. The audience laughs less with them and more at them as they establish a hierarchy like that of their betters, and Stephano happily throws himself into his tiny version of politics. Trinculo still succeeds in remaining aloof as becomes a jester in motley,[6] and still addresses comments on Caliban to the audience, but as the scene progresses, he becomes increasingly subdued by Caliban's new power.

Ariel has turned the tables on Caliban when we next meet the trio after the trip through the horse pond (IV.i.194). Caliban holds on to his purpose, driving Stephano towards Prospero's cell, but Trinculo distracts him by pointing out the gaudy clothes Prospero has used as temptation. The two clowns fall victim to civilization as they know it and waste time to boot. Again the possibilities for clowning are endless as Trinculo puts on clothes and Stephano pulls them off him. On another level, they demonstrate the chaos resulting when servants rebel against their betters, and how the fickleness of favor is a constant human factor. This level comically mirrors both the original plot against Prospero and the plot to murder the King of Naples. Again it is necessary for the plan of the play that the audience laughs at rather than with the clowns, and this can be accomplished by having Prospero and Ariel watch the scene along with the audience. Prospero has taken the comic reins away from the clowns and uses them for himself. He has time and space to do this, for all the threads of his plot have been lined up, ready for the final weaving. He chases the trio off with vicious dogs as a beginning punishment, and has them safely hidden for later. The use he makes of Stephano, Trinculo, and Caliban in this scene comes close to cruelty for its own sake, and comic as the punishment is, it still reminds the audience of Prospero's struggle between the man and the great magician.

Not until the reconciliations and restitutions have all been made, and Prospero has conquered himself and sworn off his magic, do we again meet what Prospero calls "some few odd lads that you remember not" (V.i.255). Now all importance has left the trio. Caliban recognizes the folly of ever having seen anything divine in Stephano, and both butler and jester fall into their old roles at the sight of their master; equilibrium is restored. Their entry gives rich opportunities for comedy. The two clowns are drunk and reeling, and probably still dressed in what tatters are left of their gaudy finery, a fine representation of a would-be king and his train indeed. The comedy is further enhanced by the contrast between real gentility and rebellious servants, so readily recognized by the rebels that order is promptly restored. The punishment Prospero metes out stresses the master-servant relationship further. The three, now lumped together as "servants," are sent off to clean the cell.

The clowns have a difficult task in this comedy, as they are given fierce competition for the audience's attention and laughter by Ariel and his fairies and sometimes by Prospero himself. The audience laughs on two very different levels, though. The function of Ariel and Prospero is not unlike that of an omniscient narrator. They take the audience into their confidence, prepare us for what is going to happen next, narrate any action not seen on stage, and give the audience an opportunity to laugh on their level. At the beginning we do laugh along with the clowns, but on a primitive level going neither beyond the action itself nor the immediate sensations of stink and noise; in fact, the clowns' first appearance is exactly what is expected. But after Caliban's influence starts working, Shakespeare uses the clowns as one of the contrasting groups of the plot. Their murder plot comically counterbalances the political one in order to demonstrate the futility of attempting to disturb the order of the world. Prospero masterminds the manipulation of individuals and groups, and to make the contrasts effective the clowns must be incorporated to a greater degree than usual, which takes away much of their power as free agents. This could be why

Shakespeare has split the clown's role into two in this play, emphasizing the cruelty of Stephano and the detached gentleness of Trinculo, so the audience never comes to expect one coherent clown performance. Without ever becoming remotely like a comic character, Prospero himself takes over much of the clown's function as he reveals truths about others and makes the audience reflect.

NOTES

1. See Giorgio Melchiori, "Peter, Balthasar, and Shakespeare's Art of Doubling," *MLA* 78.4 (1983), 777–792.

2. In IV.v Quarto 1 has "servingman," Quarto 4 and Folio have "Peter," and the two other Quartos have "Will Kemp."

3. Harley Granville-Barker, *Prefaces to Shakespeare: "Othello" and "Love's Labour's Lost* ," vol. 4 (London, 1969).

4. Marvin Rosenberg, *The Masks of "Macbeth"* (Berkeley: University of California Press, 1978), 352.

5. Glynne Wickham, *Shakespeare's Dramatic Heritage* (New York: Barnes & Nobel, 1969), 214–224.

6. See the reference to "pied ninny" and "patch," III.ii.62, but also note his name, which may allude to both the triviality of trinkets, and the tinkling of the bells on the costume.

3

Miscellaneous Clowns in *Richard III*, *Hamlet*, *Pericles*, *Cymbeline*, *The Winter's Tale*

The final group of minor clown parts could be called "miscellaneous," as it contains a mixture of many different types. What all these clowns have in common is their detachment from the plot and from true involvement with the other characters. Often they seem almost artificially placed in the play for effect only, but they manage to contribute to our understanding of the play as well as provide comedy with varying success and effect.

In *Richard III*, Richard himself makes use of many of the clown's traits, but within the play we also meet two murderers, who are clowns in the sense that they lend a jocular quality to the sinister job they are to perform and also mark a turning point for the audience. In many ways they serve as counterweights to the audience's perception of Richard, who has successfully endeared himself to us despite the gruesome things he has confided in us. We are first introduced to "Murderers One and Two" at the conclusion of I.iii, where they are sent to kill Clarence. There is nothing amusing about the murder itself, which occurs in I.iv, but the conversation between the Murderers which leads up to it makes for wonderful clowning. Both Murderers are skilled punsters, and they form a delightful pair with Murderer One playing the straight man and Murderer Two as our main clown. Murderer Two pretends to repent that he has promised to commit this murder, and Murderer One is surprised and ready to tell on him (I iv.110–120). The Murderers, despite the alleged attack of conscience, make the loss of a life a joking matter, and we are willing and ready to laugh with them because we have been so ably maneuvered into this mood by Richard. Murderer Two even has a most amusing little discourse on conscience, which assures us that he himself has none:

> I'll not meddle with it, it makes a man a coward. A man cannot steal but it accuseth him; a man cannot swear but it checks him; a man cannot lie with his neighbour's wife but it detects him. 'Tis a blushing, shamefaced spirit, that mutinies

in a man's bosom. . . . and every man that means to live well
endeavours to trust to himself, and live without it.
(I.iv.128–138)

The violent loss of life has been the center of most of the discourse in the play
so far, and we have grown accustomed to it, almost to the point of not turning a
hair. Therefore we laugh quite easily at these two clowns' antics and jokes about
death and conscience; but we still have to be faced with the reality of murder.
The banter continues until Clarence awakes and Murderer Two tells him that his
real murderer is his brother Richard. He takes pity on Clarence, but even as he
warns him, Murderer One stabs him in the back. After the murder the clowns'
paths divide. Murderer One remains unshaken and unrepenting, while Murderer
Two decides not to have any part in the reward, and exits sad and contrite.

The turningpoint comes early in *Richard III*, but the audience needs to be faced
with the finality of death and to be given this more humane perspective on the
proceedings in order to become free of Richard's spell and see and judge for
themselves. Through the rest of the play, Murderer Two's lesson will remain
with us as we follow Richard's complicated and involved way to death.

The gravedigging clown in *Hamlet* is one of Shakespeare's most important
minor clowns. At the beginning of his scene, the clown is accompanied by
another comic character, off whom he can bounce his wit. The audience knows
that here is Ophelia's grave, and the contrast between her fate, the Queen's poetic
description of her death (IV.vii.165–182), and the clown's speculations as he
throws up skulls, is vast indeed. The Clown has no feelings, though he knows
for whom he digs the grave; he is doing his job, and he takes pride in both his
work and his wit.

The beginning of the scene gives the audience ample opportunity to
familiarize themselves with the clown and his type of wit before the
confrontation between himself and Hamlet. The clown has some knowledge of
the law, at least of "crowner's quest law" as it is administered, and he can twist a
case as well as any lawyer. His "when she willfully seeks her own salvation" and
"It must be *se offendendo*" has been seen as a confusion of opposites, and this
may well be the case, but it could also be the clown's little game with the law
and his betters. The clown and the Other clearly believe that Ophelia committed
suicide, but the coroner's court finds otherwise; the two seeming malapropisms
might well be intentional, and therefore even more amusing. Social inequality is
further commented on:

> *Other*. Will you ha' the truth an't? If this had not been a
> gentlewoman, she should have been buried out of Christian
> burial.
> *Gravedigger*. Why, there thou say'st. And the more pity that
> great folk should have countenance in this world to drown or
> hang themselves more than their even-Christen.
> (V.i.23–29)

The clown continues his lack of respect. He is among the "ancient gentlemen,"
those who dig, because this is "Adam's profession" (29–31), and so he is at least

as good as the gentility. Moreover, what a gravedigger creates will stand longer than the memory of kings—his houses last till doomsday. The clown's familiarity with death has bred contempt and indifference; waiting for his ale, he sings as he digs the grave, and this gives Hamlet and Horatio occasion to comment on both his callousness and death itself.

Hamlet's feelings about mutability, death, and decay have clearly undergone a change since his last appearance. The young man is insecure of himself and his place in the world. He is no longer in the secure position as his father's son, his mother is no longer his father's wife. Yet he seems to have reached a point of rest within himself: he is growing up. His comments at the graveside could never have come from the young prince in the first four acts; his judgment has matured, and he is capable of seeing death as a natural end to life. The skull, which the clown throws up, is first used in the traditional manner as Hamlet, striking a pose and holding the skull in his hand, begins a philosophical reflection on mortality, seeing every accomplishment in life at last reduced to this common condition of nothing (74–115). In the background the clown is creating a comic contrast, lustily digging away as he sings, for Hamlet still has a way to go before he can say

> There is a special providence in the fall of a sparrow. If it be now, 'tis not to come; if it be not to come, it will be now; if it be not now, yet it will come. The readiness is all. Since no man, of aught he leaves, knows aught, what is't to leave betimes? Let be.
>
> (V.ii.215–220)

Only then can he feel included in the process of birth, life, and death, and come to terms with mortality, his own and others'. In the meantime, the clown serves his purpose and teaches him one of the lessons which will build the prince's maturity.

The clown's banter, punning, and quick wit show that he has been listening to Hamlet's philosophical tirade on death. He has probably given the audience a clear understanding of his thoughts on this young whippersnapper, for he replies to the prince's questions much in the same vein, only he never leaves the ground in which he is firmly planted. He demonstrates that the grave is his more than the future occupant's, for the dead are nothing and own nothing as Hamlet pointed out, ergo a grave cannot belong to them. The clown treats Hamlet much as he treated the Other; hardly is the opportunity given him before he demonstrates his acuity at the cost of his interlocutor. He also brings in the question of the afterlife, mentioning Ophelia's soul, probably to take Hamlet down yet another peg.

Hamlet is clearly amused and intrigued by the clown, who is now giving to him what he gave others during his pretended madness. He goes on to question him about himself, and this gives the clown an opportunity to rail at the audience a bit. In England, where mad Hamlet went, nobody would notice his madness, for "there the men are as mad as he" (V.i.149–150). The clown refuses to discuss this further, and begins talking about himself and his profession. We are back at the link he created between Hamlet and himself (139–144); he became a sexton on the day of Hamlet's birth. His talk of the state of the corpses at burial, and the fact that he recognizes Yorick's skull, certainly gives him the opportunity for jokes, but also teaches the lesson that death may not be as final as all that. The dead will last for a certain time in the earth and may even reach out and touch the living. The accusations of his father's ghost could have been a figment of Hamlet's imagination, but Yorick's skull is a concrete thing.

It is an interesting trick of Shakespeare's that he lets this clown remember one greater than himself (V.i.170–175), one who bested him; our witty clown was reduced to a country clod like the Other by Yorick's wit. This skull is what greatness comes to, yet memory is sweet. The clown fondly remembers the "whoreson mad fellow," the "mad rogue" that was Yorick. Hamlet feels the same way when he dwells on his childhood memories of the jester. His behavior with Yorick's skull is markedly different from his first philosophizing. He loved Yorick, and beyond the obvious, unavoidable fact of change and mortality there lurks the remembrance of the good times and the jokes shared. Here Hamlet is able to joke with mortality, though he still does not let himself be nearly touched by it. "[His] gorge rises" (181) at the smell of death and decay, but memory is still sweet. This is a lesson indeed.

Beginning with Act V, a maturing Hamlet emerges. Shakespeare may well have timed the appearance of the gravedigging clown to give us much more than release in laughter after Ophelia's madness and drowning and before the final scenes of carnage. The presence of the clown signals that Hamlet is back in character, and that whatever doubts we may have had about his state of mind we can leave behind. The clown marks a turning point in the play; the conversation between himself and Hamlet, utilizing both abstract and concrete images of death, helps Hamlet come to terms with fundamental questions of life and death.

The Gravedigger's part is a find for any comedian. There is ample opportunity for audience contact, for example when the riddles are asked, and why not let him have his pint while he disputes with the young gentleman, whose identity is unknown to him? Hamlet refers to beer-barrels in line 205, why not let his remark be prompted by the clown's mug? And beneath the jokes and puns there is matter of moment to be communicated. Though there are no more lines to speak after the discovery of Yorick's skull, the presence of the clown is still needed to finish digging and clear away the bones, and it makes reason for him to wait to fill the grave after the mourners leave, so again he has great opportunities for silent communication with the audience, continuing to underscore the contrast between his own matter-of-fact work and the artificial-seeming confrontation between Hamlet and Laertes. The clown makes Hamlet laugh as he learns his lessons, and his laughter only ends when the King and Queen approach and he remembers his purpose. Simultaneously, the spectators' laughter dies as we remember the unnecessary death of Ophelia.

The scene of the Fishermen in *Pericles* recalls the beginning of the Gravediggers' in *Hamlet*. Mixed authorship has often been discussed for *Pericles*, but there has been little doubt about Shakespeare's responsibility for the comic scenes for the Fishermen (II.i) and the Bawds (IV.ii and vi). Both groups consist of three comic characters, and the same three actors could double the parts. The star clown would then be the caustic Second Fisherman and Boult, the procurer for the brothel.

In II.i the Fishermen have the opportunity to discuss social inequalities and injustices. They compare misers to all-devouring whales, discuss politics generally, and comment on the various kinds of beggars and how well off they are in comparison with honest laboring men; and here, as in *Hamlet*, they are overheard by a prince. When Pericles hails them, he speaks in verse to their prose, making him appear one of the "drones, that rob the bee of her honey" (II.i.46–47), and they treat him with some hostility, until he throws himself upon their mercy. Here Pericles is at the lowest point of his career. After his disastrous wooing and subsequent shipwreck, he has lost everything except his life. Now the Fishermen first give information about the tournament for the hand of Thaisa, then by sheer luck retrieve his father's armor from the sea, and though they clearly do not think that Pericles belongs among the "princes and knights" (107) who court Thaisa, they help him to the rest of the trappings. The meeting with the Fishermen is a turning point for Pericles.

There is much comedy in this scene. First of all, the common man's earthy attempt at politics is always funny, even though a few, thought-provoking home truths may be hidden beneath the mirth. The Fishermen's dealings with Pericles contradicts their political stand. At first they tend to shrug him off, but when they see that he is worthy of their charity, their generalizations give way to kindness; even Second Fisherman, who tries to drive a bargain for quite some time, has to give in.

> *2. Fisherman* [to Pericles]. Ay, but hark you, my friend; 'twas
> we that made up this garment through the rough seams of the
> waters: there are certain condolements, certain vails. I hope,
> sir, if you thrive, you'll remember from whence you had them.
>
> . . .
>
> We'll sure provide; thou shalt have my best gown to make
> thee a pair [of bases], and I'll bring thee to the court myself.
> (147–151; 161–163)

He cannot get financial recompense for his labor at the present time, but the future might yield something if Pericles is successful.

The three Bawds come on stage at another protagonist's lowest point, this time Marina's (IV.ii). Like her father she has lost everything material, and now stands to lose even more, as the Pirates are about to sell her to the brothel at Mytilene. The Bawds are in a sad situation. The market is ripe, but they have few goods to offer, so Boult is sent to find new merchandise and comes up with Marina. "She has a good face, speaks well, and has excellent good clothes" (44–45), but unfortunately she proves difficult. The bawds cannot make her accept her fate; neither the promise of a life of pleasure and "tast[ing] gentlemen of all fashions" (74–75) nor the flattering response to Boult's advertisements in the market place has any effect. Innocent she is, and chaste she is resolved to remain.

Much of the comedy is created by the three Bawds' total absorption in their "trade." Both the prostitutes presently in their employ and Marina are treated like objects and joked about for their sorry condition and diseases; Marina is cried in the marketplace like a piece of meat, and her fate discussed in front of her as if she were indeed no more. This can seem very cruel to a reader, but on stage the comedy comes to life. The sexual banter among the Bawds accompanied by pinching and slapping becomes broad comedy, and Boult's description of the reactions in the market place gives him a rich opportunity to impersonate the Spaniard and the French knight and their respective follies (IV.ii.97–111). Boult demonstrates a rich variety of traditional clown traits. He does not mind working as long as there is a profit in the offing, and he boasts of his every accomplishment; he mocks his betters, needing to display some tumbling ability; his interest in the female sex is expressed in food terms—Marina is pictured as a roast on the spit, and Boult asks for a morsel (128–130)—but greed is more important, and he does not mind waiting his turn, so he is no imminent threat to Marina. She herself is the object of the audience's pity, but she has only lately been introduced as a character in the play. There has been no opportunity to build real rapport with her, since she has not yet made any active contribution or had much influence on her own fate. It is easy for the audience to enjoy the comedy and the clowning, partly because we do not know Marina well, partly because we do not expect anything truly horrible from the three Bawds.

Our expectations are confirmed in IV.vi. The scene opens on three very frustrated Bawds, who have not been able to subdue Marina the virgin, "she's able to freeze the god Priapus and undo a whole generation. . . . she would make a puritan of the devil" (IV.vi.3–9), and even Boult's threats to rape her cannot be taken seriously. The tone changes to hope when a highborn customer appears, and the Bawds' cautious remarks only whet his appetite; but he, too, becomes a convert of Marina's.

The comedy of this scene is concentrated at the end, and again its substance is contrast. Boult's bid for a "morsel" in the previous scene has been turned into the unpleasant duty of raping Marina. Boult is customarily played as a villain, but it is interesting to see him as the main clown and investigate clown traits and opportunities in the last part of Act IV. Boult is servant to the Bawds (132, 195), and it can easily be seen from their conversation that, like all servant clowns, he has great freedom of speech. But his bark is worse than his bite, especially where sexual matters are concerned. Boult consents gallantly enough to undertake the rape of Marina as he is bid, but although "ploughing" (145) is a word often used about the sexual act in Elizabethan times, here it takes on an added meaning; it comes to smack of hated manual labor. And when the two are left alone, Boult is not overly eager to accomplish the rape, for it is only slightly less unpleasant to him than the prospect of going to the wars and becoming mutilated (169–172). The idea that there are only three levels of possibility for a man in this world, peasant, warrior, or bawd, and that the position preferred is the one with least work involved, shows typical clown thinking. The clown's sexual prowess traditionally is in the boasting rather than the performance, and it proves true again despite Boult's mighty swagger. A villainous character would certainly have been enraged already by the behavior of a girl like Marina, and his rage would have grown with her resistance. Not so here: Marina easily persuades Boult to let her pursue an honest trade (182–186), and there is no sign of regret as the "morsel" slips away, only surprise at her accomplishments (187).

Boult's plight should be apparent in his acting, as he reluctantly grasps Marina (IV.vi.152) and becomes shy once the two other Bawds are out of earshot. His relief should be apparent and great once he lets himself be persuaded to let her escape. Where a villain would override a physically weak little thing, Boult enters into discussion with her. He even tries to engage in a typical clown's altercation with Marina, but is cut short:

> *Marina*. What canst thou wish thine enemy to be?
> *Boult*. Why, I could wish him to be my master, or rather, my mistress.
> *Marina*. Neither of these are so bad as thou art.
>
> (IV.vi.157–160)

Marina refuses to play his game in this as in all other matters, and Boult is brought to heel. He is made defensive by one sole speech (160–168), thus making this attempted rape a parody of all the gentlemen's conversions. Boult's relief should gradually grow while Marina speaks, and be totally apparent in line 169 where the argument begins. He could well lie at her feet, talking up at her, admiring her after the pattern of the other gentlemen before him; this position gives him added opportunity to signal his great relief to the audience.

The spectators can thoroughly enjoy this scene, which is the second turning point for Marina, and hails happier things in store for her father as well. From the outset there is no substance in the threats against her. The Bawds' pleasure in their new acquisition has turned to frustration, and they have been reduced to seeing her as a person rather than an object. The scene with Boult gives us an opportunity to laugh at all the gentlemen, whose "conversions" we have hitherto had to imagine. Marina's whole bearing has changed too, and there can be no doubt that the balance of power has shifted, another rich source of comedy.

In *Pericles*, Shakespeare uses all three clown scenes as significant turning points. Both the Fishermen and the Bawds have one fixed opinion about world order, and both groups are swayed when somebody worthy turns up. In both cases, the clown scenes are used to bring out significant traits in a protagonist's character. The gravity of both father's and daughter's plight is lessened by the use of comic characters, and the audience will expect only good as the ultimate result. When the clown role is divided, the clown's freedom is restricted, and this is important in a play with a plotline of *Pericles* 's complications. There is use for the clown, the connotations his role carries, and the release he provides, but he cannot be permitted to take up much space. Still he succeeds in delivering pointed comments directed at the common man's view of the larger things in life.

Cymbeline is another late play with an extremely complicated plotline and many threads left to be sorted out at the end. Cloten has been thought of as the clown of the play by several critics, and he is indeed a tempting choice, but he is far too involved in the intricacies of the plot, and he is too easily bested. Nothing should be allowed to interfere with the audience's perception of Imogen's character, and Cloten, rather than complicate our view of her as a clown would, only succeeds in confirming it. Also, the effect of having Imogen grieve over the stage clown's dead body would be ridiculous. *Cymbeline* does not afford much opportunity for a clown's part, especially since so much of the comedy is reserved for Cloten and the situations surrounding him, but after his death, and near the end in V.iv, Shakespeare introduces the First Gaoler and his mate.

The two Gaolers leave Posthumus bound on stage to dream the dream of his ancestry and Jupiter's oracle. When they come to fetch him, he has not understood the oracle and is eager to die though the dream has left a hopeful message. The clown first presents him with all the wonderful aspects of death, choosing, not uncharacteristically, the images of the tavern-bill (V.iv.158–172). When Posthumus does not react satisfactorily to these attempts at comfort, the clown tries to sow doubt in his soul: "you know not which way you shall go" (177–178). Posthumus refuses to be disturbed by this line of attack also, and the clown becomes disgusted and cross with him; there is no reaching this fellow. When Posthumus is freed, the tables turn on the Gaoler,

> *Posthumus.* . . . I am call'd to be made free.
> *First Gaoler.* I'll be hang'd then.
> *Posthumus.* Thou shalt be then freer than a gaoler; no bolts
>   for the dead.
>
> $\qquad\qquad\qquad\qquad\qquad$ (V.iv.195–199)[1]

The clown's own language is thrown right back at him. When left alone on stage, the clown speculates on the desire to live, which Posthumus lacks, but which he himself shares in spite of his tribulations. In a truly good world there would be no need of his profession, yet such another world would be better and probably more profitable.

Jupiter's prophecy will come true, and at the end of the play we seem to have reached a purged world order. Again, Shakespeare has placed a clown scene at a turningpoint, here accentuated by the prophecy. Imogen and Posthumus will be reunited, Cymbeline will have his family back, evil will be punished, and all will be well. The surly Gaoler-clown may still see some vision of a better world come true, though for him better equals more profitable. In the meantime, the grumpiness and dissatisfaction is used comically to show the audience his world picture and the size and nature of his problems. Small as they are in comparison with the problems of the play itself, they are still wonderfully realistic and easy to identify with, albeit comically presented. At the same time, his treatment of Posthumus is not offensive; the audience knows that Imogen is alive and as faithful as can be desired, and Posthumus' reprieve signals the happy end to come.

The Winter's Tale in many ways resembles both *Pericles* and *Cymbeline*. All three plays show a generation gap, children lost to parents, and a final and happy reconciliation brought on by outside elements. There is a marked difference, though, in the use Shakespeare makes of his clown. In *Pericles*, the comic groups are used to draw parallels between father and daughter at their lowest points; in *Cymbeline*, the clown is connected to the most offended party, and used to signal a better world to come; but in *The Winter's Tale* can be found an autonomous, Protean bundle of energy named Autolycus.

In this play Shakespeare has a character titled "Clown," but he and his father are rustics, who will follow Perdita throughout the play as her adoptive family. The son is the epitome of goodness, kindness, and rustic density, and so the perfect target for Autolycus, not his rival. Autolycus himself does not appear until Perdita is fully grown, in love, and blooming. He enters singing a song of winter defeated, of spring, sexuality, freedom, and the life of the rogue. He has "served Prince Florizel," a statement to be taken with a grain of salt since Florizel does not recall him when they meet, and since his father also was "a snapper-up of unconsidered trifles" (IV.iii.26). The audience is now prepared for the ease and unconcern with which Autolycus moves among people of all classes. He values his freedom, lives in and of the present, and lets nothing concern him. The audience has been informed that fifteen years have passed; in Autolycus we have the change confirmed. Winter, sadness, and cruel misunderstandings have yielded to spring, freedom, and lightness of heart. Autolycus's endearingly frank self-portrait is an excellent preparation for the superiority he will demonstrate in all his coming scenes. He is changeable like a chameleon, he is among the best of actors, and his knowledge of his fellow man is superb.

The Clown is Autolycus's contrast. He is thinking about honestly earned money, has been sent on an errand, has brought a list of things to buy, and is very busy indeed. Moreover, he serves the plot in bringing the audience up-to-date and preparing them for the sheep-shearing scene to follow, and for Perdita, the grown young woman. Autolycus immediately knows how to treat a person like the Clown. During the speech he has probably prepared the audience for the act he will put on, or at least for fun to come. Now he rudely tears him away from his pleasant contemplations of profit, food, and festivities, confronting him with an impersonation of a poor, robbed gentleman. His rags, a minute ago the proud legacy of his devil-may-care life, now become his passport to pity, and as the Clown carefully helps him up, he has a chance to pick his pocket in full view of a delighted audience. The joke is capped a bit later, when the Clown offers Autolycus some of the very money he has just had stolen. The audience thrills with the delightful hope and fear that Autolycus may be discovered; of course he is not. When asked about his assailant, Autolycus lights on the happy idea of describing himself as the culprit, and even giving his own name and a believable description of his career. There is great comedy in their discussion of Autolycus the rogue, whom the Clown knows well by reputation. They part in the most amicable manner, and Autolycus is given yet another moment alone with the audience. Seemingly speaking to the departing Clown's back, he prepares them for his next appearance and his plans for the sheep-shearing.

Besides providing the audience with a welcome moment of relief after Leontes's jealousy and its dire consequences, Autolycus's introduction hails a lighter mood for the rest of the play. His devil-may-care attitude to life in general and to the consequences of his actions strike a youthful cord. From this point the play is on its way towards reunion and reconciliation.

The robbing of the Clown apparently has had no consequences to speak of, for when the next scene opens the feast is beginning, and we hear no immediate complaints. On the contrary, he welcomes Autolycus when he appears disguised as a pedlar, but his remarks in anticipation (IV.iv.204–218) remind the audience of the earlier encounter with Autolycus and raise delighted expectations. Again Autolycus enters singing, this time praising his goods, but he must have changed his clothes and has possibly changed his beard or added one, for the Clown does not recognize him. On the contrary, in front of Autolycus he tells Mopsa how he was "cozened by the way and lost all [his] money" (253–254), but he assures Autolycus that there will be good business for him anyway. The audience's expectations are fulfilled indeed as Autolycus pulls the wool over the Clown's eyes and gets away with his peddling, praising his wares. The subject matter of his ballads is as fantastical as himself, and he vows that it is all true: "[w]hy should I carry lies abroad?" (272). His on-stage audience is happily cozened while the play's audience enjoys Autolycus's ability to adapt himself to the situation in hand. He clinches the deal when he sings a ballad "in three parts" with the shepherdesses, and exits to complete it with yet another song, this time about the money a man will spend for his sweetheart. There is no doubt that he will make a profit.

Autolycus's deceit prepares for another of great importance to the plot. Florizel and Perdita see elopement as the only possibility for a life together, and they are helped along by Camillo. The audience's trust in the success of the venture is strengthened by Autolycus's success:

> Ha, ha! what a fool Honesty is! and Trust, his sworn brother, a
> very simple gentleman! . . . I saw whose purse was best in
> picture; and what I saw, to my good use I remembered. . . .
> 'twas nothing to geld a codpiece of a purse; . . . had not the old
> man come in with a whoo-bob against his daughter and the
> king's son, and scared my choughs from the chaff, I had not
> left a purse alive in the whole army.
>
> (IV.iv.596–620)

With the young lovers and Camillo in the background planning their escape, Autolycus's speech becomes a commentary on the elopement. The conspirators are knowingly robbing the king, defying his authority, and planning to make use of his name in Sicily, and though love is a grand excuse they are no better than Autolycus. This is emphasized further when they plan to make use of his just fear of hanging to get him to change clothes with Florizel for a disguise. Autolycus in turn comes off the better. Not only are his clothes richer than ever before, he also has gained knowledge of the elopement, and knowledge is power:

> I understand the business, I hear it. . . . I see this is the time
> that the unjust man doth thrive. What an exchange has this
> been without boot! What a boot is here with this exchange! .
> . . The prince himself is about a piece of iniquity . . . if I
> thought it were a piece of honesty to acquaint the king withal,
> I would not do't: I hold it the more knavery to conceal it; and
> therein am I constant to my profession.
>
> (IV.iv.670–683)

A parallel has been drawn between the prince and the pedlar, and if ever Autolycus served Prince Florizel, now is the time. Indeed, Autolycus considers himself to be in his service again, thinks of him as "my master" (IV.iv.710), and is ready and willing to cover his flight once the rustics come back on stage.

His transformation is complete. Not only are his clothes different, he must have done something about his face again[2], and his style of speech has become courtly. Now we see him in his third impersonation, that of a person of authority, a soldier and courtier:

> *Autolycus.* . . . I am a courtier. Seest thou not the air of the court in these enfoldings? hath not my gait in it the measure of the court? receives not thy nose court-odour from me? reflect I not on thy baseness, court-contempt? Think'st thou, for that I insinuate, or toaze from thee thy business, I am no courtier? I am a courtier *cap-a-pe.* . . .
> *Clown.* This cannot be but a great courtier.
> *Shepherd.* His garments are rich, but he wears them not handsomely.
> *Clown.* He seems to be the more noble in being fantastical ...
> (IV.iv.730–751)

The act is good enough to cozen the Clown, but not quite good enough for the Shepherd who, in this last half of the play, has shed some of his rustic simplicity and gained in dignity. Still, the offhand manner in which Autolycus outlines the gruesome fate in store for the Shepherd and his son at court and his pretense at having the king's ear make their belief in him complete. The Clown is ready to offer him gold as a bribe, and so the end result of this impersonation is again money. Autolycus sees a hint from fate in this:

> If I had a mind to be honest, I see Fortune would not suffer me: she drops booties in my mouth. I am courted now with a double occasion—gold, and a means to do the prince my master good; which who knows how that may turn back to my advancement.
> (IV.iv.832–837)

In the fourth act, Autolycus has been the master of ceremonies, mostly through his own seeking, but the role has also been thrust upon him. His happy-go-lucky ability always to swim, never sink, and always come off the richer for each experience, takes the seriousness out of the act and makes the audience willing and happy accomplices as well as Autolycus. The audience knows that Perdita is not a shepherd's daughter and that she is a worthy wife for Florizel, and it is most understandable that Camillo urges on the young people. This is his chance to come back to Sicily. Many complications seem about to be resolved, and Autolycus's growing success can only boost expectations. When we meet him again in Act V, scene ii, the resolutions are underway, and he is an almost silent audience to the Gentlemen's dialogue, but he is not passive. He is gathering information and storing it for later use. He sees no possibilities for his own advancement, for though "I brought the old man and his son aboard the prince" (V.ii.114–115), still "'tis all one to me; for had I been the finder out of this secret, it would not have relished among my other discredits" (121–124). Autolycus is well aware of his limited social prospects. When the Shepherd and the Clown enter, Autolycus has one last chance at those he has "done good to against [his] will" (124–125). They have become gentlemen since the last time we met them, but greatness sits strangely upon them. Still, behind their newfound pride and nobility their hearts are simple, and Autolycus uses this obvious discrepancy to draw laughter from the audience,

> *Autolycus.* I know you are now, sir, a gentleman born.
> *Clown.* Ay, and have been so any time these four hours.
> *Shepherd.* And so have I, boy.
> *Clown.* So you have: but I was a gentleman born before my
> father.
>
> (V.ii.136–140)

Autolycus further draws them out by promising to mend his ways, and they willingly forgive him everything. Here, Autolycus gives his final impersonation, that of a penitent. He relies more upon action than words now, and his only reward is the laughter of the audience. He seems to be fading from the play in this act, and this is indeed the last time we see him.

Autolycus has no significant influence on the plot; he seems to be wandering in and out of it at will, unchangeable despite his many impersonations, and unlike almost everybody else in the play his disguises never catch up with him. He often demonstrates how willing people are to believe what meets the eye, and in this capacity he underscores a major theme of the play, apparent from the outbreak of Leontes' jealousy and not resolved till Hermione's statue comes alive. His mastery of changing shape consciously and at will without changing substance brings out the folly of the Clown, who immediately responds to the disguise and behaves appropriately, as do indeed many of his betters at court. Autolycus lends youthful energy to the last two acts of the play, transforming winter into spring so wrath and regret may be transformed into calm and happiness. For the audience he becomes a catalyst, which signals the transformation of tragic into comic. When he is drawn into the plot, he has no true function, and there is never any change of direction because of his influence. Autolycus's contact with the plot serves to expose the other characters and their behavior to the scrutiny of the audience. He becomes the intermediary between us and the stage, a critical factor in our understanding and indispensable for our amusement. Autolycus's presence does not so much present the audience with hitherto unknown facts; rather his attitude to his fellow characters and his way of handling them determine the mood of our experience.

The plays in which Shakespeare makes use of the stage clown in a limited part show considerable variety in his importance and nature. However, the appearance of the clown characters is always carefully timed to produce the greatest effect, usually to emphasize a turning point in the action or in a major character's fate or development or to set major events and themes of the plot in relief.

In the course of Shakespeare's production there is no development in his way of presenting a small clown part or the effect he aims for, but clearly in some plays, notably the great tragedies and the romances, can be seen an expertise in handling the clown, effectively if sometimes untraditionally, which cannot be found among the earlier plays. In almost every case the minor clown part provides the audience with an interesting possibility for a more flexible and ambiguous interpretation of the plot. Tragedies seem to be the most fertile ground for the presentation of a minor clown who allows the audience to gain deeper insight into plot and characters, while the romances invite experimentation and also show Shakespeare's triumph with the both traditional and innovative character of Autolycus. Not surprisingly, there is hardly a minor clown to be found in any of the comedies. The tragedies provide the minor clown figure with an opportunity to influence the audience through manipulation of mood and tone, a subtlety rarely needed in the comedies. His presence and comments often allow us to see characters and events from yet another angle, lending greater scope to our experience and more depth to our interpretation.

NOTES

1. Here, Folio 2 has "exeunt," which leaves the Gaoler alone on stage for a monologue. The First Folio gives no directions.

2. J. H. P. Pafford's notes to the Arden Edition believably postulates a false beard. The explanation of the meaning of the word "excrement" (714) for (facial) hair in Shakespeare makes this conjecture very convincing, and there is much possibility for comic action in the peeling off of a false beard.

Part II

Major Roles: Expanded Function

4

Bottom in *A Midsummer Night's Dream*, Dogberry in *Much Ado About Nothing*

Bottom, Dogberry, the Dromios, Grumio, Launce and Speed, Costard, Launcelot, and Pompey all have a name of their own and differ from their brethren in small parts by repeated appearances, making them into expected and welcome figures. Their impact becomes greater because they become fixed in our imagination, and their contributions reach beyond the marking of a turning point. Again there is no clear correlation between the degree to which the clown figure is developed and the time at which the play in question was written. Always the roles of these more major clowns are tailored to fit a particular function within the play. They too are the audience's bridge between play and interpretation; their doings and comments serve to facilitate the appropriation of major themes or the understanding of protagonists and their interrelations. Often they function as catalysts, furthering events but remaining unchanged by them.

We may find these clowns engaged in a plot parallel in time to the main plot, as in *A Midsummer Night's Dream* and *Much Ado about Nothing*, alerting the spectators to the comic aspects of lofty things in life such as romantic love and courtship. The two plots need not share much; indeed, a strong link between the two is often the clown's ability to move freely from one social group and plot to another. Bottom, for instance, can be seen doing this.

There is a close parallel in the use of the servant clown, whom we may find in *The Comedy of Errors*, *The Taming of the Shrew*, *The Two Gentlemen of Verona*, *The Merchant of Venice*, and to some degree in *Love's Labour's Lost*, where we see a wide variety of servants, some more sophisticated than others, some mere country clods, but all underlings. One of the greatest advantages of a servant clown is his closeness to the master and the opportunities thus created for parallel comic behavior, mockery, exposure, and silent communication with the audience. The role of the servant may be seen to lead into another category, that of the commentator, whose effect on the audience's interpretation can be created by the comments made in participation in the plot, or by using direct address, bringing about an almost choric effect at times. Finally, there is the group of clowns working as court jesters, "licensed" or "wise fools," whose fooling is a conscious choice and whose lack of understanding is artificially put on.[1] This is the group most commonly written about by critics, probably because their involvement in the main plot seems the most significant, and their written parts are large and complicated and thus readily accessible for literary analysis.

In *A Midsummer Night's Dream*, Shakespeare uses a comic group of characters, led by Bottom the Weaver and engaged in histrionic activities, to set off and comment on the main plot. The world of *A Midsummer Night's Dream* is a strange one, divided into four layers as it were. At one end of the scale we have the magical night-world of the fairies; in the middle the two different groups of human lovers, the authoritative and rational group of Theseus and Hippolyta, and the group of the four "doting" Athenian lovers; and at the bottom-end of the scale the Mechanicals, the clownish group. Much of the comedy depends on the consequences of mixing the night-world with the day-world and the court circles with the common people, and thus the sets of laws and rules by which each group abides. Much is made of the common man's expectations of the higher classes, and of the rules governing their lives.

Shakespeare makes use of the combination of a main clown and a large comic group. Often, the Shakespearean clown may be found with one or several other comic characters, a trait we have already seen in *The Tempest,* sometimes a group of two clowns of almost equal weight will make each other's wit sparkle, but more often the clown will use one or more characters off whom to bounce his own wit. In *A Midsummer Night's Dream* we have an interesting combination, which Shakespeare also uses in *Love's Labour's Lost*, a group of clownish characters which seemingly includes the main clown of the play. Bottom, however, is in a curious position between the comic group, the fairy world, Hippolyta and Theseus, and the audience. As the main clown of the play he cannot be allowed to be swallowed by the relative anonymity of the group of Mechanicals, he has to stand out. Still, he cannot be allowed to remove himself too far from his group, because a major portion of the comedy depends on his interrelation with his peers. Shakespeare manages this by employing him in several capacities. When he is functioning in the group, he usurps leadership whenever possible; when he cannot manage that, he always puts himself forward, either offering his services or complaining. When the Mechanicals' play is finally put on, he manages to function in all camps simultaneously, being part of the theatricals but also apart from them. In addition, he is given ample time alone with the audience to manifest himself as their catalyst, and he alone is allowed or forced to enter fully into the fairy world, a permission he chooses not to avail himself of wholeheartedly, because he, the clown, cannot truly enter into any close relationship.

A group of apparent clown characters like the Mechanicals can never in itself fulfill the role of a stage clown. The true clown's effect depends on his ability to move freely among groups in order to provide the audience with a kind of magnifying glass. The aim of a comic group is very different; the comedy it provides rests in itself. There may be elements of parody, and some of the audience may come to see other characters on stage in a different light because of the comic characters, but when the clown himself provides such a shift the effect is intended, and the change of focus happens on a conscious level. The subtleties of the clown's revelations are potentially available to everyone, and the popularity of the stage clown with all groups of his Elizabethan theatre audience indicates a widespread recognition of this effect. Finally, a group can never become the audience's confidant and communicate with the spectators directly; only a single character can provide the needed close contact, especially if his function involves the breaking of illusion, which happens often in *A Midsummer Night's Dream*.

Love is represented as never being easy or straightforward. Theseus and Hippolyta, whose relationship is set up as the perfect example, have had bitter experiences with a world turned topsy-turvy by their emotions, which had to be normalized before they reached their present harmony:

> *Theseus.* Hippolyta, I woo'd thee with my sword,
> And won thy love doing thee injuries;
> But I will wed thee in another key,
> With pomp, with triumph, and with revelling.

> (I.i.16–19)

The rulers of the fairy world, Oberon and Titania, are in the throes of a bitter quarrel at the beginning of the play (II.i.18–31; 60–145), and the four Athenian lovers are confused to such a degree that the mere idea of loving seems more important than its object. The clown group has no love troubles, but they choose to deal with such problems in the play they are rehearsing and hoping to present at Theseus's wedding; moreover Bottom becomes innocently involved in the fairy-world problems.

Shakespeare's choice of having Bottom and his comic group produce a play and hold up a mirror to the one in which they are characters creates a delightful, much needed distance between play and audience. It will not do for us to become involved in too personal a manner with the lovers, though their situation seems grave enough. In the first scene of Act I the audience is led to expect a traditional pattern of comedy, the climax of which will be young love triumphant over law and parental authority. These expectations are disturbed, both by the seriousness of the law as represented by Theseus, and by the appearance of not one but two other lovers on the scene. This "lovers' square" opens many more possibilities for combinations than would the triangle, and the comic potential is much greater. Though Hermia and Lysander have made plans to elope that night through the woods, our next introduction is not to the forest and the fairy world, but to the first meeting of the Dramatic Society of the Mechanicals.

The placement of this scene serves a dual purpose. The fact that these comic characters have chosen to present the doomed love of Pyramus and Thisbe allows the audience to view the four lovers of the previous scene in a new light. The discrepancy between these would-be performers and their choice of play and lack of knowledge about the roles and sex of Pyramus and Thisbe respectively,[2] reflects on and belittles the violent passion of the lovers of the previous scene. It also draws attention to the artificiality of love on a stage where all women's roles were taken on by boys.[3] The scene also draws attention to the fact that this is all theatre; the preparation of a production is often long and arduous, and ridiculous to the outsider looking in. Probably the London audience had seen productions of a quality close to this.

> *Bottom.* . . . I will move storms, I will condole in some measure. . . . I could play Ercles rarely, or a part to tear a cat in, to make all split.
>> The raging rocks
>> And shivering shocks,
>> Shall break the locks
>>> Of prison gates;
>> And Phibbus' car
>> Shall shine from far
>> And make and mar
>>> The foolish fates.
> This was lofty. . . . a lover is more condoling.
>
> (I.ii.22–37)

Bottom draws attention to accepted and recognized playing styles in a very amusing way indeed, leaving his lofty pose to address the audience as well as his fellow players. The parody functions on many levels.

Bottom immediately becomes the focus of the audience's attention. Peter Quince is the one who has taken the initiative to produce this play, but Bottom grabs the first opportunity to thrust himself forward and take over, behaving like a the comic stereotype of the ham turned critic. He pretends to know the play (I.ii.13–14), wants to play every single part (47, 66), and demonstrates how each part should be played before he is persuaded yet again to remain Pyramus. He even begins to speculate about his costume before he has read his part (83–89). His enthusiasm knows no bounds, and each time Quince makes a rational, helpful comment, Bottom must have the last word, often talking in happy malapropisms from sheer eagerness: "We will meet, and there we may rehearse most obscenely and courageously" (100–101).

The Mechanicals, like the lovers, intend to resort to the forest for reasons of secrecy. The two complementary groups will leave the day-world of Athens for the night-world of fairy magic where the most unlikely combinations will be tried out. The first and fifth acts belong in the rational day-world where known laws function, and where the consequences of actions are foreseeable and defined. The middle acts enter a magical kingdom where nothing is predictable, and where everyone but Oberon and Puck will blunder about blindly, confused, and frightened.

When next we meet Bottom in III.i, he remains unchanged, retaining the predictability of behavior and speech patterns established in I.ii. A great part of the clown's effect is his ability to remain constant and react predictably in the most unlikely situations, bringing out the comic aspect in any given constellation and lending familiarity and equality of importance to the lofty, the sordid, and anything in between. In this respect Bottom never disappoints the audience.

By the end of the second act, doubt has been cast upon the value of all love. Puck, who is happily asexual and has no pity for the mortal lovers, has filled in for the clown. Through direct address, he establishes a link of understanding between the audience and the mysterious fairy world, and we come to see both Oberon's cruel treatment of Titania and Puck's own mistakes over the lovers as all in the day's work, because it has no personal importance to either Puck or the audience. Seen with mortal eyes, the doings of Act II are cruel indeed, but seen from a Puck perspective it is all an exposition of the folly of love. We have need for a figure like Puck in the night-world. Bottom, who would be the natural point of ingress for the audience, is on unfamiliar ground. He serves to expose the folly of love only through Puck's mediation, for Puck exists by the laws of the fairy kingdom and can comment on the folly of all mortals, lovers and clowns alike.

An interesting problem is whether Bottom remains a true clown when he becomes Oberon's pawn in the fairy plot. Suddenly he is no longer in control, and Puck treats him like any other mortal and gets away with it. Once Bottom has been equipped with the ass's head, he becomes one step removed from direct contact with the audience. For a while, the clown function of mediator is almost neutralized, and he is used like any other comic character while a master puppeteer takes over. But Puck is no clown. He does his master's bidding, and amuses the audience with many of the same effects as the clown, but still he remains controlled by Oberon and is never a free agent. The way in which Oberon's orders are carried out are to some extent controlled by Puck; Bottom's ass's head, for instance, is a product of Puck's fertile brain. But Bottom is the one who has established himself in our hearts and minds as our mediator, and he succeeds in remaining our link. The vast difference between him and the delicate fairies is the main tool Shakespeare uses to keep the contact alive, moreover, Bottom's ability to enter and leave the plot of the play when the need arises is the mark of a true stage clown. The fact that he steps as freely in and out of the "Pyramus and Thisbe" play as he does of A Midsummer Night's Dream itself gives his character all the flexibility needed to make him a useful clown tool.

The beginning of the Mechanicals' first rehearsal seems completely free of fairy influence, but still the sleeping figure of Titania has to be on stage as a reminder. Bottom creates problems only to solve them again with varying degrees of awareness of the theater, but with ever-present ingenuity.[4] All his problems stem from his and his friends' expectations of their prospective audience, a joy indeed to the audience present at the actual play. All the alterations proposed by Bottom aim for better reviews by having his audience truly understand that the play is fiction, and so he leaves very little up to the imagination and simultaneously stretches it to the limit. Bottom strives for two things that cannot be reconciled, total realism and total reassurance of his audience. The final combination becomes totally ludicrous. The discrepancy comes out most clearly in the case of Moonshine, Wall, and, to some degree, Lion. Quince, ever the serious producer, brings up the problems of Moonshine and Wall for discussion, and Bottom's solutions are diametrical opposites. Moonshine is most easily dealt with:

> *Bottom.* A calendar, a calendar! Look in the almanac; find out
>   moonshine, find out moonshine!
> *Quince.* Yes, it doth shine that night.

> *Bottom.* Why, then may you leave a casement of the great
> chamber window, where we play, open; and the moon may
> shine in at the casement.
>
> (III.i.49–54)

Indeed a realistic situation, but not thought through very carefully. Quince comes up with a viable alternative, that "one must come in with a bush of thorns and a lantern, and say he comes to disfigure or to present the person of Moonshine" (III.i.55–57). This trick may not convince anybody that the moon is present, but it could work. Bottom is silently impressed by the possibilities of having a person represent a nonperson, and when Quince brings up the problem of Wall, Bottom immediately shows that he has learned his lesson:

> *Snout.* You can never bring in a wall. What say you, Bottom?
> *Bottom.* Some man or other must present Wall; and let him
> have some plaster, or some loam, or some roughcast about
> him, to signify wall; and let him hold his fingers thus.
>
> (III.i.61–66)

Bottom has understood what emblems are about, but he takes it to a ludicrous extreme. While a man may well carry a bush of thorns and a lantern, and by these attributes signal that he presents Moonshine, his colleague, covered with masonry from top to bottom, will have trouble getting himself on stage.[5] Moonshine's props may be considered symbols, but by no means could Wall's be so justified. Bottom oversteps the line between appealing to the audience's imagination and insulting it. The contemporary audience would certainly recognize this dilemma, remembering when they were faced with similar treatment, and enjoy this peek behind the scenes tremendously. A modern-day audience, familiar with the Theater of the Absurd, has no trouble either.

A similar problem of stage conventions has to be faced when Lion is created, but the reasons are different. At the first meeting, Bottom wanted to present Lion because he could do it realistically, but was quickly convinced that such a performance would entail great costs for the performers personally ("That would hang us, every mothers' son" [I.ii.73]), and this thought has apparently fermented in his fertile brain. In addition to the Prologue, which is to reduce the audience's fear of the horrid matters to be presented, something extra must be done about Lion, for

> you ought to consider with yourself; to bring in (God shield
> us!) a lion among ladies is a most dreadful thing; for there is
> not a more fearful wild-fowl than your lion living; and we
> ought to look to't.
>
> (III.i.28–32)

The problem can be solved by ruining the illusion totally, having the man's face seen in the lion's mask, and also letting him address the ladies to calm them before his performance begins. The idea of having the group of comic characters perform "Pyramus and Thisbe" is amusing indeed, but the addition of Bottom's imaginative contributions makes the whole effort delightfully ridiculous to the audience, whose imaginations will fill in where Bottom's descriptions leave off.

Once the first rehearsal is begun, there is yet another wonderful discrepancy, this time between Bottom's vain pretense while the play was discussed and the disastrous delivery of his very first line, "*Thisbe, the flowers of odious savours sweet —*" (III.i.78). We expect malapropisms from Bottom, and we get them even when he is quoting written text! His acting style, full of sound and fury, further underscores his histrionic shortcomings, his vanity, and his boundless enthusiasm.

So far, Shakespeare has used his clown in a twofold capacity. His function has been to demonstrate the distance between the play and the audience, but he has also exposed to us most of the problems of writing and performing a play; we are drawn back even further, behind the play itself. At the same time Bottom has become very dear to the spectators. The Pyramus play is in itself a comment on love in an exaggerated form, but Bottom the clown typically is not wholly alert to the amorous aspects of the proceedings, only to the more practical ones. This trait is carried over into the second half of the forest scene, which provides the audience with yet a second comment on the ridiculous aspects of love. Bottom, now with an ass's head, is courted by the infatuated queen of the fairies, forming the most unlikely couple the list of *dramatis personae* could bring together. Giving Bottom an ass's head should not be seen as Shakespeare's comment on his capabilities, nor as an unsubtle hint to the audience; the trick is Puck's, who seizes any opportunity for a practical joke to expose the folly of any mortal. But the ass's head joke becomes significant in relation to Titania's folly; it recalls Oberon's list of animals she might encounter and fall in love with (II.i.180–181). Still, whichever head Bottom is wearing, he remains unchanged and hardly ruffled by events.

Finding himself alone and left by his companions in the forest dark, Bottom decides not to act frightened. He sings in a loud, carrying voice—this is, after all, a demonstration of courage, and maybe his friends could hear him:

> *The ousel cock, so black of hue,*
> *With orange-tawny bill,*
> *The throstle, with his note so true,*
> *The wren with little quil . . .*
> *The finch, the sparrow and the lark,*
> *The plain-song cuckoo gray . . .*

                                              (III.i.120–126)

Birdsong evokes thoughts of melodious sweetness, but this very fact invites the clown actor to use a loud, gruff voice to create more comedy. Titania's reaction,

> What angel wakes me from my flowery bed
>
> . . .
> I pray thee, gentle mortal, sing again;
> Mine ear is much enamoured of thy note;

                                              (III.i.124,132–133)

further demonstrates the discrepancy and adds to the comedy. Her woman's voice is speaking in delicate verse, while his gruff man's voice rumbles on in coarse prose.

An interesting point is Bottom's lack of interest in sexuality. Even with the ass's head with its connotations of heightened sexuality and stupidity on his shoulders, Bottom does not live up to Titania's expectations. Instead he indulges in a maddening display of common sense of the special Bottom variety which the audience has come to expect from him. He sees no reason why Titania would love him, but then "reason and love keep little company together nowadays" (III.i.138–139). Bottom does not become a "bestial lover"; the ass's head only affects his personality in the most practical manner. His inclinations are still down-to-earth, only now he wants hay instead of human food, and the comfort of being scratched, though not by Titania. In fact, it is quite difficult for Titania to get any response from her lover. Bottom's orders to the fairies suggest that he takes to this kind of comfortable living as if it were his due in the present situation, but Titania herself seems like one of the ladies at Theseus's court, and her love makes him feel, if anything, uncomfortable.[6]

With the small fairies Bottom feels much more at home, and he can joke at their expense. Much of the comedy depends on the difference in size between Bottom and the fairies, and the speed with which Bottom manages to wrench the poetry from their names; Cobweb is good for staunching wounds, Peaseblossom belongs in the vegetable garden, and like Mustardseed he is wonderful on the dinner table. This pattern continues in IV.i, though Bottom now has grown more used to his new status and takes doting more in his stride. An addition to the comedy of this scene are Bottom's own asinine allusions; he is "such a tender ass" (25). Shakespeare has made use of his metamorphosis to demonstrate that the clown's love of creature comforts transcends anything. Even in his waking-up speech the emphasis is on the sensory input he has received: "The eye of man hath not heard, the ear of man hath not seen, man's hand is not able to taste, his tongue to conceive, nor his heart to report what my dream was" (IV.i.209–212). The clown remains essentially unchanged, no matter what he is put through. This immutability serves as a comment on the four lovers and their many changes. The final pairing-off happens to them more than it is a personal choice, and it can be staged so Puck, enlisting the help of the audience, finally accomplishes it. In comparison, Bottom seems like a rock of integrity.

The First Folio has the stage direction "They sleep all the act" for the four lovers,[7] and Bottom, too, is asleep as his own head is restored to him and the fairies leave the scene at dawn, while the representatives of rationality, Theseus and Hippolyta, enter the forest. The audience sees the five sleepers, all victims of the night-world's strangeness, together on stage, and have an opportunity for direct comparison. The parallel continues upon their waking up. All five feel that they have dreamt, and Bottom remembers most keenly of all. He is almost ashamed that he could dream such dreams. "Methought I was—and methought I had—but man's but a patched fool if he will offer to say what methought I had" (IV.i.207–209), he tells the audience, grasping his head, but he cannot quite bring himself to mention the ass. Still, a great impression has been made:

> I have had a most rare vision. I have had a dream, past the wit
> of man to say what dream it was. . . . I will get Peter Quince
> to write a ballad of this dream: it shall be called 'Bottom's
> Dream', because it hath no bottom.
>
> (IV.i.203–215)

Already Bottom is bouncing back while he is processing the experience. He
decides to have a ballad made of his dream because this is the stuff art is made of,
and he will present his ballad at court after the play. The everyday world has
already taken precedence, and Bottom will find a way to make himself look good,
even after the episode of the ass's head. The monologue can be said to constitute
the turning point of the play. The night's adventures are over; the day-world will
return with all its realism and reliability, and whatever insights and glimpses
Bottom may have had will disperse as will the lovers' confusion. He is his own
bubbling, exuberant self when he returns to warn his fellow actors to prepare for
the performance at court (IV.ii.25–43), and as down-to-earth and practical as ever:
"[L]et Thisbe have clean linen; . . . let not him that play the lion pare his nails,
. . . eat no onion or garlic, for we are to utter sweet breath" (37–41).

Bottom's awakening monologue, directly addressed to the audience, is a
traditional stable of the clown's act. The clown actor has the audience to himself,
and can confide in them as he philosophizes on some puzzling problem or
something ridiculous coming to mind. In this case Bottom has been puzzled by
his experience, and uses the audience as a silent conversation partner to come to
terms with it. In other cases a similar confidential moment can be created by
looking away from Titania, say, to address a philosophical remark to the
audience directly, freezing the action in the meantime: "And yet, to say the truth,
reason and love keep little company together nowadays. The more the pity that
some honest neighbours will not make them friends. Nay, I can gleek upon
occasion" (III.i.138–141). Bottom does not feel comfortable enough with Titania
to address such remarks to her, but the audience is used to such fare and has come
to expect it. The part of the clown demands these sudden leaps back and forth
between the play proper and the role of mediator to the audience.

In the fifth act, an equilibrium has been reached. The three couples, now at
peace, prepare to see the Pyramus and Thisbe play presented by the unlikely
actors. As a performance the play is as much a disaster as could be expected, and
both audiences, the on-stage one and especially the one in the theatre, enjoy
themselves to the full. The audience in the pit has the further pleasure of seeing
the four lovers and their follies exposed by the Pyramus and Thisbe play. Their
comments on the folly of Bottom and his fellow actors comically reflect on their
own actions in the night-world. Moreover, there is the performance of the
company clown, who without a care slips back and forth between his role as
Pyramus and his role as commentator and critic, teaching his audiences about the
finer points of theatre and performance:

> *Theseus.* The wall, methinks, being sensible, should curse
>   again.
> *Pyramus.* No, in truth, sir, he should not. 'Deceiving me' is
>   Thisbe's cue: she is to enter now, and I am to spy her

> through the wall. You shall see it will fall pat as I told you:
> yonder she comes.
>
> (V.i.180–185)

Bottom probably uses reproaching glances and gestures without number as well; there certainly are numerous opportunities throughout the play-within-the-play. At the end, Bottom is back to his own character almost before Thisbe is quite dead, to offer a choice between Epilogue and Bergomask.

Bottom the clown moves freely and unconcernedly from his own world among the workingmen of Athens to the fairy world to the world of the court, but he is never in enough contact with the concerns of the main plot to have any influence in its shaping. He belongs in the subplot, which exposes the main plot rather than becoming its parallel, in order that the audience may gain a deeper insight and enjoyment. The two love-intrigues in which he is involved, one of them literary, the other fantastical, and even his metamorphoses, leave him unruffled and unchanged. Whatever he is faced with he has the ability to digest and comment on. He functions as the audience's catalyst and provides mirth and laughter along with greater understanding.

Bottom's function and effect is not unlike Dogberry's in *Much Ado About Nothing*. They are of the same type, employ similar speech patterns and the same type of malapropisms, enjoy social mobility, and have a high opinion about themselves and their abilities. Their doings are also roughly similar, but Dogberry finally has a great, unmerited effect on the main plot.

Dogberry and his shadow Verges are constables, and typically for the clowns' stage appearance they are not called upon to appear before there is a crime for them to solve. Up until III.ii, Don John, the prince's bastard brother, has done his best to sow the seed of jealousy in Claudio's mind, and the audience is guided to see that this otherwise sunny and humorous play will have a darker side. A poisonous plot to thwart Claudio's marriage is hatched in II.ii, and in III.ii the news of Hero's alleged inconstancy is broken to him. By this time the situation is ripe for Dogberry and the members of his Watch. Now there is need for the clown figure to serve as a counterweight to Don John and his plot, and indeed Dogberry is as light as Don John is dark. The balance is achieved and made clear by the placing of the scenes; first we get the plot complete with time and place, then we are presented with the Watch, who will be at the same place at the same time, and eventually undermine the plot and restore order.

The impression made by Dogberry, Verges, and the rest of the Watch is chaotic confusion and lack of organization, but tremendous dedication to the tasks at hand because the work is light. They are most unlikely representatives of law and order, but will in their fuzzy way eventually succeed in serving both. The presence of comic figures at a dark moment becomes a comforting factor, which puts the audience at rest and assures us that nothing truly tragic is about to occur. Dogberry knows all the technical terms of his trade, but is, like Bottom, unfortunately inclined to malapropisms, and because his fellows know no better, the resulting confusion becomes delightfully funny. This is a Watch for peaceful times, Don John's diametrical opposite. The problematic situations the Watch discuss are of the most ordinary variety:

Second Watch [8]. How if a will not stand?
Dogberry . Why then, take no note of him, but let him go, . . .
and thank God you are rid of a knave.

. . .

Watch. How if [the drunks] will not?
Dogberry. Why then, let them alone till they are sober . . . If
you meet a thief, you may suspect him by virtue of your
office, to be no true man; and for such kind of men, the less
you meddle or make with them, why, the more for your
honesty.
Watch. . . . shall we not lay hands on him?
Dogberry. . . . The most peacable way . . . is to let him show
himself what he is, and steal out of your company.
(III.iii.27–30, 44–59)

This, along with the hushing of babies, is all these men expect. After his admonitions to the Watch, Dogberry plans to retire, but he leaves word to be called if anything extraordinary happens (III.iii.82–83). Dogberry should play this scene partly to the audience, addressing them as well as the Watchmen whenever a problem is brought up. He clearly implies that he has a knowledge of the world and invites the spectators' indulgence with his ignorant underlings. We are reconfirmed in our belief that this play is basically sunny, and that all will be well. Verges,[9] who does his best to impress everybody with his own knowledge and willingness, does not have this close audience contact. It is the prerogative of the main clown of the play to exhibit this degree of command.

By a happy chance the Watch, who had planned to do no more than "sit here upon the church-bench till two, and then all to bed" (III.iii.87–88) overhear Borachio and Conrade discuss their villainy, and they make the arrest, albeit on quite a different charge than could be expected. It should be noted that Dogberry has had nothing to do with this and only makes an appearance later when he is called.

This happens in III.v. Dogberry and Verges try unsuccessfully to tell Leonato about the apprehended criminals, but Leonato is preoccupied with the coming wedding and has no time for them. The contrast between Dogberry's long-winded straying from the subject and Leonato's more or less polite attempts to get rid of the two serves a dual purpose: the plot is not interrupted and brought to an untimely conclusion, and the audience is reassured. Leonato is clearly not aware that this case can be of serious concern to him, so he orders Dogberry to conduct the interrogation. This scene is another example of the mobility of the clown; though the social gulf between Leonato and Dogberry is large, the clown bridges it unconcernedly, full of his own importance as he is, using Verges, who is as far below Dogberry as he himself is below Leonato.

The interrogation is ingeniously placed as a reassuring contrast to the gruesome scene in the church. Dogberry's examination is a beautiful parallel to the accusation of Hero in the previous scene; the criminals are assumed guilty, and they are not allowed to defend themselves. This parallel is hard to miss, and the comedy is all the greater because Borachio and Conrade are known to be guilty where Hero was known to be innocent. Moreover, a voice of reason and order and a further basis for comedy is provided by the Sexton, who clearly knows what he is talking about. He handles the interrogation seriously, providing the organization needed and setting off the performance of the clown. Dogberry still blunders delightfully on, proudly sporting his wit and knowledge:

> *Sexton.* Which be the malefactors?
> *Dogberry.* Marry, that am I and my partner.
> *Verges.* Nay, that is certain, we have the exhibition to
>   examine.
> *Sexton.* But which are the offenders that are to be examined? ...
>   Master Constable, you go not the way to examine, you
>   must call forth the watch that are their accusers.
> *Dogberry.* Yea, marry, that's the eftest way.
>
> (IV.ii.3–33)

Throughout the interrogation Dogberry asks irrelevant questions and gets irrelevant answers. The only incriminating answers are given because of the Sexton's prompting and ability to act (57–63). Finally, mortified by being found out and irritated by Dogberry's stupidity, Conrade calls Dogberry an ass and prompts a wonderfully pompous monologue which, if anything, proves Conrade's point. The irate Dogberry manages to cram every known aspect of his character into these fourteen lines (71–84), providing the audience with a fireworks finale to the fourth act. His pride of place, his inflated ego, and his unshakeable belief in his own knowledge are mixed with malapropisms to create an irresistible piece of comedy, especially when addressed alternately to Conrade and the audience. Dogberry should appeal to the audience and demonstrate the appalling conditions under which he has to labor. Here he is, doing his duty excellently, and this treatment is what a man of his importance is to be exposed to!

Much Ado About Nothing is a play with much contact between stage and house. Most of it takes place when a character is alone on stage using the audience as a confidant, and often presenting us with the opportunity to laugh both with and at the character in question. In the case of Dogberry's monologue appealing for sympathy, our laughter becomes ironic; we laugh at Dogberry, and maybe realize that we have never had a chance to laugh with him, because of his monstrous pomposity. Dogberry is confident that the house sides with him and understands him, but at this point our laughter becomes a rejection, and he is saved only because he ultimately serves the cause of justice. As we have seen, Shakespeare sometimes needs to create a distance between clown and audience, and to a lesser extent the same feeling of rejection surfaces at the end of *The Tempest*. But among the more well developed clown parts, Dogberry stands alone. There is never a question of the audience rejecting Bottom, for example. When Dogberry appears again with Verges in V.i, the audience will react differently to the comic traits that amused them earlier; Shakespeare even lets Don Pedro echo such feelings in his ridiculing of the Dogberry style (215–218), which leaves Dogberry speechless for a surprisingly long time.

The light mood disappears with the opening of the fifth act, but the gloom is dispersed by the entrance of the prisoners dragged by the Watch and by Dogberry, who delivers the solution to every problem in one sentence:

> *Dogberry.* Marry, sir, they have committed false report, moreover they have spoken untruths, secondarily they are slanders, sixth and lastly they have belied a lady, thirdly they have verified unjust things, and to conclude, they are lying knaves.
>
> (V.i.210–214)

Once all these unmistakably Dogberrian tangles have been cleared up, there will remain nothing to hinder a happy ending to the play; indeed Borachio immediately confesses, unable to bear another lengthy performance by Dogberry. This very brief speech marks the true turning point we have come to associate with the clown's part. The audience is now free to enjoy Claudio's "punishment" and the restitution of his beloved, watching him from the outside instead of suffering along with him. Also all doubt as to the happiness of Beatrice and Benedick is removed. Nobody truly cares about the fate of Don John, but even he is dealt with, if somewhat briefly, in the end (V.iv.123–126). Dogberry is rewarded, amply it seems from his reaction, but not according to his deserts. Again he has done nothing to accomplish the solution to the problems, but he is happy to reap the benefits. Dogberry's function, like Bottom's, is that of a catalyst. At dark moments he serves to remind the audience that this is after all a comedy, and he reassures them that the outcome will be happy. Moreover, his little world, in which he is so very important and

> a wise fellow, and which is more, an officer, and which is more, a householder, and which is more, as pretty a piece of flesh as any is in Messina, and one that knows the law, go to, and a rich fellow enough, go to, and a fellow that hath had losses, and one that hath two gowns, and everything handsome about him.
>
> (IV.ii.77–83)

has a tremendous impact on the resolution of the main conflict of the play, as well as on its tone and mode. Like Bottom, he remains unalterable whatever is dished out for him, even his flashes of hot temper are very much in character.

Bottom and Dogberry may be said to form a link between Shakespeare's minor clowns and their function and the major clown parts. Though these two characters are much more integrated than the minor clowns, their impact on the main action is coincidental. They are unconscious of their effect on the plot, and their self-important foolishness and total predictability is what makes them endearing to the audience. Also, they unknowingly mark the turning point of the plot but do nothing to provoke it. What distinguishes them most markedly even from Autolycus, the shape changer, is the degree to which they imprint themselves on the audience's consciousness. Their very self-importance promotes an alliance with us, and their predictability helps create the distance needed to enjoy a comedy, because they are used often enough to call forth a Pavlovian reaction of warm reassurance whenever they appear. The quality of their lines is enough to make any comedian successful, but the effect will be multiplied manifold by using a well-known comic actor who knows his company and their mannerisms well like Shakespeare's company clowns did.

NOTES

1. *All's Well That Ends Well, As You Like It, Twelfth Night,* and *King Lear.*

2. *Bottom.* What is Pyramus? A lover, or a tyrant? (I.ii.19); *Flute.* What is Thisbe? A wandering knight? . . . Nay faith, let not me play a woman: I have a beard coming (I.ii.41–44).

3. Shakespeare often draws attention to this fact, but not always for comic effect. We have already met Christopher Sly and his page-as-wife in *The Taming of the Shrew.* In *Hamlet,* the comedy is obvious when Hamlet banteringly addresses the youth in the players' group (II.ii), but in *Antony and Cleopatra* (V.ii.218–220) the reference, among other things, serves to emphasize the impossibility of Cleopatra's situation. In *A Midsummer Night's Dream* the effect should be pure comedy, and the purpose to create a further distance between the lovers and the audience.

4. C. L. Barber gives a good analysis of this aspect of the play in the section "Moonlight and Moonshine: The Ironic Burlesque" in his book *Shakespeare's Festive Comedy*: A Study of Dramatic Form and Its Relation to Social Custom (Princeton: Princeton University Press, 1959).

5. When the play is finally produced, Moonshine appears with all these attributes, and even a dog has been added. The point of the joke is in presenting a figure so overloaded with symbolic props that he can hardly move. Bottom's imagination should be pictured at work here.

6. Modern productions have depicted Bottom as very sexual indeed, but this writer obviously disagrees with such interpretations.

7. At the end of what is the Arden Edition's III.ii.

8. According to the Arden Edition of 1988. The lines of the individual members of the Watch seem readily interchangeable, and are switched around in different editions.

9. In the Quarto, Dogberry and Verges are called "Kemp" and "Cowley" respectively in speech headings in IV.ii. Cowley, too, was a comic actor.

5

The Dromios in *The Comedy of Errors*, Grumio in *The Taming of the Shrew*, Speed and Launce in *The Two Gentlemen of Verona*

When the clown takes upon himself the role of servant to a master, a new world of possibilities is opened. It can be debated whether the clown in some of his other capacities is a servant as well, but a loose definition of service rules out the very special set of dramatic circumstances created when a master and servant pair move as a unit;[1] sometimes they are mirror images of each other, but always we find the servant in an advantageous position when it comes to exposing the master. We find this constellation in five of Shakespeare's comedies, *The Comedy of Errors, Love's Labour's Lost, The Taming of the Shrew, The Two Gentlemen of Verona,* and *The Merchant of Venice*, all comparatively early plays, and all to some degree deriving from and influenced by the *Commedia dell'Arte*.

In the case of *The Comedy of Errors*, Roman comedy itself becomes the source,[2] and Shakespeare makes use not only of the traditional servant/master relationship, but expands the servant into a clown; he even adds much to the comic effect by creating a pair of identical slave/servant twins, one for each of the master twins, and thus doubles the comic potential for mistaken identity and confusion. Though Plautus's *Menaechmi* and *The Comedy of Errors* share numerous scenes and effects, the addition of twin servants gives Shakespeare possibilities without number, and it is especially in these purely Shakespearean sections of the play that the clown has an opportunity to shine; however, because of the intricacies of Shakespeare's plot, the clown is given limited possibility to relate directly to the audience.

The Comedy of Errors is permeated by a farcical atmosphere of physical violence, and the effect is a chain reaction of master's violence to servant which breeds servant's violence to any underling in the given situation. The servant clown mirrors his master's actions. The Ephesian and Syracusian Dromios are both repeatedly beaten and given little or no opportunity for defense. These beatings, most often administered by the hot-tempered Antipholus of Ephesus, are the result of the mistaken identity plot, upon which the comedy of the play depends, and the beaten Dromio most often suffers for what his double did. There is hardly a scene in which one Dromio or the other finds no opportunity to complain about ill treatment, a pattern they have known since birth, when their service began.[3] But in III.i. Dromio of Syracuse is able to lord it over somebody else, ironically enough his own brother and Antipholus of Ephesus, who have come to their home for dinner only to find their places taken by the other master-servant pair:

> *Syracusian Dromio.* . . . to-day here you must not; come again
>   when you may.
> *Ephesian Antipholus.* What art thou keep'st me out from the
>   house I owe?
> *Syracusian Dromio.* The porter for this time, sir, and my name
>   is Dromio.
> *Ephesian Dromio.* O villain, thou hast stol'n both mine office
> and my name;
>   The one ne'er got me credit, the other mickle blame.
>
> (III.i.40–45)

Not only does the Syracusian Dromio find himself in a position of power and enjoys denying the house to these people, he also has an excuse to accuse his twin of wenching and spares no insult. The altercation goes on at length, and though no physical violence takes place, plenty is threatened between the Dromios. The insistence with which Dromio keeps the gate shut cannot be attributed to pride of place as much as to finally having found a way to get back at the world for all its mistreatment.

In *The Taming of the Shrew* we find two parallel situations. Grumio, Petruchio's servant, has his share of abuse from his master. The subject of their very first conversation on stage in I.ii. is actually "knocking." Petruchio talks about knocking at doors whereas Grumio presumes all knocking happens to his own or someone else's head, and his belief is soon confirmed:

> *Petruchio.* . . . Here, sirrah Grumio, knock, I say.
> *Grumio.* Knock, sir? Whom should I knock? Is there any man
>   has rebused your worship?
> *Petruchio.* Villain, I say, knock me here soundly.
> *Grumio.* Knock you here, sir? Why, sir, what am I, sir, that I
>   should knock you here, sir? . . . My master is grown
>   quarrelsome. I should knock you first. And then I know after
>   who comes by the worst.
>
> (I.ii.5–14)

Grumio establishes himself as servant stereotype, but also manages to establish a rapport with the audience which is closer than most created by the Dromios. He understands his master and helps us do so. But Grumio can be as fierce as his master and has a chance to prove it, first in IV.i, later in IV.iii, his two last scenes.

IV.i opens with a short monologue in which Grumio voices the now familiar complaints about abuse on the journey: "Was ever man so beaten? Was ever man so rayed? Was ever man so weary? I am sent before to make a fire, and they are coming after to warm them" (IV.i.2–5). After this cold treatment he is ready for his fellow servants. He flatly refuses to give Curtis any information about the wedding, the journey, and the new mistress, but in the process reveals everything anyway. He even cuffs Curtis's ear; Grumio's ill-treatment is passed on to one over whom he has power. When he inspects the other servants, he answers their greetings very uncivilly, giving quite a good imitation of Petruchio's manner:[4]

> *Nathaniel.* Welcome home, Grumio.
> *Philip.* How now, Grumio.
> *Joseph.* What, Grumio.
> *Nicholas.* Fellow Grumio.
> *Nathaniel.* How now, old lad.
> *Grumio.* Welcome you. How now, you. What, you. Fellow,
>   you. And thus much for greeting.   (IV.i.96-102)

His lordly manner, however, disappears immediately and turns to excuses the minute Petruchio enters. Later, in IV.iii, Grumio again mirrors Petruchio, this time in his treatment of Kate. He is obviously under orders, but enjoying himself and drawing the audience into the fun, gesturing and winking when he offers and then refuses food to his starving mistress (IV.iii.17–32). His only reward is another beating, this time from Kate, but he probably bears it happily. In this case the servant has successfully abused the mistress to prepare her for Petruchio's next attack, but Grumio's enjoyment is no smaller for that.

The purpose served by having the clown servant mirror and even parody his master's violence is easily seen if we imagine the Ephesian Antipholus without any servant. The violence he displays is part of a pattern set in the very first scene when the harsh laws of Ephesus are explained to his father. Antipholus himself is the greatest exponent of violence; he both executes and attracts it. Without Dromio for a lightning rod, the audience would have to take the violence without any grain of salt, which would spoil the comic effect. Instead of being ridiculous because of his part in the general confusion, Antipholus would emerge as a tyrant. With the servant in the play, everything suffered by Antipholus or at his hand can be measured with Dromio's suffering and his reaction to it. In Grumio's case, this effect is less obvious. Petruchio's violence towards Grumio himself seems no more than what could be expected from a spirited master to a stupid servant, and the violence he exhibits in response to Kate is calculated to match her own. Grumio's mirroring serves to underscore the comic effect rather than help shaping it.

The Comedy of Errors is an early play. The part given to the servant clown is quite predictable, his use of verse stiff and labored in many cases, and his response to his treatment soon becomes stereotypical. But in one particular instance the Syracusian Dromio sparkles like a true Elizabethan stage clown. He is given a prose passage on courtship and marriage (III.ii.71–163), which does indeed mirror his master's courting of Luciana but also is a brilliant piece of comedy in its own right. It has more room for audience contact than most of the

Dromio part. Not only does Dromio display the clown's fear of sexuality, but he has been set upon by a regular dragon and the quaking seems justified. She has frightened him so badly that he begins to doubt his identity, reminding us of his master who has just declared himself ready to be transformed, at one with Luciana (39–40 and 61–69). Hard on the heels of romantic courtship comes Dromio, running:

> *Syracusian Dromio.* Do you know me, sir? Am I Dromio?
> Am I your man? Am I myself?
> *Syracusian Antipholus.* Thou art Dromio, thou art my man,
> thou art thyself.
> *Syracusian Dromio.* I am an ass, I am a woman's man, and
> besides myself. . . . besides myself, I am due to a woman, .
> . . she would have me as a beast, not that I being a beast she
> would have me, but that she being a very beastly creature
> lays claim to me.
>
> (III.ii.72–86)

A greater contrast could hardly be imagined. After the traditional flowery wooing with the maiden preserving a distance and the man entreating in romantic terms, in flies Dromio, certain that he is being chased by an aggressive woman, who will indeed have him "as a beast." The sexuality, which Luciana fears to be incestuous, comes to hideous flower in Dromio's predicament. The comedy of the parallel is all the greater because the audience knows that no previous marriage stands between Antipholus and his love. But the confusion of identities, which has Dromio suffering also, makes us smile at the certainty with which Antipholus says that Dromio is "[his] man" and "[him]self"; Antipholus has made enough mistakes already.

The banter which follows and calms down Dromio is not needed to create the mirroring effect and has clearly been added for the sheer enjoyment of having the clown display his art. Nell, the gargantuan kitchen wench, is depicted as if she were a globe comprising all of the known world: "No longer from head to foot than from hip to hip; she is spherical, like a globe; I could find out countries in her" (III.ii.111–113). And he proceeds, prompted by his master, to go through her geography, cutting off at the Netherlands, for "[he] did not look so low," though she was able to tell him "what privy marks [he] ha[s] about [him]" (138, 140-141). This makes his master fear witchcraft, and he decides to flee Ephesus that very night. Here the clown, in the safety of his master's presence, can ridicule the intimidating feminine element to expose his master's passion for Luciana, but mostly for the sheer joy of clowning.

In the last act, where violence threatens to overwhelm comedy, everything is saved by Emilia playing *dea ex machina*, and a happy end is achieved. For the first time we see the two pairs of twins together on stage to the wonder of everyone. At the first sight of each other, the Dromios display their usual clinging to their own identity:

> *Duke.* . . . And so of these, which is the natural man,
> And which the spirit? . . .

> *Syracusian Dromio.* I, sir, am Dromio, command him away.
> *Ephesian Dromio.* I, sir, am Dromio, pray let me stay.
>
> (V.i.335–336)

Later, when everything has been explained, the twin servants are left on stage to end the play. They use each other as a mirror and like what they see (418), but have to sort out which of them is the elder and should have precedence; even this question is resolved in harmony: "We came into the world like brother and brother, /And now let's go hand in hand, not one before another" (V.i.425–426). Again the servants mirror the masters with the addition of the traditional comic business of offering each other precedence.

While the Dromios gain in comic effect because they are twins and constantly mistaken for each other, they do not have many chances to expose anybody directly. Grumio, on the other hand, is given two wonderful opportunities in crowded scenes to expose other characters directly and indirectly to the audience (I.ii. and III.ii). Once the knocking dispute has been resolved, Grumio stops taking part in Hortensio and Petruchio's conversation about marriage, instead directing his remarks to the audience. The more people come on stage, the more daring becomes Grumio's comments and the more cutting his remarks. First, when the two young men begin plotting, he addresses the audience: "Here's no knavery. See, to beguile the old folks, how the young folks lay their heads together" (I.ii.137–138), and as soon as Gremio, the old, ridiculous wooer of Bianca, comes on stage, Grumio remarks: "A proper stripling and an amorous. . . . O this woodcock, what an ass it is!" (I.ii.142, 159), which is overheard by Petruchio. Grumio comments on the importance Gremio attaches to money (176), and echoes his master's courageous replies, making them sound like so much bragging:

> *Gremio.* . . . But will you woo this wildcat?
> *Petruchio.*   Will I live?
> *Grumio.* Will he woo her? Ay, or I'll hang her.
> *Petruchio.* . . . Tush, tush, fear boys with bugs!
> *Grumio.*   For he fears none.
> *Hortensio.* . . . [We'll] bear his charge of wooing, whatsoe'er.
> *Gremio.* And so we will, provided that he win her.
> *Grumio.* I would I were as sure of a good dinner.
>
> (I.ii.194–216)

Grumio has a game going between house and stage, juggling Petruchio's braggadocio and then throwing it to the audience for a response. His remarks in this scene are few but his effect large, and it should be augmented by mimicking the person he ridicules. He may stand directly behind Gremio and copy his every gesture and make a great show of bravado behind his master, only to fall back to his true self at the end of the scene when food and drink are proposed. Grumio's position here is an interesting one. He acts consciously, steps out of his play and contacts the audience directly, placing himself in a mediating position both verbally and physically. Many of the things he says and does cannot be overheard or seen by the other players, who are still in the world of *The Taming of the*

Shrew which he has temporarily left. Grumio's level of consciousness is lower than the court jesters' and Falstaff's, but it is remarkable. His knowing contact with the audience is close to the satirist clowns'.

In III.ii, where Petruchio is late for his own wedding and where Gremio narrates the events at the church itself, it is unclear exactly when Grumio is on stage. He is listed in the Folio text as entering with Petruchio after line 83, and probably exits with his master at line 121. In the meanwhile, there is no line written for him. Petruchio and Kate appear after line 181, but the Folio has no mention of Grumio, who does speak, however, at line 203. The logical thing would be for him to follow his master and exit at line 237. This would give him two periods of time on stage in which he has only one nonsensical line to speak but ample opportunity for silent clowning. The role as comedian in this scene belongs to Gremio, the pantaloon, who is so carried away by his chance to win Bianca that he waxes quite clownish. The enjoyment is doubled because the audience knows about the other plans made for Bianca, and so can enjoy Gremio's remarks and simultaneously laugh at the old man's stupidity. Grumio's role again is that of overreacting to what he hears, augmenting the audience's enjoyment by drawing attention to special remarks and situations, pretending fear when Petruchio is strongly criticized, then bravado as Petruchio sails through his problems. He constantly reminds the audience that Petruchio is putting on an act. There is indeed enough business for a clown.

The greatest effect of both the Dromios and Grumio is their mirroring of their masters' behavior. They have few opportunities to use any of the clown's other comic tricks, but these plays do not need any other behavior. In both plays the mirroring augments the comedy, though not to educate the audience; both depend on the stereotypical characters of the *Commedia dell'Arte lazzi*, where the servants display intense, stylized physical activity. There is no need for any depth to achieve maximum comic effect.

The servant clowns of *The Comedy of Errors* and *The Taming of the Shrew* are confined to the role of the master's double, but already in *The Two Gentlemen of Verona*, another early play, we find a much more independent clown as a part of a psychologically more well developed plot.

The Two Gentlemen of Verona has no less than two comic servants, Speed, servant to Valentine, and Launce, servant to Proteus. Quickwitted Speed, who is often referred to as small and slight, and who engages in humorous battles of words with his master, is more of a comic page, whereas Launce is our true clown, a bumbling country clod with a strong affection for his one prop, Crab the dog. Shakespeare uses the two to set off each other's wit, but Launce especially to create a contrast to his master. It is no coincidence that loyal Launce serves the scheming, deceitful Proteus.

Launce appears relatively late in the play when the plot is well under way and Valentine is already deeply in love with Silvia. Launce is introduced in a long, rambling monologue on parting (II.iii.1–32), which can only endear him to the audience.[5] He comes as far downstage as he can, addressing the audience directly, and his explanations are so convoluted that everything becomes terribly mixed up. One purpose of the monologue is to prepare the audience for the character of Proteus. Launce declares that "'twill be this hour ere I have done weeping," but Crab, his dog, "this cruel-hearted cur," never shed one tear, though the whole family, even the cat, was weeping along with Launce. One thing rarely found in Shakespeare, which makes this monologue so effective, is Launce's use of props. Crab has to be on stage in some form, as he has to be first himself, then Launce (21–23). Besides Launce takes off his shoes to represent his parents, uses his staff for his sister, and his hat for the maid.[6] All the props are part of his costume, but they are taken off and positioned about the stage, and attention is drawn to the state and significance of each of them in turn:

> This shoe is my father. No, this left shoe is my father; no, no,
> this left shoe is my mother; nay, that cannot be so neither.
> Yes, it is so, it is so: it hath the worser sole. This shoe with
> the hole in it is my mother; and this my father. A vengeance
> on't, there it is.
>
> (II.iii.14–19)

Much comedy is crammed into this little section. Launce forgets his sorrow in his eagerness to get the shoes exactly right, and brightens visibly when things come out to his satisfaction. He manages to comment crudely on his mother's sexuality, maybe even her character.[7] The shoes are used again when Launce proceeds to take leave of them, but kissing them good-bye is most unpleasant. Their smell is more than he has reckoned with:

> now should I kiss my father (*he picks up the shoe, notices its*
> *smell, puts it back down*); well, he weeps on; now come I to
> my mother. . . . Well, I kiss her (*kisses the shoe*). Why there
> 'tis: here's my mother's breath up and down.
>
> (II.iii.25–29,[Suggested stage directions mine.])

The discrepancy between the protestations of deep sorrow and the copious weeping, feelings like those displayed in the previous scene when Julia and Proteus part, and the down-to-earth disgust provoked by the smell of well-worn shoes make for delightful clowning.

Panthino disturbs Launce in his explanations of sorrow, and Launce immediately clings to the idea of maybe losing his Crab, as he scrambles to get his shoes and hat back on. The clown, pulling on shoes amid talk of "fil[ling the river] with [his] tears" and "driv[ing] the boat with [his] sighs" (II.iii.52–53) is another delightful piece of comedy, obviously echoing the language of romantic love from in the previous scene.[8] Such language may not be consistent with the image Launce has created of his own character, but the echo of Proteus's language will provoke more laughter when coming from the lips of the clown.

Launce's own attitude to love seems ambivalent like that of any other clown. In II.v, a scene with Speed, he succeeds in equating a "lover" with a "lubber" (37, 40), but in III.i Launce confesses himself to be in love. He is aware of his master's treachery and of love as the cause of it, and he goes about discussing his own passion in a more sedate but no less secretive manner:

> I am in love, but a team of horses shall not pluck that from
> me; nor who 'tis I love; and yet 'tis a woman; but what

> woman I will not tell myself; and yet 'tis a milk-maid; yet 'tis
> not a maid, for she hath had gossips; yet 'tis a maid, for she's
> her masters maid, and serves for wages. . . . Here is the cate-
> log of her conditions.
>
> (III.i.264–272)

Again his honest address to the audience, his only confidants, creates a contrast to his master's treacherous treatment of Valentine. His "cate-log" shows that his feelings have been thought through time and again, and that the qualities of the milkmaid, have been weighed and weighed again. Speed comes upon him as he works his way through his list, and the two proceed to discuss the various qualities of womankind through the example of the milkmaid. Launce the lover is ever ready with a positive interpretation, which makes the whole scene into a comment on love in general and Valentine's love and Proteus's infatuation in particular. After the long list of virtues and vices has been studied thoroughly, the milkmaid's professed wealth tips the scales in her favor, and Launce declares that he will have her. This, however, is the last we hear regarding this match; Launce's clownish love relationship cannot transcend the verbal stage. Still, Launce brings up two aspects of love never mentioned by the gentlemen lovers, sexuality and material gain. Both are probably main ingredients in Proteus's feelings for Silvia. The audience needs a person like Launce to demonstrate these aspects of Proteus's infatuation, and we keep them in mind in the next scene, where Proteus proceeds in villainy.

In Launce's final scene, IV.iv, his function remains constant. He exposes Proteus's negative characteristics while he shows his own gentle qualities. He has lost the lapdog he was to bring Silvia as a love token from Proteus, and knowing the superior qualities of his own Crab he has offered him instead. Crab, however, has cut a bad figure at court, but Launce has taken the blame for both stolen food and wet floorboards. Now he tells the audience about his loyalty to the thankless dog: "How many masters would do this for his servant?" (IV.iv.29–30). Proteus certainly will not. Through his loyalty, his straightforwardness and lumbering wit, but most of all his unconscious ability to reveal his master's character to the audience, Launce becomes very dear to us indeed.

NOTES

1. In the case of *The Comedy of Errors* and *The Two Gentlemen of Verona* even two pairs are found.

2. See Plautus's *Menaechmi* .

3. The beaten and complaining servant has deep roots in classical comedy, and especially the complaints have been integrated in the Elizabethan clown's part.

4. Mimicry is very much part of the servant's relationship to his master, and may even be said to be a key characteristic of the nonrustic servant clown. The Dromios echo their masters, Launcelot Gobbo of *The Merchant of Venice* echoes Shylock, and Speed of *The Two Gentlemen of Verona* often sounds almost like Valentine, quite deliberately so in II.i.7.

5. See J. L. Styan, *Shakespeare's Stagecraft* (Cambridge and New York; University Press, 1967), 74.

6. His predicament resembles Bottom's plans for the "Pyramus and Thisbe" props. Launce, however, has no idea that he is creating a piece of theatre; he only wants to help the audience.

7. Eric Partridge, in *Shakespeare's Bawdy*, (New York: Dutton, 1955) does not miss this. Besides the notorious "hole," there is a pun of sole/soul.

8. In II.ii.14–15, Proteus says, "The tide is now; nay, not the tide of tears./That tide will stay me longer than I should."

6

Costard in *Love's Labour's Lost*, Launcelot Gobbo in *The Merchant of Venice*

Two other servant clowns have a function similar to that of Launce, namely exposing negative or ridiculous aspects of their betters in particular situations; they are Costard of *Love's Labour's Lost* and Launcelot Gobbo of *The Merchant of Venice*. Neither is closely connected to one master, but the variety of their service and the versatility of their function allow them to stand forth as commentators on their entire world. Both Costard's and Launcelot's roles are untraditional in several ways, but both display numerous clown traits.

John Barton has said in relation to playing the role of Costard, "Until we love individual words we cannot love language, and if we don't we won't be able to use it properly."[1] Costard indeed demonstrates an unconscious savoring of language, possibly more than any other Shakespearean clown, and though his language is full of malapropisms, he has knowledge and agility in the use of synonyms and true fascination with acquiring long or complicated words. His linguistic ability, which is unexpected in a country clod like "Costard the swain" (I.i.178), manifests itself as soon as we meet him:

> *King.* But, sirrah, what say you to this?
> *Costard.* Sir, I confess the wench.
> *King.* . . . It was proclaimed a year's imprisonment to be taken
>   with a wench.
> *Costard.* I was taken with none, sir: I was taken with a demsel.
> *King.* Well, it was proclaimed demsel.
> *Costard.* This was no demsel neither, sir: she was a virgin.
> *King.* It is so varied too, for it was proclaimed virgin.
> *Costard.* If it were, I deny her virginity: I was taken with a
>   maid.
> *King.* The maid will not serve your turn, sir.
> *Costard.* This maid will serve my turn, sir.

> *King*. Sir, I will pronounce your sentence: you shall fast a
> week with bran and water.
>
> . . .
>
> *Costard*. I suffer for the truth, sir: for true it is I was taken
> with Jaquenetta, and Jaquenetta is a true girl; and therefore
> welcome the sour cup of prosperity! Affliction may one day
> smile again; and till then, sit thee down, sorrow!
>
> (I.i.274–306)

At this early point in the play, Costard's role as commentator is already well under way. Here he demonstrates the ridiculousness of the King's rules about total abstinence from women for three years. Costard tries to worm his way out of the punishment, but he does not deny the crime, for "[s]uch is the simplicity of man to hearken after the flesh."[2] He will soon be proved right; even the King will fall.

Jaquenetta, the object of Costard's passion, is also wooed by his jailor Don Armado,[3] though he describes this country girl as an unworthy object to break the law for (I.ii.157–163). Jaquenetta, however, seems to have the same attitude to love as Costard, and she is unimpressed by Don Armado's verbosity and protestations, if not by his masculinity (I.ii.124–135). Jaquenetta chooses Don Armado over Costard, it seems, but though she is pregnant she chooses to have him wait for her for three years doing peasant's work (V.ii.874–76), thus putting herself on a par with the French ladies.

Though Costard's natural longings and inclinations, mirroring the predicaments of his betters, is a general theme, he serves other purposes as well. Apart from the running puns, which are integral to the clown's part, and which Costard has more than the usual share of,[4] there is his fascination with language and learning, a comment on the King's ambition to make the court of Navarre "the wonder of the world; / . . . a little academe" (I.i.12–13). The themes are not unrelated, but Costard is living proof that intellectual and amorous pursuits do not preclude one another. The best examples of this are found in III.i and V.i.

In III.i both Don Armado and Berowne have decided to make Costard their Cupid and have him carry a love letter to their respective ladies. Both reward Costard with a tip, and in both cases Costard reacts strongly to the fancy names given Don Armado's "three farthings" and Berowne's "a'leven-pence farthing better."

> *Don Armado*. There is remuneration. . . .
> *Costard* . . . . Remuneration! O that's the Latin word for three
> farthings: three farthings, remuneration. 'What's the price of
> this inkle?' 'One penny': 'No, I'll give you a remuneration':
> why, it carries it. Remuneration! why it is a fairer name
> than French crown. . . . Pray you, sir, how much carnation
> ribbon may a man buy for a remuneration?
> *Berowne*. O what is a remuneration?
> *Costard*. Marry, sir, halfpenny farthing.

Berowne. O! why then, three-farthings worth of silk.

. . .

Berowne. There's thy guerdon: go.
Costard. Gardon, O sweet gardon! Better than remuneration;
a'leven-pence farthing better. Most sweet gardon! I will do
it, sir, in print. Gardon! Remuneration!

(III.i.128–167)

Costard, though he is disappointed that the amount is so small, is smitten with
the possibilities of words. He quite forgets to be jealous over Jaquenetta. The
sarcastic way in which he tries out the taste and sound of his new words, rolls
them off his tongue, and tries them in sentence construction and
miniconversations is delightful. And possibly his ironic fascination makes him
mix up the letters and deliver them into the wrong hands as an unconscious
revenge. In this scene, Costard displays marked awareness of his clown status
and consciously plays stage against house for effect. Nobody is left unaware that
Don Armado's word is a very large one for such a small sum of money, just as
his words of love are oversized for the kind of passion he feels.

Costard's fascination with words and wordplay is also evident in his
relationship with Moth, Don Armado's page, whose tongue is nimble indeed.

Costard. An I had but one penny in the world, thou shoulds't
have it to buy gingerbread. Hold, there is the very
remuneration I had of thy master, thou halfpenny purse of wit,
thou pigeon-egg of discretion. O, an the heavens were so
pleased that thou wert but my bastard, what a joyful father
wouldst thou make me. Go to; thou hast it *ad dunghill* , at the
fingers' ends, as they say.

(V.i.64–71)

This very fascination makes him acquit himself so relatively well as Pompey the
Great in the play of "The Nine Worthies" put on by the comic group in the last
act, where he is up against such masters of learning as Sir Nathaniel, the Curate,
and Holofernes, the Schoolmaster, whose long-winded discourse makes even Don
Armado seem lucid.

Holofernes decides that Costard "because of his great limb or joint, shall pass
Pompey the Great" (V.i.119–120), though Don Armado resents it. The interlude
of the Nine Worthies is quite similar to the Pyramus and Thisbe play of *A
Midsummer Night's Dream*. Not only are the actors amateurs and likely to
become confused, but they freely fail out of their parts and talk to their on-stage
audience or discuss matters of real life within the play. The stage audience, too,
behaves similarly; nobody hesitates to break in and make fun of the
hardworking, would-be actor, or make conversation among themselves:

Costard . I Pompey am,—
Berowne.   You lie, you are not he.

> *Costard* . I Pompey am,—
> *Boyet.*   With libbard's head on knee.
> *Berowne.* Well said, old mocker: I must needs be friends with
>   thee.
> *Costard* . I Pompey am, Pompey surnam'd the Big,—
> *Dumain.* The Great.
> *Costard* . It is 'Great', sir; Pompey surnam'd the Great; . . .
>
>   . . .
>
> *Costard* . 'Tis not so much worth; but I hope I was perfect. I
>   made a little fault in 'Great'.
> *Berowne.* My hat top a halfpenny, Pompey proves the best
>   worthy.
>
> (V.ii.541–557)

Costard is less affected by his on-stage audience than the other, supposedly more-sophisticated Worthies. Again he is a stage clown who moves unembarrassed from one social sphere to another without difficulty. The same proves true when he begins riling Don Armado as Hector a bit later, clearly enjoying the disturbance he creates, and the possibility of mimicking his betters (V.ii.662–674). This is Costard's only revenge on Don Armado for having supplanted him in Jaquenetta's affections, and superb it is in front of the King and Princess and their followers. Once Don Armado was Costard's jailor because of a similar offense, but now the tables can be turned, and publicly at that. A duel is averted only because of Armado's cowardice, which Costard knows he can depend on. The whole Jaquenetta episode within the play of the Nine Worthies serves as another parallel to the court. At this point the King and noblemen have all confessed their loves to each other and begun wooing more openly, and lo, Costard brings before them the very consequences of proximity. It would not be a bad idea to present Jaquenetta peeking out at the audience at this point.

The parallel is repeated in the song at the end of the play, where the cuckoo stands for spring and rampant sexuality, whereas the more sedate owl cries in winter and thus represents stability, domesticity, and steadiness. When the young men and Don Armado have served their terms and performed the tasks set them by their ladies, they will be more suited to the married state. Costard the clown naturally goes free of the results of amorous entanglements.

There is one indication that Launcelot of *The Merchant of Venice* has not been equally lucky, but it is an indication only and not followed up at any other point in the play;[5] still, there it is:

> *Lorenzo.* I shall answer that better to the commonwealth than
>   you can the getting up of the negro's belly: the Moor is
>   with child by you, Launcelot!
> *Launcelot.* It is much that the Moor should be more than
>   reason: but if she be less than an honest woman, she is
>   indeed more than I took her for.
>
> (III.v.34–39)

This altercation takes place in a context loaded with sexual references. Launcelot and Jessica are discussing salvation, and he touches on "the sins of the fathers," and her "bastard hopes" that her father "got [her] not." She retorts with "the sins of [her] mother" then to be visited upon her. When she says her husband has made her a Christian, Launcelot counters, "this making of Christians will raise the price of hogs," clearly referring to other aspects of Jessica's altered state (III.v.1–23). When Lorenzo enters, he jokes that Launcelot "get[s his] wife into corners," and the bawdy puns continue flying, including Lorenzo's accusations about the Mooress. Launcelot, however, does not pursue the subject once he has made his pun, and neither does Lorenzo; in fact, this is the only time Launcelot's potential for sexual prowess is referred to in the play.

It must be taken into consideration that Launcelot's whole function changes radically when he leaves Shylock's household. The Folio has the suggestive stage direction, "*Enter Iew, and his man that was the clown*," which suggests a change in the role of Launcelot. At the beginning of the play, we are faced with a typical rustic clown, but after he is employed by Bassanio, his style becomes more polished. Even his language changes, leaving out the malapropisms and adding elaborate puns, and his propensity for practical jokes disappears.[6] Moreover, he does not address the audience in monologues late in the play; indeed, his role seems diminished in comparison to clowns like Launce and Costard. Though he is still styled "clown" in stage directions and speech headings for the rest of the play, Launcelot's relationship with both his fellow characters and the audience is altered. He does not stop being "the clown," rather, the definition of "clown" changes midway through the play. Launcelot becomes more of an equal to his betters, and in this context the jokes about the Moor's pregnancy and Launcelot's evasions do not have to mean anything but banter, especially when we remember that Jessica and Lorenzo have finally been united after passionate courtship and elopement. They certainly are not among the many Shakespearean lovers who have to be reminded about their own sexuality.

The Jew and the clown are the characters counterpoised in this play, but only as long as the Jew can be thought of as ridiculous. When we reach the trial scene, Portia has taken over the function of counterweight to the now dangerous Jew. With Launcelot's change of function and style he loses impact. He is still an amusing character, but he is no longer endearing. He has not been given time or force enough to build up an image as a licensed fool or court jester, though that may be what Shakespeare halfheartedly attempts. Launcelot is more or less forgotten, and at his last appearance in V.i. he has been reduced to comic messenger. The function as jokester has been taken over by Portia, who first outwits Shylock in the trial scene and then her husband in the scene of reunion. There is apparently no more room for a full-fledged clown figure after the middle of the play, and this may be why Shakespeare departs from the tradition of the clown's inability to have a sexual relationship and lets Launcelot be accused of impregnating the Moor.

While Launcelot is the country clod, he is akin to both Launce and Costard. He is given the traditional bad master, whom he seeks to escape after a lengthy struggle with his conscience, and a family represented by his ancient father, "being an honest man's son, or rather an honest woman's son, for indeed my father did something smack, something grow to; he had a kind of taste;—"

(II.ii.14–17). Though he plays practical jokes on his father when he first appears on stage, Old Gobbo's approval and help is important to Launcelot. He reacts innocently, almost childishly, during the negotiations about his new position; he interrupts, does not let his father finish what he is saying, and displays great eagerness and joy at the prospect of sporting a gaudy livery, all traits traditionally associated with the Elizabethan stage clown.

In some ways Launcelot and Costard approach the licensed fool, the court jester. They both display the folly of their world in its entirety to the audience—Launcelot less than Costard—but because they are both formally rustic clowns, they are not entirely fitted for the jester's mental agility. Launcelot's character changes towards the jester, but never is developed enough, and Costard makes his effect by leaning heavily on members of the large comic group, especially Don Armado and Moth, but certainly also Holofernes and the Curate. Launcelot has his chance to interact in a jesterly fashion with Shylock at one point in the play (II.v) but never truly brings the sparks to fly, and Costard never gets further on this path than his argument with the King to save his own skin (I.i).

NOTES

1. John Barton, *Playing Shakespeare* (London and New York: Methuen, 1984), 48.

2. I.i.214–215. Costard shares this insight with Lavatch of *All's Well That Ends Well* and his longing for Isbel, and Touchstone of *As You Like It*, who pursues Audrey for the same reason. These three apparently have actual carnal knowledge of women, or know of what they speak. It is a strange contradiction that other clowns and clownlike figures in Shakespeare, who talk of love and sex with great scorn, all are or seem sexless.

3. Don Armado is part of a large comic group of seven. Their distribution and function of the comic group reminds one of *A Midsummer Night's Dream*, and sometimes of even *Twelfth Night* ; all three plays make use of a comic group of roughly the same size as the group of protagonists in which the main conflict of the play is mirrored.

4. Beginning with his name, and repeated often as in, for example, the "l'envoy" pun and the wealth of other puns of III.i.

5. David Wiles, in *Shakespeare's Clown* (Cambridge and New York: Cambridge University Press, 1987), analyzes Launcelot's name and links it with lechery and gluttony both (8). "Launcelot" suggests to him both jabbing wit and sexual prowess. In Leslie Hotson's book *Shakespeare's Motley* (London: Rupert Hart-Davis, 1952), it is stated that historically both the stage clown and little children often wore a wooden dagger at the back. Launcelot's wit is more like jabs with a wooden dagger, amusing, but absolutely without danger, and mocking or negating sexual prowess. The lines referring to the Moor have traditionally been cut from the text in performance. Still, the lines are there and must be examined, because they seemingly contradict the clown's fundamental attitude to women.

6. II.v. is the transitional scene.

7

Pompey in *Measure for Measure*

Another stage between the servant clown and the court jester is formed by the uninvolved commentator, who succeeds in laying bare the very structure of his society and finds it wanting. Pompey of *Measure for Measure* throws himself into the stream of events and the people involved with abandon, always molding himself to the demands of the situation. Pompey is well aware of his status as commentator and audience educator, and he wants to teach through amused laughter. He serves to expose his society with a view to baring its weaknesses, but though such a role could make us expect a surly fellow such as Thersites in *Troilus and Cressida*, Pompey's relationship with his fellow characters and with the audience is amiable indeed.

In *Measure for Measure*, the world is clearly split in two. We have the upper-class world, which concerns itself with such things as society and morality, and we find a kind of underworld, in which such notions are of no concern except when imposed from above. There is lively interaction between the two and even some understanding, and the strongest link is represented by Pompey the Clown. Technically Pompey is in service, but his job as Mistress Overdone's tapster does not last very long, and she is more partner than mistress. His stage appearances with her are few and short, and he makes little use of his association with her in his relationship with the audience. Later, again technically, he enters the service of the state, but still seems more of a free agent than a servant. Thus Pompey is given the opportunity to move freely in both worlds, and he even makes his way through the court unscathed.

When first we meet him (I.ii.78), the audience is already aware that the tensions in this play are going to arise between society and its laws on the one hand and human sexuality on the other. All levels of society will be affected by such a conflict. Pompey is given the somewhat strange task of describing the consequences of the law to Mistress Overdone, repeating the tale she has just told to the two Gentlemen, Lucio, and the audience. There is, however, a difference in tone and kind between the two parallel narratives, which lets

Pompey's retelling earn its place after all. The first telling gives the facts, and some of the feelings of the speakers (I.ii.59–67). When Pompey retells the story immediately afterwards, adding the bawdy comments to be expected from the clown, events are viewed as general to humankind:

> *Pompey.* Yonder man is carried to prison.
> *Mistress Overdone.* Well! What has he done?
> *Pompey.* A woman.
> *Mistress Overdone.* But what is his offence?
> *Pompey.* Groping for trouts, in a peculiar river.
> *Mistress Overdone.* What? Is there a maid with child by him?
> *Pompey.* No: but there is a woman with maid by him. You
>   have not heard of the proclamation, have you?
>
>   (I.ii.79–86)

During his short stay in this scene, Pompey succeeds in stating his attitude towards the law, sexuality, and prostitution. The law can impose as harsh a punishment as it may devise against human inclinations, but human nature cannot be changed, so "good counsellors lack no clients" and never shall (I.ii.98–99). With Pompey's words still on our minds, we see Claudio on his way to prison followed by the pregnant Juliet. The obvious unfairness of the law is driven home still more strongly.

Pompey is next seen in direct confrontation with the representatives of the law, Angelo and Escalus (II.i). This scene is ingeniously placed. At this point, the audience knows the reasons for the Duke's absence, and that he has chosen Angelo as his deputy because he is in need of Angelo's harshness. Moreover, we have met Isabella in the nunnery and been given a chance to form an opinion about her character, and we have been given ample opportunity to study Angelo, both through other people's opinion and through his own words. Angelo presents a picture of the unwavering sword of justice, but when he is faced with Pompey and two other members of the comic group, Froth and Elbow the Constable, the sword is not even drawn. The objects seem unworthy though the crime is grave, and Angelo cannot be bothered with such low-life characters. Ironically enough, Elbow, the representative of the law, is the one whose malapropisms, thoroughness, stupidity, and inability become too much for Angelo, especially when his thread is taken up by Pompey with much more ingenuity and more irritants added.

The argument forms a comic parallel to Claudio and Juliet's predicament. Elbow's pregnant wife has innocently ventured into Pompey's brothel, and apparently Froth, equally innocently, has taken her for a prostitute. Escalus is capable of seeing both the humorous and the human aspects in the awkward tale of the situation, and he pardons everybody where Angelo condemned their betters. Meanwhile, the altercation is exquisitely comic, and Pompey has every chance to juggle his roles as "tapster," as serious witness, as lawyer for Froth, and as stage clown to the enjoyment of the audience. Not until Angelo leaves, however, and Escalus is able to concentrate on Pompey do we get some insightful comments:

> *Escalus.* Pompey, you are partly a bawd, Pompey, howsoever
> you colour it in being a tapster, are you not? Come, tell me
> true, it shall be the better for you.
> *Pompey.* Truly, sir, I am a poor fellow that would live.
> *Escalus.* How would you live, Pompey? By being a bawd?
> What do you think of the trade, Pompey? Is it a lawful
> trade?
> *Pompey.* If the law would allow it, sir.
> *Escalus.* But the law will not allow it, Pompey; nor it shall
> not be allowed in Vienna.
> *Pompey.* Does your worship mean to geld and splay all the
> youth of the city?
> *Escalus.* No, Pompey.
> *Pompey.* Truly, sir, in my poor opinion, they will to't then.
>
> (II.i.216–230)

Pompey's line, "I am a poor fellow that would live," echoes in III.i, the scene between Isabella and her brother, as does Escalus's remark, "Which is the wiser here, Justice or Iniquity?" (II.i.169). The technique of teaching through laughter is a time-honored one, and it works well. Where Isabella's discussion of the same problem with Claudio sets the audience thinking about morality, Pompey's remarks hit their mark immediately because he goes straight to the salient point: given the choice, who would choose death over life?

Pompey has now uttered his opinion on sex, society, and morality within both worlds of the play, and he is even given a chance to enlighten the Duke himself. He is again arrested because he continues to "sell men and women like beasts" (III.ii.2), and the Duke listens to his speech about usury, which can easily be interpreted to encompass Pompey's trade as well. When the Duke asks, "Canst thou believe thy living is a life, /So stinkingly depending?" Pompey is nothing daunted, "Indeed it does stink in some sort, sir. But yet, sir, I would prove—" (25–28). He is not given the opportunity to continue his argument, but when he begs Lucio to stand bail for him, both the Duke and the audience are made to speculate on the nature of guilt, and again the scene echoes shortly afterwards in the play. Lucio has fathered an illegitimate child (III.ii.192–197), slanders people to their faces if he is their superior, and behind their backs if he is not. Now he has the power to refuse bail to Pompey and to inform against Mistress Overdone. Where and what is justice? Fresh in the audience's memory is the second scene between Isabella and Angelo (II.iv), which has proved Angelo himself capable of trying to buy a woman's favors and therefore no better than Lucio, and we also clearly remember the conclusion of the prison scene (III.i), where the Duke and Isabella plan to substitute Angelo's spurned love for Isabella, and so are no better than Pompey and Mistress Overdone. Though the argument could be made intellectually that at the time a formal betrothal equaled a legal marriage, and therefore sexual intercourse could not be regarded as sin, still everybody concerned engages in emotional as well as physical acts of prostitution on some pretext.

Pompey the Bawd has now become imprisoned and immediately changes his unlawful trade for the lawful one of hangman, though with certain reservations:

Provost. Can you cut off a man's head?
Pompey. If the man be a bachelor, sir, I can; but if he be a
    married man, he's his wife's head; and I can never cut off a
    woman's head.

(IV.ii.1–4)

His change of status is rather suddenly sprung upon the audience, but again Shakespeare's timing is superb. Claudio was to be executed for fornication, though his and Juliet's formal agreement is at least as legal as Mariana's "pre-contract" (IV.i.72) with Angelo; the Duke turns bawd and plans to assist in chopping off a maidenhead; in the scene immediately following, the bawd turns hangman but refuses to cut off women's heads.

Pompey soon finds himself as much at home as an executioner's assistant as he was when a tapster at the brothel. He opens IV.iii with his only monologue, in which he tells about, and probably physically parodies, all the rakes he used to know at Mistress Overdone's and now meets again here. Pompey is alone with the audience, and to make the most of the situation the clown will draw upon the individuals within his reach. First of all he presumes that everybody is with him in the jail, and every time he mentions a name, he will point at somebody in the house:

(*Pompey points*). . . here's young Master Rash; (*confides to
the rest of the audience*) he's in for a commodity of brown
paper and old ginger. . . . (*points*) Then is there here one
Master Caper, (*confides to the rest of the audience*) at the suit
of Master Three-pile the mercer, . . .
(IV.iii.4–10 [all stage directions my suggestions])

At the close of the monologue his pointing finger races around the house as name after name is mentioned, and still there are "forty more"! Pompey does not only make use of direct address to the audience, he draws in all of us and takes all the liberties with the spectators a clown possibly can, creating exquisite fun for everybody. We are, after all, all criminals and sinners together. Though the prisoners are in jail for various other reasons, they are all "great doers in our trade" (IV.iii.19). Still, they are small fry in comparison with Barnardine, as is indeed any other criminal in the play, for not only is he a murderer, he is untroubled by conscience (IV.ii.64–66). He cannot come to the Provost in IV.ii because he is asleep, and in IV.iii he has no time to be executed because of sleepiness. This scene is another of the many parallel scenes in *Measure for Measure*; here we are presented with a contrast between Barnardine's indifference and Claudio's deep fears of death earlier in the play. Pompey has taken the Duke's role as persuader and preparer upon himself, but has a much more difficult task on hand. Claudio was ready to admit to his crime and accept punishment, but Barnardine first refuses to be wakened and come forth, then declares that he has been drinking and is unfit to die yet, and finally refuses to leave his cell that day. He will not be executed.[1] Pompey, meanwhile, twists all and any of Barnardine's arguments, he cajoles and entices, but all to no avail:

> *Pompey.* Your friends, sir, the hangman. You must be so
> good, sir, to rise and be put to death. . . . Pray, Master
> Barnardine, awake till you are executed, and sleep afterwards....
> he that drinks all night, and is hanged betimes in the morning,
> may sleep the sounder all the next day.
>
> (IV.iii.27–46)

Pompey is playing Devil's advocate just like the Duke did to Claudio in the
prison scene. The Duke certainly does not intend Claudio to die, nor does he
accept his crime as punishable by death; yet he plays such tricks on Claudio's
conscience that he honestly accepts death as a just sentence. Barnardine is
untroubled by such niceties as repentance, and Pompey's attempts to lure him
forth have no effect. The Duke is more successful because of Claudio's
sensibility and sense of belonging in an ordered society. In the prison where the
Jester plays Death no such miracle is wrought.

This is our last encounter with Pompey the Clown. Pompey has functioned as
an important route of ingress into the main themes of the play, and has created
most of the parallel scenes that help with interpretation. He has taken much of
the tragic sting from the action in doing so, but now, however, when only the
resolution is left, there is no more need for Pompey. The comedy of the fifth act
is provided through revealing the Duke's true identity and through the
punishment by marriage of Lucio. As the play draws to a close there is no more
need of drawing the worlds together. The audience has all the necessary
information, and we know who is guilty and who is not. The clown has provided
us with the perspective we need to see the comedy in the fifth act. Lucio is the
only comic figure left; because of his personal involvement with the Duke as
Friar, he needs some comic punishment, and he is treated as an equal with all the
other sinners of the play. Claudio and Juliet are married as are Angelo and
Mariana, and Lucio is forced to make an honest woman out of his "bawd." For
the Duke there is the possibility of being paired with Isabella, though modern
productions often leave this union pending. Pompey the clown, however, has no
place in this crowd of couples. We remember his teaching as we see them all
united, but he has prepared us so well that we do not need his actual presence at
the conclusion of the play.

The role of the Shakespearean clown in his more well developed parts is not
different in kind from the smallest ones, but of course he is more noticeable, and
his effect grows when the audience is allowed to become better acquainted with
him. We are amused by the Porter in *Macbeth* but enamored of Bottom. Still,
the clown's is a somewhat stereotypical role, and this fact can be underscored by
the style of the performer, but the more there is to his part, the more effectively
Shakespeare's clown may transcend the stereotype; Dogberry, for instance,
creates an almost negative response in the audience. When we see a well-known
actor in a minor part, he will have a great impact because of the anticipation
with which he is received and the fixed way in which his performance is regarded.
The same actor in a larger part will exercise even greater control over audience
perception and response, something a clown like Pompey, who is conscious of
his effect and makes the most of it, will handle especially well. The audience
willingly participates in whatever such a clown suggests, and that will be plenty

because the greater part gives him room to draw out more of the themes of the play. The role of audience guide is much more apparent in these larger clown parts, and it becomes inseparable from and almost one with the parts of the court jesters. The larger the clown's part, the more obvious becomes his role as structural element within the play. Where the minor clown parts mainly provide the audience with a twist to the point of view as a turning point is reached, the more major clown parts provide and clarify many of the parallels necessary for an interpretation. The clown is indeed still present at crucial turning points in the plays, but the function as a signal for these points becomes more obscured as his part grows larger and his importance as teacher and guide gains ground.

NOTE

1. Barnardine is never executed; the Duke pardons him, V.i.478–483.

Part III

The Court Jesters in the Comedies

8

Lavatch in *All's Well That Ends Well*

Many clowns in Shakespeare's works have a label attached besides "clown," be it "shepherd," "servant," or "bawd." Lavatch of *All's Well That Ends Well*, Touchstone of *As You Like It*, Feste of *Twelfth Night*, and Lear's Fool of *King Lear* are formally, if not all practically, attached to one specific socially privileged household, where they fill the position of court jester, which in turn carries along with it certain obligations and privileges. Some degree of wit or wisdom is called for, and great agility in the use of language. Much of the strength of the court jesters' impact lies in their position as commentators, mirrors, and educators of the audience, a function they share with the minor clowns, and like them the jesters stand apart from the plot and have little or no hand in shaping it. In reality the difference between the court jesters and the other clowns is one of position, not of kind; the court jester clowns are employed as "fools," and their folly is artificially put on.

Lavatch is the clown who forms the link between the more major clown parts and the court jesters. His is not a large part, but he fulfills numerous functions within the play, some of them the jester's, some a mere servant's. He is granted free speech and is at home within his social sphere where he clearly belongs, but he is also employed in carrying messages and running errands, and he is probably in his mistress's confidence more than an ordinary servant clown would be. He does not function solely as his mistress's mirror, but is more of a comic mirror for general ideas within the play as they are presented by certain characters, Bertram especially. Finally, his many rhymes and songs link him firmly with the court jesters.

All's Well That Ends Well is dominated by women much more than any other Shakespearean play. Though Rosalind pulls all the strings in *As You Like It*, and Isabella is a strong character in *Measure for Measure*, Helena only is dominant. She chooses an unwilling object for her affections, and through the help and support of other strong females succeeds in snaring him. The plan which gets her Bertram as a husband is all Helena's, and the means she employs to reach the end she desires are all female. Bertram appears immature and childish, both in his choice of company, his inconstancy, and his need continually to prove his manhood at court, at war, and with women. The part of Lavatch strengthens the audience's perception of this upside-down view of power, because he constantly sides with the females of the play.

Bertram's confidant is Parolles the braggart, who shares with Lavatch the role of comic character in the play, but where Lavatch's every comment angles for our laughter, Parolles unwillingly draws it upon himself. There is no question of seeing these two as a comic pair, whose wits sparkle when in contact with each other, or whose shared stupidity carries amusement to new heights. Parolles is the victim of everybody's wit except Bertram's. The audience sees through Parolles immediately, and Shakespeare uses Bertram's naive blindness as a main ingredient in his characterization. To Bertram, everything is black or white; he has huge difficulties in seeing Helena as a person, and from the beginning he labels her as a social inferior with a given role in life, so she can be no concern of his, least of all as a marriage partner. Bertram's mother, the Countess of Rossillion, however, has no such blindness to contend with. She accepts Helena for her superior qualities, dismisses Parolles, and enjoys Lavatch, though she pretends to do so reluctantly:

> *Countess.* My lord that's gone made himself much sport out of
> him [i.e., Lavatch]; by his authority he remains here, which he
> thinks is a patent for his sauciness; and indeed he has no pace,
> but runs where he will.
>
> (IV.v.61–64)

When we first meet Lavatch in I.iii, he is a great hindrance to a wordy fellow servant, who wishes to tell the Countess about Helena's affection for Bertram but cannot do so as long as Lavatch is present. We have already listened to Helena's own confession of her love for Bertram, and have sensed more than innocent romantic fantasies in her feelings. Now Lavatch puts further emphasis on the sexual aspects and problems of love and marriage, thus preparing the Countess for what she is to hear:

> *Lavatch.* . . . if I may have your ladyship's good will to go to
> the world, Isbel the woman and I will do as we may. . . . I
> think I shall never have the blessing of God till I have issue
> a' my body; for they say barnes are blessings.
> *Countess.* Tell me the reason why thou wilt marry.
> *Lavatch.* My poor body, madam, requires it; I am driven on by
> the flesh, and he must needs go that the devil drives. . . . I
> do marry that I may repent. . . . and I hope to have friends
> for my wife's sake. . . . the knaves come to do that for me
> which I am aweary of. . . . if I be his cuckold, he's my
> drudge. . . . If men could be contented to be what they are,
> there were no fear in marriage . . .
>   *For I the ballad will repeat*
>   *Which men full true shall find:*

> *Your marriage comes by destiny,*
> *Your cuckoo sings by kind.*

(I.iii.15–61)

In this scene, Lavatch, as it were, presents us with an image of the whole conflict of the play. Lavatch has a realistic view of the relationship between the sexes. Bertram's immature view is shaped by what he perceives to be society's expectations of him, both where the choice of a partner and the proofs of sexual prowess are concerned. Still, Lavatch shows some mirroring of Bertram. "Isbel the woman" is not a beloved individual, only a means to quench the urges of the flesh, and after Lavatch's journey to the court of France, he sees that

> Our old lings and our Isbels a' th' country are nothing like your old ling and your Isbels a' th' court. The brains of my Cupid's knock'd out, and I begin to love as an old man loves money, with no stomack.

(III.ii.12–16)

During this speech, the Countess is reading Bertram's letter, which tells of his unconsummated marriage and escape. Later he will woo and think he wins Diana, whom he will then spurn publicly. To Bertram, no woman becomes more than "an Isbel" of the town or country till Helena shows him that she has bested him (V.iii.298–310). Only then does a woman become a person to Bertram. And in the meantime, though he has not realized it, he has loved "with no stomack," has spent his whole marriage "repenting," and his "love" has been as barren as that of "an old man for money."

Already in I.iii, Lavatch associates mainly with women, who are the recipients of the better part of his wit and his bawdy remarks. This pattern will continue throughout the play. He does have scenes with Parolles, but because of his character Parolles can easily be seen as effeminate, and becomes the butt of Lavatch's jokes rather than the prompter of them.[1] The Countess, Lavatch's mistress, is the main whetstone for his wit, and certainly not without wit herself. Their conversations consist of the familiar question-and-answer game between jester and interlocutor we still may see among circus clowns or on the music hall stage. The Countess takes no offense at Lavatch's language and proffered opinions, she takes everything in her stride and gives as good as she gets. In I.iii, Lavatch sets out to comment on Helena directly but also gets in some remarks about the male sex, clearly aimed at Bertram, who is ripe and ready to behave just like the "friends" Lavatch would gain from marriage to Isbel. Lavatch demonstrates that there are two sides to the sowing of wild oats. There is the young man, who is indulgently tolerated and often applauded by society, but there is also the woman, and maybe a husband, who might not "be contented to be what [he is]" (I.iii.48), like a practical clown. Lavatch also makes use of the contrast seen throughout this play between age and youth. He sees himself and the Countess as experienced people who know the world, opposite to Bertram who is just setting out to commit all the mistakes of an inexperienced youth.

Helena, on the other hand, he calls "one good [woman] in ten" (I.iii.76), holding her forth as a great prize in the lottery-game of marriage. She is neither a city- nor a country-Isbel, but a person in her own right. Lavatch exits to fetch her with the words, "That man should be at woman's command, and yet no hurt done!" (I.iii.89–90), not only referring to his own position opposite the Countess, but to all the other relationships between the sexes, extant and yet to be established within the play.

The scene in which we next meet Lavatch, II.ii, contains no true action and very little matter to comment on the plot or help its forward motion. The only concrete thing happening is the dispatching of Lavatch with a message to the court where now both Bertram and Helena can be found. Still, Lavatch and the Countess demonstrate the power of words and the way words can be employed with different ends in mind. It is a wonderful scene for the clown. He has the opportunity to set up court and city against country life with all the laughter at the expense of the court. The audience, as thrilled by the sight of kings and nobility then as we are now,[2] have their point of view turned upside down by the clown. Lavatch has only contempt for other people's professed greatness, and for court matters and manners:

> I know my business is but to the court. . . . if God have lent a
> man any manners he may easily put it off at court: he that
> cannot make a leg, put off's cap, kiss his hand, and say
> nothing, has neither leg, hand, lip, nor cap; and indeed such a
> fellow, to say precisely, were not for the court.
>
> (II.ii.3–12)

Putting on such manners is very easy business; the audience has just seen him do it, for of course he has to act out his speech. He then proceeds to demonstrate that one answer will suffice in all situations, the magic words being "O Lord, sir!" and "O Lord, sir! Spare not me!" He takes a long time to disclose his all-purpose answer, and in the meanwhile succeeds in holding up to ridicule the emptiness of polite manners and a whole way of social interaction:

> *Countess*. Will your answer serve fit to all questions?
> *Lavatch*. As fit as ten groats is for the hands of an attorney, as
>   your French crown for your taffety punk, as Tib's rush for
>   Tom's forefinger, as a pancake for Shrove Tuesday, a morris
>   for May-day, as the nail to his hole, the cuckold to his horn,
>   as a scolding quean to a wrangling knave, as the nun's lip to
>   the friar's mouth; nay, as the pudding to his skin. . . . From
>   below your duke to beneath your constable, it will fit any
>   question.
>
> (II.ii.19–30)

Not only does Lavatch compile an incredible mixture of apparently unrelated examples with which to sharpen anticipation, he chooses them from among the lowest and least savory things he can imagine: simple food, blackmail, adultery, mock marriages, country festivities and their sexual connotations, and the professed looseness of monks and nuns. His string of examples is set up to prove that manners are put-on things intended to delude one's surroundings, and that language is a game where the most skilled will win the social battle, be he highborn or lowly. Unfortunately for Lavatch, the Countess herself is equally skilled in the manipulation of language, and the audience is presented with a most amusing scene indeed.

But the idea of language as a means of delusion rather than communication remains with the audience throughout the rest of the play. We do not, of course, see everybody doing this all the time, but knowingly or unknowingly everybody takes part in the game. Parolles is an instance in point and in turn provokes this same behavior in others. The most striking instances are the scenes where he goes to fetch his lost drum and is caught and interrogated by Bertram's friends to open Bertram's eyes to his lack of substance (III.vi, IV.i, and IV.iii). Parolles himself is just as aware of his manipulations of language as Lavatch is. But Parolles is by no means the only one engaging in verbal games with intent to delude. Helena persuades Diana's mother to have her daughter do the bed-trick (III.vii), and Diana herself is not unskilled with words as she proves when she carries out the trick in IV.ii.

All the games the characters play are exposed at some point, and for this Lavatch's scene with the Countess also prepares us. He has to admit that his phrase "may serve long, but not serve ever" (II.ii.53) when the Countess traps him. Similarly, Parolles must admit that his tongue has brought him too far (IV.iii) like Diana, who exposes herself to the King's wrath (V.iii). Helena herself gets around Bertram's verbal trick of the letter. His language did not tell her "never" though he thought it did. Unlike Lavatch, who bounces back after his little verbal defeat and finds that his magic phrase "serves well again" (II.ii.56), Bertram has been totally and irrevocably caught.

Finally this scene establishes Lavatch's position in the Rossillion household. This is his scene alone with his mistress, and the two clearly are comfortable together and enjoy each other. The audience is willing to accept the Countess as the voice of sense and reason within the play, already favorably impressed with her handling of Helena's wish to go to court and her demonstration of the clarity with which she sees through her fellow creatures (I.iii). After this scene we come to love her. Lavatch with his wit and wordplay helps establish her as the deeply humane, faceted, and warm touchstone of this play.[3] The country and the genuine values found there are established as the moral center of the play's world.

Lavatch never gets the opportunity to exercise his wit or try out his all-purpose answer on true courtiers at court, but he does carry his message there, and in II.iv we meet him, giving his message to Helena and being interrupted in a very traditional bit of punning by Parolles. This sparks yet another of Lavatch's ingenious comments on the use of language and how speech characterizes people:

> *Parolles.* Why, I say nothing.
> *Lavatch.* Marry, you are the wiser man; for many a man's
> tongue shakes out his master's undoing. To say nothing, to
> do nothing, to know nothing, and to have nothing, is to be

> a great part of your title, which is within a very little of
> nothing.
>
> (II.iv.21–26)

After this shrewd piece of advice from Lavatch, Parolles proceeds to tell Helena about Bertram's intended departure and pass on his orders to her in florid verse; instead of saying nothing and knowing nothing, Parolles involves himself more deeply in the deception (II.iii.261–296). Lavatch is present till the end of the scene, where Helena calls for him to depart with her. Back at Rossillion, he is able to comment on Bertram's behavior and character from his own observation (III.ii). The Countess is happy, because apparently "It hath happen'd all as I would have had it" (III.ii.1), which in turn prompts Lavatch's comments on what he calls Bertram's melancholy:

> I take my young lord to be a very melancholy man. . . . Why,
> he will look upon his boot and sing; mend the ruff and sing;
> ask questions and sing; pick his teeth and sing. I know a man
> that had this trick of melancholy sold a goodly manor for a
> song.
>
> (III.ii.3–9)

Bertram has indeed done his best to "[sell] a goodly manor for a song," when he chose Parolles as an advisor, and casually left Helena. Lavatch carries the idea of the whim even further, choosing sexuality as his example. He addresses the audience directly, while the Countess reads her letter, and declares that the sight of the ladies at court has cured him of his longing for Isbel (III.ii.11–16). This statement reflects the clown's traditional avoidance of physical contact with the female sex; now, back from court, Lavatch is no longer interested in Isbel. But the statement also reflects how carelessly Bertram throws away the King's favor, his mother's approval, and a loving wife.

He leaves the Countess to comment on her letter alone and express an uninterrupted opinion of her son to the audience. When he returns to announce Helena's arrival, he has more scathing comments about Bertram, disguised as comfort. The Countess does not rebuke him, for she sees the truth of his words. According to Lavatch, there is some virtue in running away, at least "your son will not be killed as soon as I thought he would . . . if he run away, as I hear he does," but there will be no "getting of children" either, because there is no "standing to't" (III.ii.36–41). Here again Lavatch favors the women in the play, because strength and goodness are concentrated there.

After this scene, Lavatch and Rossillion retreat into the background, while the play is given over to the young people. The audience witnesses the truth of many of Lavatch's observations, but does not need the actual presence of a court jester to promote laughter. When events are ripe, everybody again converges upon Rossillion for the conclusion of the play.

The courtier Lafew has come there to offer his daughter in marriage to Bertram, and he is happily accepted (IV.v). Now Lavatch demonstrates his license and ability as a court jester, and though Lafew's wit is great, Lavatch succeeds in besting him. The humor is of two varieties. First of all there are the traditional bawdy exchanges, where Lavatch professes to be "[a] fool . . . at a woman's service, and a knave at a man's" (22–23), but there is also a darker side to the fun, represented by Lavatch's jokes about Hell and the devil, deftly linked with sexuality. This association lingers in the audience's mind at the conclusion of the scene, where Lavatch announces the arrival of Bertram:

> *Lavatch.* O madam, yonder's my lord your son with a patch of
>   velvet on's face; whether there be a scar under't or no, the
>   velvet knows. . . .
> *Lafew.* A scar nobly got, a noble scar, is a good liv'ry of
>   honour; so belike is that.
> *Lavatch.* But it is your carbonado'd face.
>
>   (IV.v.90–97)

Here, the romantic notion of noble scars won in war and the unromantic scars acquired under the surgeon's knife in an attempt to cure syphilis become united, and the dark side to sexuality is stressed once again. So is Bertram's faulty character: this is the young man Lafew wanted for his daughter.

Following the pattern of his fellow clowns in smaller parts, Lavatch disappears before the resolution at end of the play. We meet him for the last time in V.ii with Parolles. Parolles is at a low point, and Lavatch is in a position to call him names as Parolles begs him for a favor:

> *Parolles.* Good Master Lavatch, give my Lord Lafew this
>   letter; . . . I am now, sir muddied in Fortune's mood, and
>   smell somewhat strong of her strong displeasure.
> *Lavatch.* . . . I will henceforth eat no fish of Fortune's
>   butt'ring. Prithee, allow the wind.
> *Parolles.* Nay, you need not stop your nose, sir. I spake but by
>   a metafor.
> *Lavatch.* Indeed, sir, if your metafor stink I will stop my nose,
>   or against any man's metafor. Prithee, get thee further. . . .
>   Prithee stand away. A paper from Fortune's close-stool, to
>   give a nobleman!
>
>   (V.ii.1–17)

Lavatch then proceeds to speak of Parolles to Lafew as "not a musk-cat," "[a] carp," and finally "rascally knave" (20–24). Parolles has tried to make use of Lavatch in his capacity as a messenger, but he is brushed off soundly and kept waiting so long that the very Lord he seeks sees him in his plight. Many modern editions give the stage direction *Exit* for Lavatch after line twenty-five, but there is no *Exit* for him here in the Folio. In this as in so many other instances it would be effective to keep the clown on stage in full view, making gestures and faces behind the backs of the others. Lavatch has been able to assume Parolles's affected mannerisms at the beginning of the scene, holding his nose and waving his hand to clear the air of the horrible stink of the braggart. Probably Lafew will use these very gestures himself, mirrored by Lavatch.

But Parolles is saved by Lafew and assured of food. We have here a foreshadowing of the end, where

> "the time will bring on summer"—
> When briars shall have leaves as well as thorns
> And be as sweet as sharp . . .
> All's well that ends well.

(IV.iv.31–35)

This is not necessarily an unquestionably happy end even for Helena but she can be content. In his last scene Lavatch is back to pure joking, and there is no sinister layer of meaning under his name-calling. Now even Bertram has seen through Parolles and been made free of his influence, but even Parolles deserves to live, if not in splendor.

Bertram himself is pulled down like Parolles in the last scene. Lafew no longer wants him for a son-in-law after he has been exposed, and the King is ready to execute him as Helena's murderer, but Helena herself offers him a new life as her husband. Parolles's words "I praise God for you" (V.ii.52) sounds much like Bertram's "If she, my liege, can make me know this clearly/I'll love her dearly, ever, ever dearly." They both accept their fate.

Lavatch the clown has not been truly involved in the development of the play itself, but he has been an important instrument for the audience to understand the characters and their motivations, and create audience sympathy. The role of Lavatch is necessary for the clarification of the moral structure of *All's Well That Ends Well*.

NOTES

1. In performance, Parolles is almost invariably overdressed and trimmed in lace, constantly conscious of his appearance. Moreover, there are character traits like his cowardice, his fear of pain, his special variety of hypocrisy, and his way of associating with other males to mark him as effeminate.

2. The cover of any popular magazine will prove this point; today we have the added spice provided by the less blueblooded celebrities as well.

3. In all scenes of importance for the outcome of the plot, the Countess is present or has given consent. Helena "woos" Bertram with her blessing, and even the conclusion of the play with its numerous resolutions takes place at Rossillion.

9

Touchstone in *As You Like It*

Touchstone of *As You Like It* is probably the clown who has had most attention from critics. He is so well integrated in the play that at times he can seem to be a real participant. His part is undoubtedly a large one, and he is on stage regularly throughout the play. Touchstone is indeed an interesting object of analysis, and at times we may feel that we know him well and intimately, but what we really know is the pattern of the clown's part, and such predictability may mislead us.

Rosalind and Celia first prepare us for Touchstone. Rosalind uses the term "Nature's natural" (I.ii.47), for as Touchstone enters the ladies have been sporting their own wit and skill at punning, playing with the word "nature." A term like this comes easily to Rosalind's nimble mind. Celia speaks of "the dullness of the fool [which] is the whetstone of the wits" (52–53), but neither remark describes Touchstone's abilities, and his very first mental capers are far from "dull":

> *Touchstone.* No, by mine honour, but I was bid to come for you.
> *Celia.* Where learned you that oath, fool?
> *Touchstone.* Of a certain knight, that swore by his honour they were good pancakes, and swore by his honour the mustard was nought. Now, I'll stand to it, the pancakes were naught and the mustard was good, and yet was not the knight forsworn. . . . Stand you both forth now: stroke your chins, and swear by your beards that I am a knave.
> *Celia.* By our beards, if we had them, thou art.
> *Touchstone.* By my knavery, if I had it, then I were. But if you swear by that that is not, you are not forsworn.
>
> (I.ii.57–71)

Touchstone takes his examples from two widely different worlds, the common man's table with its pancakes and mustard and the lofty spheres of knights and unreliable honor. We are reminded of our knowledge of the very court in which we stand with Touchstone. He needs no "transformation" from the lowly to the witty, his wit is ready, sharp, and to the point from the very beginning. He grasps the opportunity to rail at the two witty ladies, "The more pity that fools may not speak wisely what wisemen do foolishly," and now he is acknowledged by Celia, "By my troth, thou sayest true" (I.ii.80–82). Touchstone is far too involved in the court circles to be "Nature's natural," he is an allowed or artificial fool and can therefore be expected to have considerable intelligence. But first and foremost he is a brilliant stage clown, and his duty as such is in serving the interests of the audience.

Touchstone, more than any other of Shakespeare's jester clowns, works well paired off with another player. Our first experience of him in this capacity is at the opening of II.iv, the arrival of the disguised travellers in Arden, where Rosalind sparks his wit: "O Jupiter, how weary are my spirits!" and Touchstone replies, "I care not for my spirits, if my legs were not weary" (II.iv.1–2). The audience has already developed an affection for Rosalind. We know of her background, her sweetness and resolution, and with Touchstone we have seen her falling comically in love.[1] We have thoroughly enjoyed her worry during the wrestling match, her giving Orlando a favor, and her unwillingness to part from him. Now Touchstone reminds us of this scene as he comments on the unhappy love of Silvius the shepherd:

> *Rosalind.* Alas, poor shepherd, searching of thy wound,
>   I have by hard adventure found my own.
> *Touchstone.* And I mine. I remember when I was in love I
>   broke my sword upon a stone, and bid him take that for
>   coming a-night to Jane Smile. . .
>
>   (II.iv.41–45)

Silvius's lament is in conventional verse, and lovesick Rosalind echoes him. When Touchstone breaks in with his mock lament in prose, using the most down-to-earth examples, the audience is alerted to the empty ring of Silvius's conventional phrasing, but also made aware that Rosalind's love needs maturing if it is to become real and lasting. Touchstone uses a wonderful technique, taking the lofty and making it ridiculous by putting the conventions to lowly use. The challenge to a duel becomes a sword broken on a stone, so at this point Touchstone will be brandishing his wooden sword furiously.[2] The reason for the challenge is not romantic, it is a direct accusation of sexual congress, and moreover it is not delivered to the rival but, as if practicing, to a mere stone, which cannot come "a-night" to anyone. Still the stone proves to be his superior and breaks the sword. In the wording of this monologue there are innumerable suggestions to the actor on how to behave on stage. The prime purpose, though, whether or not props are involved, must be heavy underscoring of the sexual aspects of love and courtship, so different from Silvius's stilted nonsense. Touchstone's sword can serve excellently as a prop to embody each and every reference to the penis. It will be a good batler, a fine peascod, could even be milked and kissed like the udder, and naturally serves grandly for a sword. The whole idea of romantic love is summed up at the very end of the speech: "We that are true lovers run into strange capers;[3] but as all is mortal in nature, so is all nature in love mortal in folly" (II.iv.51–53), and Rosalind replies, "Thou speak'st wiser than thou art ware of." This point can and should be debated. Rosalind and Celia, and later Jaques, interact with Touchstone the court jester and treat him like the inferior he is supposed to be. His wit is expected to be brilliant, but as far as intelligence is concerned he is seen as belonging on a lower plane. To the audience there can be no question that Touchstone is constantly aware of and adjusting to the people he associates with, and he lays bare their every folly at such an early point in time that we can anticipate what our protagonists will be doing next. Touchstone lifts the audience to a higher level, from which they can view the "strange capers" on stage from the delightful distance this new transparency brings. After all, there is no joke quite as enjoyable as the one we have seen through beforehand.

But Touchstone does not even have to be present on stage for him to make his points and for us to enjoy his mirror of the world. In II.vii Jaques comes to the court of Duke Senior and reports a meeting with "a motley fool" in the forest. Jaques, the self-established malcontent, who "[him]self [has] been a libertine" (II.vii.65), has been made "ambitious for a motley coat" (43); he exposes himself and his ulterior motives to the audience by quoting what Touchstone has said to him, and his own overjoyed reactions. In his delight he repeats Touchstone's by now familiar actions and style as best he can, but instead of becoming parallel to the fool, maybe even his successful rival, he is an abuser of the license to which he aspires. Touchstone's mirror shows us Jaques's distortion.

What Jaques has marked most clearly is the clown's opportunity for castigating comments. First of all there is the famous "dial speech" with all its punning, which is made unsavory by Jaques's approach;[4] moreover, Touchstone is said to have exposed the conceit of the young ladies at court (37–38), but we already know Touchstone's views. Jaques envies the freedom of expression of the court jester. In the speed of performance every aspect of the mirroring and distortion may not emerge clearly, but an audience does not have to be consciously aware of every little tool of Shakespeare's trade for it to work. Duke Senior speaks to a well-prepared house when he chastises Jaques (II.vii.64–69). To any audience Touchstone's mission, even when he is absent, is perfectly clear.

The Forest of Arden itself and its symbolic function as representative of a golden age is also utilized, mirrored, and mocked by Touchstone. It is interesting to note that the character of Touchstone is one of few additions Shakespeare made to Lodge's *Rosalynde* , the main source of this play, and that the idea of comic mirroring is Shakespeare's own. It serves to expose the reverse of life in Arden to any who might be romantically inclined, and later it will serve to castigate Rosalind and her romantic sentiments to the joy of the audience.[5] In III.ii, paired off with Corin, Touchstone describes life in Arden:

> [I]n respect of itself, it is a good life; but in respect that it is a
> shepherd's life, it is naught. In respect that it is solitary, I like

it very well; but in respect that it is private, it is a very vile
life. Now in respect that it is in the fields, it pleaseth me well;
but in respect it is not in the court, it is tedious. As it is a
spare life, look you, it fits my humour well; but as there is no
more plenty in it, it goes much against my stomack.

(III.ii.13–21)

Touchstone even succeeds in cornering Corin and delivering the final blow to the
innocence of a shepherd's life, and at the same time he prepares the audience for
the love scenes to come:

Corin. . . . the greatest of my pride is to see my ewes graze
and my lambs suck.
Touchstone. That is another simple sin in you, to bring the
ewes and the rams together, and to offer to get your living
by the copulation of cattle; to be a bawd to a bell-wether,
and to betray a she-lamb of a twelvemonth to a crooked-
pated old cuckoldly ram, out of all reasonable match.

(III.ii.74–81)

Touchstone's railing against the conventionally pure and innocent life in an
unspoilt setting invests even the ideal life of a shepherd with rampant sexuality.
The comedy is delightful when Rosalind enters with one of Orlando's
conventionally romantic verses, which is extremely badly written. To the
modern-day audience her disguise lends extra comedy to the scene, and
Shakespeare's audience had the added spice of knowing that they were watching a
boy playing a girl dressed up as a boy, sexually a most confusing and amusing
combination; but any actress delivering a rapt reading of this awful doggerel will
provoke laughter:

From the east to western Inde
No jewel is like Rosalind.
Her worth being mounted on the wind,
Through all the world bears Rosalind.

(III.ii.86–89)

Touchstone, never in the mood for this kind of nonsense, proceeds to
demonstrate what these verses lack:

If a hart do lack a hind,
Let him seek out Rosalind.
If the cat will after kind,
So be sure will Rosalind.

(II.ii.99–102)

The audience cannot help seeing Touchstone's point; amidst our laughter at this
sheer nonsense, delivered partly to us, we realize that any healthy human union
cannot thrive on airy nothings. Touchstone could be supported by Celia, who

could give a scathing reading of the next Orlandian verse; but Rosalind still has her head buried in a pink cloud, and Touchstone leaves in disgust (157–159). Rosalind/Ganymede's scene with Orlando in III.ii certainly demonstrates how "all nature in love [is] mortal in folly."

Rosalind is about to have Orlando woo her in her boy's disguise, a most comic situation, but despite the fun the audience sees Rosalind's feelings mature during the courtship. Orlando's views are also expanding, and his perception of the female sex is becoming less romantic. The comedy of the wooing is delightful, and it is made even more so by the contrast provided by Touchstone's wooing of Audrey. The two share the remainder of Touchstone's scenes; he has been furnished with a living prop, not unlike Launce's dog Crab.

The very fact that Touchstone admits to having sexual feelings and is willing to act upon them sets him apart from most of his brother clowns, and only Costard goes further than Touchstone. They both use their own sexuality to teach the audience about the world of the play. In *Love's Labour's Lost*, Costard's admission comes early because the audience needs this pointer to bring home the futility of the king's decree. We are being guided into an interpretation, and the rest of the play will be seen and understood accordingly. Lavatch and Launce also demonstrate some interest in women. Lavatch claims to be "driven on by the flesh" (I.iii.26–27) and to want "issue of [his] body" (23), but his interest in "Isbel the woman" disappears soon enough. Launce of *The Two Gentlemen of Verona* reads us the catalogue of his milkmaid lady-love (III.i.263–360) to show us the role of calculated wooing in this play. But both Launce and Lavatch keep their sexuality within the accepted bounds for a clown; everything remains at the verbal stage, and the "lovers" are never seen together. Costard's and Touchstone's sexuality is more intricate, but specifically because their respective plays demand this. Shakespeare keeps the clown type unblemished, however, by never having a true love scene between Costard and Jaquenetta, and never letting Touchstone accomplish anything physical because of Audrey's prudishness. But the couples are together on stage, and this opens up the possibility for various forms of comic clown courtship, which could well become quite rowdy. Still, both Costard and Touchstone stay within tradition. Their sexuality—blatant indeed for a clown—serves to create understanding of and distance from the madness of a world which has willfully chosen celibacy, or where male and female are totally intermixed and indistinguishable to the lover both in appearance and behavior.

The lady loves of Lavatch and Launce can be seen on stage only at the discretion of a director. Jaquenetta is more substantial with a sizable part and a comic effect of her own, but Audrey is quite another matter. She can well be seen as Touchstone's comic partner after the pattern of Dogberry and Verges or Stephano and Trinculo. Audrey is the passive, Touchstone the active partner of the relationship, which serves as an ingenious mirroring of the Rosalind-Orlando courtship. Where Rosalind is in control of the maturing love between herself and Orlando, Audrey is in control of the static relationship between herself and Touchstone; and Touchstone is mirroring Rosalind who ought to remain passive, being beloved and female. The clownish lovers constantly remind the audience of the physical aspects of love, a purpose elegantly served by the Celia-

Oliver union as well. Moreover, the more foolish aspects of the wooing and winning of Orlando are held up to ridicule.

The parallels between the Touchstone-Audrey and the Rosalind-Orlando unions are legion, for example the lovers' use of their mistresses' names. The first nine lines of the fifth act has Touchstone use the name "Audrey" no less than four times, and Orlando uses "Rosalind" constantly. Rosalind's name can be spoken in many ways, as we see from Orlando's and especially Touchstone's rhymes, but Audrey's, which is connected with goats and sheep in our consciousness, can be given a baa-ing or lowing sound which will suit her slovenly appearance, her occupation, and the affair generally.

In III.iii, Touchstone and Audrey discuss poetry, recalling Rosalind's reading of Orlando's verses:

> *Touchstone.* When a man's verses cannot be understood, nor a man's good wit seconded with the forward child, understanding, it strikes a man more dead than a great reckoning in a little room. Truly, I would the gods had made thee poetical.
>
> *Audrey.* I do not know what 'poetical' is. Is it honest in deed and word? Is it a true thing?
>
> *Touchstone.* No truly; for the truest poetry is the most feigning, and lovers are given to poetry; and what they swear in poetry may be said as lovers they do feign.
>
> *Audrey.* Do you wish then that the gods had made me poetical?
>
> *Touchstone.* I do truly. For thou swear'st to me thou art honest. Now if thou wert a poet, I might have some hope thou didst feign.
>
> (III.iii.9–23)

Where Orlando's poetry is written as an outlet for passion, Touchstone sees the medium as a route of ingress into the fortress of the female. Orlando innocently expresses his infatuation, Touchstone sees poetry itself as devious, as a means of subtle communication. Only once is Touchstone directly involved with poetry itself. In V.iii he may or may not join in the singing of "There Was a Lover and His Lass," but he is certainly listening with Audrey. The song has the usual *carpe diem* theme, which Audrey could have been expected to comment negatively upon, but she refrains. The word "poetry" is not included in even her passive vocabulary.

While there is no doubt that Rosalind is intended to be a beautiful and admirable specimen of womanhood, Audrey is her opposite. She admits to ugliness herself (III.iii.29), and Touchstone is by no means blinded by Cupid: "A poor virgin sir, an ill-favoured thing sir, but mine own; a poor humour of mine sir, to take that no man else will" (V.iv.57–60). This, however, is not quite true. In V.i, Audrey's professed lover William appears on stage. William is a country clod, totally devoid of wit and an unworthy rival of Touchstone's. Audrey, who is always keeping up her image of the pure and honest woman, denies any relationship with William; still she is flattered to have the attention of two males. The audience sees an amusing parallel to another lover's triangle in the forest, the one between Silvius, Phebe, and Rosalind/Ganymede (III.v), with Touchstone acting comically in Rosalind's part, that of the omniscient controller. The difference between Touchstone and the two rustics is just as great as the one between Rosalind and the shepherds, but where Rosalind uses her knowledge of the hopelessness of Phebe's infatuation to punish kindly, Touchstone becomes intimidating:

> *Touchstone.* . . . Now you are not *ipse*, for I am he.
> *William.* Which he sir?
> *Touchstone.* He sir that must marry this woman. Therefore
> you clown, abandon—which is in the vulgar leave—the
> society—which in the boorish is company—of this female-
> -which in the common is woman. Which together is,
> abandon the society of this female, or clown thou perishest;
> or to thy better understanding, diest; or, to wit, I kill thee . . .
> Therefore tremble and depart.
> *Audrey* . Do, good William.
> *William.* God rest you merry, sir.
>
> (V.i.43–59)

There is wonderful opportunity for Touchstone to clown in this scene, and for Audrey to contribute her share. In close contact with the audience, Touchstone has gradually worked his way from feigned friendliness to equally feigned frenzy, and he delivers his challenge capering about William and brandishing his wooden sword, making himself as large and dangerous as possible. Touchstone often uses his "superior learning" to best an opponent or score a point, and he never hesitates to use his "courtly" ways against the inhabitants of the forest. We know from Jaques that Touchstone's dress is "motley."[6] Whatever a director chooses to dress Touchstone in, there should always be an element of the comic in his garb to set him apart. When he blows himself up with words, the ridiculousness will be underscored and magnified by his clothes. Whatever such a fellow claims to intend, he will never convince his audience of ill intentions, we know that such wordiness never produces action. William's polite leave-taking, cap in hand, makes Touchstone's victory almost ridiculous, but still we love him. Audrey, though proud of her lover's prowess, must show some concern for William's welfare, so she hastens his departure and may even shoo him along, for a duel would stain her reputation.

The placing of the comical lovers' triangle lays the foundation for the audience's perception of the confrontation with the shepherds (V.ii.76). The four voices repeating their refrain would be amusing even without a Touchstone, but after we have just seen the thoroughly comic lovers in action, this sighing and moaning becomes doubly ridiculous:

> *Phebe.* . . . . tell this youth what 'tis to love.
> *Silvius.* It is to be all made of sighs and tears,
>   And so am I for Phebe
> *Phebe.* And I for Ganymede.
> *Orlando.* And I for Rosalind.

Rosalind. And I for no woman.
Silvius. It is to be all made of faith and service,
    And so am I for Phebe.
Phebe. And I for Ganymede.
Orlando. And I for Rosalind.
Rosalind. And I for no woman.

                                                    V.ii.82–92)

The rhythm of the repetitions may suggest a dancelike choreography, which
would add to the comedy. Still, amidst our amusement, we can see that Rosalind
is playing her tricks with greater and greater skill, not only exposing the
conventionality of the shepherds but also her beloved Orlando, who joins in the
sighing; she herself does not.

Throughout the last half of the play there is much talk about marriage.
Marriage is always a part of Rosalind's and Orlando's wooing, but Touchstone's
ideas are of another stamp. He knows that marriage is the only way to gain
ground with Audrey, and because his intentions are far from honorable he tries to
get around the conventions as best he can. His whole ploy is set up and fails in
III.iii:

> *Touchstone.* . . . sluttishness may come hereafter. But be it as
> it may be, I will marry thee; and to that end I have been with
> Sir Oliver Martext, the vicar of the next village, who hath
> promised to meet me in this place of the forest and to couple
> us.
>   .   .   .
>
> *Audrey.* Well, the gods give us joy!
>
>   (III.iii.34–41)

Both Touchstone's choice of words and the vicar's name clearly indicate to the
audience what his true intentions are, and he reveals as much a short while later
in conversation with Jaques:

> *Touchstone.* As the ox has his bow sir, the horse his curb, and
>   the falcon her bells, so man has his desires, and as pigeons
>   bill, so wedlock would be nibbling.
> *Jaques.* . . . Get you to church and have a good priest that can
>   tell you what marriage is. This fellow will but join you
>   together as they join wainscot; then one of you will prove a
>   shrunk panel, and like green timber, warp, warp.
> *Touchstone* [*aside*]. I am not in the mind but I were better to
>   be married of him than of another, for he is not like to
>   marry me well; and not being well married, it will be a good
>   excuse for me hereafter to leave my wife.   .   .   . Come,
>   sweet Audrey,
> We must be married or we must live in bawdry.
>
>   (III.iii.70–88)

Touchstone only seeks sexual gratification. The wife is not the bow, the curb, and the bells; his desires are. The woman he will deal with later if necessary. Sexual desire is present, unpleasant, and must be served. His feelings for Audrey are summed up well in the final rhyme on her name.

When next we see the couple, marriage is still under discussion (V.i). Apparently Touchstone has fled Sir Oliver in fear of being truly bound, for Audrey was willing enough to accept the vicar, "the priest was good enough, for all the old gentleman's saying" (3–4). Apparently Audrey's decision to remain chaste until marriage stands firm, for Touchstone repeatedly returns to the subject. In the scene with William it is, "I am he . . . that must marry this woman" (V.i.43–45), and the opening lines of V.iii are

> *Touchstone.* Tomorrow is the joyful day, Audrey, tomorrow
> will we be married.
> *Audrey.* I do desire it with all my heart; and I hope it is no
> dishonest desire, to desire to be a woman of the world.
>
> (V.iii.1–5)

Rosalind's plotting gradually solves problems and slowly imposes order on her self-created chaos, and likewise Touchstone is brought to order by Audrey; no mean feat, and a very comical one. Where before he was all for bawdry, now he seems to be all for Audrey, and in performance this comes out clearly. At the beginning he is the active partner in the relationship, wooing her in a mock-pastoral, mock-conventional manner by helping with her goats and sheep (III.iii). All the while the audience is well aware of his sexual innuendo and attempts at seduction; goats are notorious lechers as we all know. But in the fifth act Touchstone has given in, and more comedy is created. Audrey may even lead the way in this act. She can come in trailing him behind in her relentless pursuit of marriage and honesty, which now begins to sound like female blackmail. In other regards Touchstone seems himself to the very end. As the problem-solving marriage ceremony approaches, all the protagonists are assembled on stage and Touchstone delivers his famous speech on "[the] lie seven times removed" and "the degrees of the lie" to Jaques (V.iv.67–102). Touchstone in the forest was somewhat out of depth amidst fatigue and hardship and maneuvered about by a woman. Touchstone at the court is quite another matter. Here he may sport his wit and be understood and praised. He is in his element as a court jester. But even Touchstone is not allowed to escape from the sea-change Arden works upon everybody who enters, and he emerges saddled with a wife. Still, his last remark is in praise of the great "virtue of If" (102).

Touchstone is not allowed to escape the stage. He has to be present with his Audrey at both the wedding ceremony and the final dance, and he will make his mark on both. Hymen addresses Touchstone and his wife with "You and you are sure together/As the winter and foul weather" (V.iv.134–135); and Jaques says, "And you to wrangling, for thy loving voyage/Is but for two months victuall'd" (190–191). Winter and foul weather may not promise the brightest of prospects, but they are suited to each other. Seeing Touchstone and Audrey with the three other couples will demonstrate to the audience that the four unions are seriously joined, not just a two months' venture as Jaques suggests, and this makes the impression even more comical. Here is our sprightly Touchstone tamed by a female, and what a female! But so was Orlando and Oliver, and both Silvius and Phebe for that matter. Audrey gradually gains the upper hand in the battle between the sexes, and she can make a wonderful, comic contribution to the clown partnership in the process. Fortunately Touchstone is not diminished by his sexual defeat, and during the final dance if not during the marriage ceremony he and Audrey must stand for the purely physical aspect of marriage, where Silvius and Phebe represent the tensions of the power struggle, and Celia and Oliver the true accord, all of which are elements of Rosalind's and Orlando's ideal union.

NOTES

1. In I.ii Touchstone last speaks the lines 127–129, but he is given no exit. It is an excellent idea to let him remain with the two young women and let him underscore the comedy of Rosalind and Orlando's falling in love by parodying their gestures, looks, and sighs in intimate detail.

2. There are many indications that the clown's sword was indeed made of wood, the most famous example being Shakespeare's own; he lets Feste sing of it in *Twelfth Night*, IV.ii.125–132. Why mention a "dagger of lath" if the clown was not brandishing one at the time?

3. His "we" will not include Silvius, but will include Rosalind and himself and everybody in the audience.

4. "And so from hour/whore to hour/whore we ripe/search, and ripe/search, /And then from hour/whore to hour/whore we rot and rot (from syphilis),/And thereby hangs a tale/tail/penis" (26–28). See H. Kökeritz, *Shakespeare's Pronunciation* (New Haven: Yale University Press, 1953), 58–59.

5. Duke Senior himself is well aware of the hunger and cold this world may offer its people. Touchstone is wary, already on entering it: "now I am in Arden, the more fool I; when I was at home I was in a better place, but travellers must be content" (II.iv.13–15).

6. For a competent discussion of what "motley" probably looked like, see Leslie Hotson, *Shakespeare's Motley* (London: Rupert Hart-Davis, 1952); and Guy Butler, "Shakespeare and Two Jesters" (*Hebrew University Studies in Literature and the Arts* 11 no. 2, 1983).

10

Feste in *Twelfth Night*

Feste more than any other Shakespearean clown works and plays with the use and abuse of language. In *Twelfth Night* the audience is brought into a world of paradoxes and contradictions in terms of the world in which we live and operate, physically as well as linguistically. As in *The Tempest*, the outside world is represented by intruders, but in *Twelfth Night* there is no returning to an unromantic reality outside Illyria.[1] The outsiders, Viola and Sebastian, are absorbed and integrated. Illyria contains only two layers, that of the Duke and the Lady Olivia and their circles, and that of Sir Toby and his comic group. The two layers cannot be termed social, for Sir Toby is the Lady Olivia's cousin, and he and Sir Andrew are both "knights." Still, Sir Toby, dragging Sir Andrew with him, has chosen to operate on a level socially beneath him. Between the groups, with total social, mental, and physical mobility, we find Feste, Olivia's court jester and the clown of the play.

Feste's clowning primarily consists of two levels, the sophisticated verbal acrobatics he performs with the court circles and the more earthy interaction with the comic group. He is equally at home operating alone and as an element in a group. The comic group's mirroring of the higher level is to a large extent made available to the audience by Feste's interaction and mediation, as is the interplay between the two courts. In one way, however, Feste distinguishes himself totally from his brother court jesters; he remains completely aloof from the love intrigues, he does not take sides, and the only time he actively participates he does so to punish. He is most often presented on stage as a wizened, gnomelike man, and in several respects he is a reflection of an earlier, less complex stage clown, often almost vice-like. His jesting has many malicious elements. Also, Feste more than any other of Shakespeare's clowns makes use of what might be called utter nonsense and indeed calls himself "not [the Lady Olivia's] fool, but her corrupter of words" (III.i.36–37). His attitude to language is a reflection of what serves his best interests at the time. He begs diligently, he twists the meaning of words, and he uses them to expose the protagonists of the play.

Feste has little time to lavish on the audience alone in the form of monologues and must constantly perform a balancing act between the stage, where he is actively involved in conversation, and the audience, who needs and enjoys his mediation, but because of his verbal—and presumably physical—agility this distance is neatly bridged.

In *Twelfth Night*, it is perfectly possible for the audience to fall into the trap comedies often set for us, identifying all too readily with values and attitudes so excessive as to be ridiculous. Both Orsino and Olivia are representatives of such things. Orsino's love is ludicrous in its conventional sentimentality, for he is in love with the idea of love more than with his lady and thoroughly enjoying it.[2] Olivia's errors are also in the vein of conventional sentimentality, but she isolates herself and protests immunity to love because of grief. Feste's function is as the audience's guide; he stops us from adopting any of these viewpoints by demonstrating their comic hollowness.

Music is highly prized at Orsino's court for its effects on the Duke's feelings. The value he assigns to any piece of music is as subjective and changeable as his attitude to love:

> That strain again, it had a dying fall:
> O, it came o'er my ear like the sweet sound
> That breathes upon a bank of violets,
> Stealing and giving odour. Enough, no more;
> 'Tis not so sweet now as it was before.
>
> (I.i.4–8)

Feste, who is given more songs than any other Shakespearean clown, is in a wonderful position to use Orsino's moods in the interplay between stage and audience. In II.iv Orsino longs for a particular song, which has "relieved [his] passion much" (4), but he is unable to remember who sang it. While a courtier, who does remember, goes to find Feste, whose very name awakens the audience's anticipation, Orsino discusses sentimental love with Viola, who has already learned how to handle him:

> *Duke.* . . . play the tune the while.
> . . . How dost thou like this tune?
> *Viola.* It gives a very echo to the seat
> Where love is thron'd.
> *Duke.*   Thou dost speak masterly.
>
> (II.iv.14–23)

The song is described at length while Feste is present. He should demonstrate considerable unwillingness to stand idle while the Duke lectures Viola, and his first remark indicates two things to the audience: he is impatient with Orsino's sentimentality, and he knows Orsino well. His "Are you ready, sir?" (49) can be delivered with scathing irony and a heavy stress on "ready." The song itself, "Come away, come away death" (51–66) certainly does not conform to Orsino's description, an indication that the feelings he superimposes on every available object clouds his judgment.

The song is not what "[t]he spinsters and the knitters in the sun, /And the free maids that weave their thread with bones" (44–45) would sing, and there is no dalliance with "the innocence of love" (47) as promised. Feste delivers beautiful lyrics, but it is a man's song and it describes Orsino and his protested passion to perfection. The preoccupation with death, being "slain by a fair cruel maid," the black, unadorned coffin, and the lonely grave are all part of conventional love lyrics. But this sophisticated little gem is delivered by the Clown, which reflects on both Orsino's infatuation and on love in general.[3] When Feste sings this song, it can easily be made into a joke between him and the audience. Feste does not have to present the lyrics straightforwardly; he is free to add his own element of parody to it and could easily make an exposition of Orsino's "pain" and his whole attitude to love.

Because of the contrast between the contents of the song and the context in which it is delivered, Feste immediately creates a wonderful piece of mockery, a great distance where criticism may thrive, between Orsino and the audience. Indeed the Duke is oblivious to what Feste has accomplished, so Feste repeats the lesson as he is rewarded, still with no effect on Orsino but to the delight of the audience:

> *Duke*. There's for thy pains.
> *Feste*. No pains, sir, I take pleasure in singing, sir.
> *Duke*. I'll pay thy pleasure then.
> *Feste*. Truly sir, and pleasure will be paid, one time or another.
> *Duke*. Give me now leave to leave thee.
> *Feste*. Now the melancholy god protect thee, and the tailor make thy doublet of changeable taffeta, for thy mind is a very opal. I would have men of such constancy put to sea, that their business might be everything, and their intent everywhere, for that's it that always makes a good voyage of nothing. Farewell.
>
> (II.iv.67–79)

Feste's last lines have elicited much comment and many explanations from editors and critics, but when delivered with speed on stage they become very clear. The audience catches certain fertile images, which all add to Feste's picture of the shallowness of Orsino's passion and character. First there is the contrast between "melancholy god" and "tailor," all delivered in one breath, then the visual impact of "changeable taffeta" and "opal," and finally the powerful cluster of associations connected with "sea," "business," "voyage," and "nothing." Orsino is all shimmering surface with no fixed course of action. We are not allowed to stop and think or analyze, we do not need to. Because there is no attempt to answer Feste, it can be assumed that he speaks directly to the house, a little apart from the others, probably jingling his money for further emphasis.

There is much potential for comedy in this scene, and especially the song can be delivered in a variety of ways. The best rendition would use rather too many conventional gestures. Feste should be copying and exaggerating Orsino's mannerisms without making him totally ridiculous in the mirroring. Feste's most important quality is his aloofness, and that should never be jeopardized.

Feste has only this one scene totally concentrated on Orsino, and only one with Olivia, Viola, and Sebastian, the other parties in the love plot.[4] In each case he brings out important qualities that the audience should know, and employs a wide variety of means to reach this goal. The audience has been prepared in advance for Olivia by both Orsino and Maria, and we expect a strict and not totally pleasant lady. Maria tries to strike fear into Feste as he is about to be ushered into Olivia's presence:

> *Maria.* [M]y lady will hang thee for thy absence.
> *Feste.* Let her hang me: he that is well hanged in this world
>   need fear no colour.
>
> .   .   .
>
> *Maria.* Yet you will be hanged for being so long absent; or to
>   be turned away—is not that as good as hanging to you?
> *Feste.* Many a good hanging prevents a bad marriage: and for
>   turning away, let summer bear it out.
>
> (I.v.3–20)

Feste addresses the audience as Olivia enters and invokes Quinapalus, a philosopher of his own invention, to prepare us for the methods he is about to use. Olivia is indeed angry with him, but he takes a philosophical, mock-logical approach and mollifies her:

> *Olivia.* Take the fool away.
> *Feste.* Do you not hear, fellows? Take away the lady.
> *Olivia.* Go to, y'are a dry fool: I'll no more of you. Besides,
>   you grow dishonest.
> *Feste.* Two faults, madonna, that drink and good counsel will
>   amend: for give the dry fool drink, then is the fool not dry:
>   bid the dishonest man mend himself, if he mend, he is no
>   longer dishonest. . . . Anything that's mended is but
>   patched. . . . If that this simple syllogism will serve, so: if
>   it will not, what remedy?. . . The lady bade take away the
>   fool, therefore I say again, take her away. . . . Good
>   madonna, give me leave to prove you a fool.
> *Olivia.* Can you do it?
> *Feste.* Dexterously, good madonna.
> *Olivia.* Make your proof.
>
> (I.v.36–59)

During the catechism that follows, Feste proves Olivia a fool for mourning her brother, who is blissful in heaven. The important interplay between Feste and the audience takes place as he dexterously catches Olivia's attention and shows us a delightful young woman underneath the black gown of mourning. Feste calls the true Olivia forth to such a degree that she criticizes Malvolio, "O, you are sick of self-love" (89), and defends Feste and his brethren, "There is no slander in an allowed fool, though he do nothing but rail" (93–94). Feste's catechism is also the preparation for Olivia's "catechism" by Viola later in the same scene. The mollified Olivia finds herself falling in love.

Viola meets Feste in III.i, and again Feste suits his clowning to the situation and the intelligence of his interlocutor. On the Shakespearean stage, a disguise is always impenetrable to anybody but the audience and the few people in the know. Feste addresses Viola as he would a young man, and there is no attempt on his part to make her come forth and confess herself a female. Viola has great intelligence and is able to hold her own against Feste's punning for quite a long time, and Feste does make her demonstrate her verbal dexterity, her intelligence, and her great ability to act the young swaggerer. Both Feste and Viola are in close contact with the audience, and Viola even addresses us directly. Feste himself is restricted to more traditional aspects of clowning, winking at the audience and by other means catching our attention whenever he is about to make a good joke. There even is an opportunity to remind the audience of the scenes with Orsino and Olivia, and given the love triangle of which Viola is now a part the reminders are exquisitely funny:

> *Viola.* Art not thou the Lady Olivia's fool?
> *Feste.* No, indeed sir, the Lady Olivia has no folly. She will
>   keep no fool, sir, till she be married[5], and fools are as like
>   husbands as pilchards are to herrings, the husband's the
>   bigger. I am indeed not her fool, but her corrupter of words.
> *Viola.* I saw thee late at the Count Orsino's.
> *Feste.* Foolery, sir, does walk about the orb like the sun, it
>   shines everywhere. I would be sorry, sir, but the fool should
>   be as oft with your master as with my mistress: I think I
>   saw your wisdom there.
>
> (III.i.32–42)

Viola appreciates Feste and values his abilities. She rewards him with money, and he begs for more as he is expected to, and is rewarded further. When Feste leaves she describes what the work of a brilliant jester is like, and the audience cannot help but relate this description to her own situation:

> This fellow's wise enough to play the fool,
> And to do that well, craves a kind of wit:
> He must observe their mood on whom he jests,
> The quality of persons, and the time,
> And like the haggard, check at every feather
> That comes before his eye. This is a practise
> As full of labour as a wise man's art:
> For folly that he wisely shows is fit;
> But wise men, folly-fall'n, quite taint their wit.
>
> (III.i.61–69)

Viola herself lives in this same precarious situation. Because this short monologue to the audience, represents both a reversal from the comic to the serious and an abrupt shift from prose to verse, the message is brought home very strongly.

Feste's scene with Sebastian (IV.i) is short but delightful. Sebastian is a stranger in the world of Illyria and therefore can show us how bizarre things have become. He does not waste time jesting with Feste. He is irritated and does not understand why he is approached. Feste himself puts on an equally irritated facade and talks back at Sebastian in the same language, though in prose to Sebastian's verse, and sharing his puzzlement with the audience:

> *Sebastian.* I prithee vent thy folly somewhere else,
>   Thou know'st not me.
> *Feste.* Vent my folly! He has heard that word of some great
>   man, and now applies it to a fool. . . . tell me what I shall
>   vent to my lady. Shall I vent to her that thou art coming?
>   (IV.i.10–17)

Sebastian also gives Feste money, if only to be rid of him. It is amusing to see Feste at a disadvantage here, for he, like the rest of Illyria, is unable to adjust himself to Sebastian, whom he believes to be Viola. There is no common jesting, no sharing of level or medium; all Feste's expectations are thwarted, and it is impossible for him to do anything but latch on to Sebastian's vocabulary and use it back. Shakespeare manages a doubly comic effect from this encounter. The joke is originally on Sebastian, but the misunderstandings make Feste's confusion another source of laughter, and so Feste is not allowed to steal the scene in his usual way. Sebastian is a wild card, one who crosses everybody's expectations and intentions. Here he almost disables Feste, who expects the other twin.

Feste succeeds in keeping aloof from the problematic love relationships in the upper layer of Illyrian society, but he remains equally detached from the comic group at the lower layer. This can seem strange, for the comic group is large, lively, and delightful, and seemingly there would be a lot of business for Feste to attend to. Still, only once (IV.ii) does he allow himself to become actively involved in any of the comic group's business. His time is spent in commenting and exposing rather than participating. When Feste interacts with the comic group, his language, behavior, and style are markedly different from his courtly manner, and the Falstaffian Sir Toby and his echo Sir Andrew clearly enjoy him and treat him like one of the group. Orsino's court has no comic group, but then Viola is associated with this court, and she succeeds admirably in enhancing Orsino's comic side; his derogatory comments about the strength and constancy of women become delightfully amusing when directed at Viola, whose very being denies their truth. Moreover, it would never do to make Orsino too much the fool. He is after all the object of Viola's affection, and having her in love with a foolish character would spoil the love and trust the audience must feel for her to make this comedy work.

Olivia's household, on the other hand, can well bear having the comic group about, even having Sir Andrew in love with the mistress, for here we find

Malvolio the Puritan, who attracts the comic attacks and diverts them from the lady of the house. Olivia, who has sworn to live for sorrow rather than love, is remarkably beset by Cupid, loved as she is by Orsino, Sir Andrew, Malvolio, and Sebastian. Her own love for Viola/Cesario could well have been used as a means of ridiculing her decision to remain chaste, but instead it serves to bring out her warmth and determination, making her ready for Sebastian. When in the presence of the comic group, Feste delights in enhancing its disruptive effect on Olivia's household to the pleasure and benefit of the audience. In II.iii a late and rowdy night becomes noisier and more irritating to the household because of Feste's participation. He also brings out the benign foolishness of Sir Andrew and the more sinister one of Malvolio. Sir Toby treats Feste like an old acquaintance; Sir Andrew dotes on Feste and what he thinks Feste represents, and Feste kindly obliges:

> *Sir Andrew.* Here comes the fool. i'faith.
> *Feste.* How now, my hearts? Did you never see the picture of
>   'we three'?
> *Sir Toby.* Welcome ass. Now let's have a catch.
> *Sir Andrew.* By my troth, the fool has an excellent breast. I
>   had rather than forty shillings I had such a leg, and so sweet
>   a breath to sing, as the fool has. In sooth, thou wast in very
>   gracious fooling last night, when thou spok'st of
>   Pigrogromitus, of the Vapians passing the equinoctial of
>   Queubus: 'twas very good i' faith: I sent thee sixpence for
>   thy leman: hadst it?
> *Feste.* I did impeticos thy gratillity: for Malvolio's nose is no
>   whipstock, my lady has a white hand, and the Myrmidons
>   are no bottle ale-houses.
> *Sir Andrew.* Excellent! Why, this is the best fooling, when all
>   is done. Now a song!
> *Sir Toby.* Come on, there is sixpence for you. Let's have a
>   song.
> *Sir Andrew.* There's a testril of me too: if one knight give a
>   [text presumably dropped from Folio] . . .
> *Feste .* Would you have a love-song, or a song of good life?
> *Sir Toby.* A love-song, a love-song.
> *Sir Andrew.* Ay, ay. I care not for good life.

(II.iii.15–39)

The interchange is short and quick, but the relationship of the two knights and Feste is perfectly clear. Sir Andrew's lack of brains and wit and his knowledge of his own imperfection come out in his admiration of Feste. We see that Toby is the leader, he the follower. His praise waxes more elaborate after Feste's song, "O mistress mine," a beautiful little love song, again used as a joke, but he is equally eager to sing the proposed catch with the two others, "I am a dog at a catch" (62–63).

The uproar calls forth first Maria, then Malvolio. Malvolio has already voiced his contempt for Feste, calling him a "barren rascal" who is "gagged" unless you "laugh and minister occasion to him" (I.v.81–86), and though there is as much reason to reproach Feste as Sir Toby, and though both of them keep singing, Malvolio hardly deigns to notice the jester. In this scene there has been much competition to face for Feste, for

> the knight's in admirable fooling.
> *Sir Andrew.* Ay he does well enough, if he be disposed, and so
>   do I too: he does it with better grace, but I do it more
>   natural.
>
> (II.iii.81–84)

The two drunken knights form a natural magnet for the comedy and the attention of the audience; Feste himself can only add to their noise and goad them on, something they hardly need to make this scene a success. Feste's presence is a delight, but apart from singing his lovely song he adds little comedy to the scene; most of the initiatives are Sir Toby's. Still, it is necessary to associate Feste with the comic group in preparation for his later appearance as the Curate, just as it is necessary to establish Malvolio as a stereotypical Puritan.

In the Folio, Feste is given no stage direction to exit, but it would be effective to have him leave before the plot against Malvolio is hatched. There is no obvious business for him and no comic or instructive function after his last remark. The trio formed by Maria, Sir Toby, and Sir Andrew becomes a unity, which will stand at the core of the plot for the destruction of Malvolio for the rest of the play. The trio also shows the beginnings of a mock lover's triangle to echo that of Olivia, Viola/Cesario(/Sebastian), and Orsino. Feste's later participation only adds to the comedy, it adds nothing to the plot.

Feste is not seen with the comic group again until IV.ii, when he plays his role as Sir Topas. It may seem strange that he does not participate in the three most exquisitely funny scenes: the "letter" scene, where Malvolio discovers Maria's lure (II.v); the "midsummer madness" scene, where Malvolio comes to woo Olivia according to instructions (III.iv); and the "mock-duello" scene, where both Viola's and Sir Andrew's lack of manhood is amply demonstrated (III.vi). But Feste's role, comic though it is, is used for more than out-and-out comedy. His social and spatial mobility is clear, as is his connection with the four lovers. He constantly shapes himself to his company, and except with the mysterious Sebastian he succeeds in bringing forth traits the audience will need to know the better to enjoy the play. Shakespeare makes very limited use of him in what could seem to be his element, the topsy-turvy layer of pure comedy represented by Sir Toby's group. All the sexual innuendo, the spur-of-the-moment practical joking, and much of the comic monologue and dialogue traditionally associated with the stage clown is given to Sir Toby's group. Shakespeare has split the clown's role between the Falstaffian Sir Toby, whose earthy temperament provides the belly laughter, and the wrenlike Maria with ingenuity and brains on the one hand, and Feste on the other. Feste the clown represents a development into something like a puppet-master, and rarely do we see this more clearly than in IV.ii.

There is a sinister side to the comedy of this scene. Malvolio is in darkness in his prison, and repeatedly states that he cannot see. Therefore it will make bad sense dramatically to have Malvolio visible to the audience. Seeing him while listening to his complaints of darkness and isolation would make him too comic; it would impede the impact of the text, and most certainly make the mood lighter than it is intended to be.

Maria provides Feste with a costume at the very beginning of the scene: "Nay, I prithee put on this gown, and this beard; make him believe thou art Sir Topas the curate; do it quickly" (IV.ii.1–3). It will be necessary for Feste to be able to get into and out of the costume with ease as he has to do so numerous times and very quickly, so the gown will have to be voluminous, best of all open in front so it can be thrown back, and the beard must also be removable, perhaps mounted on a stick so it can be held to Feste's face and put behind his back. Of course Feste dresses up for the benefit of the audience alone. Malvolio will not be able to catch a glimpse of him, and Maria herself points this out to him and us: "Thou might'st have done this without thy beard and gown, he sees thee not" (IV.ii.66–67). Within the realm of the stage this is perfectly true, but the costume makes a world of comic difference to both Feste and the audience. With the costume Feste dons an aura of sanctimoniousness, apparent in his stance and carriage as well as his voice. He points this out to us while he dresses up to make quite sure we will not miss it. He has a rare moment completely alone with the audience as he says,

> Well, I'll put it on, and I will dissemble myself in't, and I would I were the first that ever dissembled in such a gown. I am not tall enough to become the function well, nor lean enough to be thought a good student; but to be said an honest man and a good housekeeper goes as fairly as to say a careful man and a great scholar.
>
> (IV.ii.4–10)

During this speech his whole personality as well as his garb should change as he readies himself for this new part, and the metamorphosis should be complete when Sir Toby enters and addresses him as "Master Parson." The audience is thoroughly prepared to enjoy what follows.

The first encounter between Feste and Malvolio is watched by Sir Toby and Maria as well as the audience. Malvolio complains bitterly about the darkness and the way he has been abused, and Feste counters in mock-logic, making fun of the whole world of learning as well as of Malvolio. The fact that Toby and Maria are present and visible while Malvolio is not takes away some of the serious aspects of the dialog. Malvolio has been sorely abused given cruel treatment, but the memory of him reading the letter and later appearing cross-gartered and in yellow stockings still lingers with the audience and softens the impact. Besides Sir Toby and Maria provoke the self-same Pavlovian reaction as the stage clown himself, that of almost automatic laughter. Only when Toby and Maria leave, giving Feste the idea of addressing Malvolio in his own person, does Feste's real torture of the unfortunate Puritan truly begin.[6]

Feste pretends to approach the prison, so he sings to identify himself. The song is chosen both to goad Malvolio and to remind us all that love has led to his madness:

Hey Robin, jolly Robin,
Tell me how thy lady does.
My lady is unkind, perdie.
Alas, why is she so?
She loves another—

(IV.ii.75–82)

During the song Malvolio calls "Fool!" no less than three times, and having finally caught Feste's attention, he has to submit to a typical example of clown joking:

> *Feste.* Alas, sir, how fell you besides your five wits?
> *Malvolio.* Fool, there was never man so notoriously abused: I
>   am as well in my wits, fool, as thou art.
> *Feste.* But as well? Then you are mad indeed, if you be no
>   better in your wits than a fool.

(IV.ii.89–93)

During the song, Feste will probably dance about in his best jesterly manner, and while he is discussing sanity and madness with Malvolio he will get as close to the prison or cage as he can and speak with great simplicity, offering himself as confidant. Once Malvolio has stopped begging and found his former manner again, Feste pounces on him:

> *Malvolio.* They have here propertied me; keep me in darkness,
>   send ministers to me, asses[7], and do all they can to face me
>   out of my wits.
> *Feste.* Advise what you say: the minister is here.[*As Sir
>   Topas*] Malvolio, Malvolio, thy wits the heavens restore:
>   endeavour thyself to sleep, and leave thy vain bibble babble.
> *Malvolio.* Sir Topas!
> *Feste* [*As Sir Topas*]. Maintain no words with him, good
>   fellow! [*As himself*] Who, I, sir? not I, sir! God buy you,
>   good Sir Topas! [*As Sir Topas*] Marry, amen! [*As himself*]
>   I will, sir I will.

(IV.ii.94–105)

The technique adopted by Feste serves several purposes. First it confuses Malvolio totally. He thinks he is alone with Feste and that it is safe to vent his rage, but is immediately plunged back into abject fear by the presence of Sir Topas, who has a say in proving him mad and keeping him confined. Second, Feste finds the opportunity to create wonderful stage business. For the benefit of the audience, he goes through one personality-cum-costume change after the other. Sir Topas is situated on one side of Malvolio's prison, Feste on the other. As he changes clothes he also has to change location, and the result is an amazing display of gymnastics, an entire farce in itself. When Sir Topas finally "leaves," Malvolio is reduced to begging Feste for "some light and some paper" (ll.109–110);[8] he now wheedles where he scorned before, and Feste gets a revenge which begins to seem petty:

> *Malvolio.* . . . I am as well in my wits as any man in Illyria.
> *Feste.* Well-a-day that you were, sir!
> *Malvolio.* By this hand, I am! Good fool, some ink, paper, and
>   light, and convey what I will set down to my lady. It shall
>   advantage thee more than ever the bearing of letter did.
> *Feste.* I will help you to't. But tell me true, are you not mad
>   indeed? or do you but counterfeit?
> *Malvolio.* Believe me, I am not, I tell thee true.
> *Feste.* Nay, I'll ne'er believe a madman till I see his brains. I
>   will fetch you light, and paper, and ink.
>
> (IV.ii.110–122)

Again Feste creeps close to Malvolio's place of confinement to be as confidential and secretive as possible. The audience is constantly reminded of Malvolio's earlier experience with a letter as he himself begs to be allowed to write one; we can only expect disaster to come from this communication as well. We fear, with good reason, that the reader of the letter will be "seeing a madman's brains," and indeed Feste, the bearer of the letter, gets the task of reading it aloud later.

The mood of this scene, where Feste is the instrument of torture for Malvolio, is markedly different from the Puritan's earlier scenes. When he interrupts Sir Toby's revels—a scene in which Feste is present—much of the comedy is provided by his appearance. Malvolio is ridiculous in his night shirt, probably in bare feet, with a nightcap askew on his head, and carrying a candle. When he discovers Maria's letter, his black Puritan's dress provides a comic clash with the strutting motions of making love and assuming power. And finally, cross-gartered and in yellow stockings with a huge grin pasted on his face, he becomes our laughing-stock. So much of our laughter at Malvolio has been provoked by his looks and the clash between manner and personality. In this his last scene with Feste where he is invisible we are not distracted by looks. His voice carries far more appeal than his physical presence ever could. We do laugh, but there is guilt in our laughter for Malvolio is unjustly imprisoned and accused, even deprived of light. Feste and the church he represents take on an aura of evil, an impression Feste underscores in the song with which he exits. He equates himself with the Vice, a character whose characteristics Shakespeare and his audience must have been well aware of. Feste plays Vice to the devil possessing Malvolio, to whom Sir Topas has already referred: "Out, hyperbolical fiend! . . . thou dishonest Satan!" (IV.ii.26–32), but the innocent he is leading into temptation is the fiend's host, Malvolio himself. The irony is stressed at the beginning of the next scene, where Sebastian is also troubled by "madness," but of the happy variety though it is brought on by love.

Though Shakespeare has created a distance between Feste's role and our traditional expectations of the stage clown, he is capable of traditional clowning, all of which is centered around word-play, or "corruption" of words, as he himself says. He can use different voices and personalities as well as twist his opponents words, often into the unintelligible. We see him in this well-known capacity towards the end of the play in the fifth act, where he banters first with Fabian, then with the Duke:

> *Fabian.* Now as thou lov'st me, let me see his letter.
> *Feste.* Good Master Fabian, grant me another request.
> *Fabian.* Anything.
> *Feste.* Do not desire to see this letter.
> *Fabian.* This is to give a dog, and in recompense desire my
>   dog again. . . .
> *Duke.* . . . How dost thou, my good fellow?
> *Feste.* Truly, sir, the better for my foes, and the worse for my
>   friends.
> *Duke.* Just the contrary: the better for thy friends.
> *Feste.* No, sir, the worse.
> *Duke.* How can that be?
> *Feste.* Marry, sir, they praise me, and make an ass of me. Now
>   my foes tell me plainly I am an ass: so that by my foes, sir,
>   I profit in the knowledge of myself, and by my friends I am
>   abused.
>
>   (V.i.1–19)

This is the kind of clowning we know well from the smallest clown's part through to the court jester clowns, and though Feste is verbally more nimble than most and is again well rewarded for his skill, it is still the kind of clowning that puts the spectators at ease and reassures them. Feste is sent to fetch Olivia, thus bringing three of the participants in the love-"triangle" together on stage. The next time we meet him he brings Sir Toby on stage wounded, thus heralding the arrival of Sebastian, the fourth member of the "triangle." Only when it has been discovered that Sebastian/Viola are two people, which makes enough lovers for two happy couples, do we see Feste again.

This time Feste appears in a most interesting capacity for a clown. He is out for public revenge. He has waited a long time to deliver Malvolio's letter, for "as a madman's epistles are no gospels, so it skills not much when they are delivered" (285–287), but here it finally is. Olivia, belatedly concerned for Malvolio, has no idea that the contents may be private, and asks Feste to read aloud. Now Feste's talent for interpretation through use of voice comes forward again with a vengeance:

> *Feste.* By the Lord, madam—
> *Olivia.* How now, art thou mad?
> *Feste.* No, madam, I do but read madness: and your ladyship
>   will have it as it ought to be, you must allow *vox*.
> *Olivia.* Prithee, read i' thy right wits.
> *Feste.* So I do, madonna. But to read his right wits is to read
>   thus.
>
>   (V.i.290–298)

When the letter is finally read to all of us by Fabian, Malvolio is released and the plot against him revealed. Feste has another opportunity to play with voices, this time Malvolio's:

> *Feste.* Why, 'Some are born great, some achieve greatness, and some have greatness thrown upon them.'9 I was one, sir, in this interlude, one Sir Topas, sir, but that's all one. 'By the Lord, fool, I am not mad.' But do you remember, 'Madam, why laugh you at such a barren rascal, and you smile not, he's gagged'? And thus the whirligig of time brings in his revenges.
>
> (V.i.369–376)

Time's whirligig, however, has nothing to do with this revenge. The clown steps beyond his usual boundaries and admits to having personally influenced the plot. This is the only time in Shakespeare's whole production that a stage clown takes events into his own hands and creates a lasting, uncomic effect on any other character. Feste's parody of Malvolio can only show how long planned this revenge is; Malvolio's remarks about the "barren rascal" echoes back as far as I.v. The dark tone of this comedy may not have been something Shakespeare's first audiences noted, but modern spectators can hardly avoid taking it into consideration.

Possibly because of Feste's unique revenge on Malvolio we may feel uncomfortable with him. Though he possesses innumerable clown skills and uses them in wonderful ways, he has few moments truly alone with the audience and does not use this time to come close to the spectators. There is a marked distance between Feste and ourselves which we never see in the other jester clowns. Feste is a thing apart, who becomes more puzzling and elusive because of the unfamiliar ways in which he makes use of the clown part's familiar elements. His approach to the audience and the function he fills for them is the same as that of any other major clown, but Feste's angle is different. Touchstone invites us to see folly and laugh goodhumoredly with him; Feste lends us a magnifying glass to observe the movements of the specimens, so we can laugh at them because "we know better." Feste has little of the clown's immediacy and warmth, but so much more professional gloss and slipperiness.

One final thing which sets Feste apart is the number and quality of his songs, another sign of professionalism. He is even given the Epilogue, the play's last word, which is also a song, a "normalizing" comment on the entire play. We, the audience, have just witnessed something delightfully impossible, unique to the comedy: the resolution of conflict and a happy end. Feste's song reminds us of a more down-to-earth existence, where love and marriage do not automatically entail everlasting happiness, and where the Malvolios of this world are more common than the Orsinos and Olivias. Here time progresses and people grow from childhood to old age. Life has its problems, but they are only "rain," not flood waters, and can be dealt with. His final call for applause like his use of the term "whirligig" is a reminder of Fortune's wheel, which will turn in repetition, not freeze at one supreme point such as the end of *Twelfth Night*. Still, endings like this please the audience, which is what the company wants, so "we'll strive to please you every day" (V.i.407). Even here, alone with the audience, Feste demonstrates that this is a play, not the real world.

Roberta Mullini says of the clown in action:

> [D]uring the performance fools always work on the two dynamic levels of illusion and reality, between the stage and the audience. On the former level their word operates as a kind of litmus paper of the character's folly, on the latter it shows and proclaims the dialectical balance with the fool's wit. The fool's word, and not his action, interacts with the other characters.[10]

This is particularly true of the court jester clowns, who are given sufficient space for this type of action. Not only is the spectator affected by the clown's function on an unconscious plane, he can actually become aware of the clown's pattern of twofold interaction and feel elevated to a higher level of perception, a kind of omniscience which only the clown can provide. The audience will feel great delight at seeing through the characters of the play with the help of the clown's mediation, and they happily pay their debt of laughter to the one who brought them this knowledge. At the same time, the clown never makes us his dependents. We are allowed to keep Touchstone with us throughout *As You Like It*, and Feste is there for us during all of Twelfth *Night*, but we never miss Lavatch once he has vanished from our sight. Early or late, the departure of the clown, our catalyst, always leaves the audience with a deeper understanding and an ability to create for themselves a richer experience from the play.

NOTES

1. *As You Like It* has some of its protagonists absorbed by the Forest of Arden and its world view, whereas others return to the outside world, presumably to attempt to make it better.

2. A common theme, especially in comedies; Shakespeare also uses it in the still-happy beginning of *Romeo and Juliet* to contrast Romeo's first love interest with his feelings for Juliet, and in *A Midsummer Night's Dream* where the four lovers go to extremes in interchangeability.

3. The audience is reminded of this in lines 11–13: "Feste the jester, my lord, a fool that the Lady Olivia's father took much delight in." We may suspect that Feste's connection with Olivia plays a great part in Orsino's enjoyment!

4. Olivia's is I.v, Viola's III.i, and Sebastian's IV.i.

5. The word "fool" here can refer to both the poor husband and the folly of marriage generally, as is suggested in the Arden note to the line, but it should not be forgotten that babies were referred to fondly as "fools" too.

6. The Folio has an *Exit* for Sir Toby after line 74, none for Maria; but it would make no dramatic sense to leave her on stage after he has left. The two must leave together as the couple they will shortly become.

7. The "asses" must refer to Sir Toby and his group, into whose custody Malvolio has been given.

8. Earlier he was specific: "a candle, and pen, ink and paper" (84).

9. Feste has not actually heard Malvolio read these words from Maria's letter, or heard him quote them to Olivia, but the audience is unlikely to remember this as they see the performance. This is another instance of the unrealistic elements in Elizabethan comedy and the stage clown's personality.

10. Roberta Mullini, "Playing the Fool: the Pragmatic Status of Shakespeare's Clowns," *NTQ* 1.1 (1985), 102.

Part IV

The Clown as "The Bitter Fool"

11

Thersites in *Troilus and Cressida*

In two plays Shakespeare uses the clown in the role of the jester-as-critic. Thersites in *Troilus and Cressida* and the Fool in *King Lear* are very different, but they share a critical attitude to events around them, which affects and colors their jesting. Both their worlds are dark and forbidding. *King Lear* is a full-fledged tragedy, and though it may seem strange to find a jester in such a play, Shakespeare creates a union of the Fool and his tragic world, which serves to guide the spectators and help them profit from their experience. *Troilus and Cressida* presents more of a problem with genre. It has long shared the label of "problem comedy" with *Measure for Measure* and *All's Well That Ends Well*, and indeed these plays all present love struggling with greater problems than parental opposition, be it social convention, legal complications, or the fortunes of war. But where the other two problem comedies end in acceptable solutions to the lovers' trials, *Troilus and Cressida* concludes in augmented bitterness and sadness. In Thersites, Shakespeare has created the perfect clown to match his play, bitter, biting, ironic, and repellent as he is.

The worlds of *Troilus and Cressida* and *King Lear* both show us bonds broken, and people we have come to sympathize with are betrayed and disillusioned. Somewhat unexpectedly in two such plays we still find a large part for the clown in his role as mediator between stage and audience. When present he is always ready with a remark to help us see through the betrayals and interpret the things shown us. However, few characters with much the same function could be more different than Thersites from Lear's Fool. Thersites' style of jesting has isolated him from his fellow characters, and he apparently does not want a different status, for he is always aggressive and ever ready with insulting remarks, not sparing even his present patron. Lear's Fool is also isolated, but his loneliness is not of his own choosing. He, too, can be aggressive and has biting jests to spare, but his isolation stems from Lear's, and his aggression is always directed at Lear's enemies. Lear is certainly not spared, but then Lear is often his own worst enemy. Where Thersites is bristling with enmity towards mankind in general and lovers and braggarts in particular, Lear's Fool's jesting, even when caustic, shows deep compassion and understanding of the human condition.[1] Different as they are, the jesting of these two clown figures is tailored to their individual function as audience guides within the frames of their respective worlds.

Thersites is a strange clown figure. At first glance it would seem that the title of clown would go better with a figure like Pandarus, for he provokes much laughter of the quality we usually associate with the clown's part. His jokes are on sexuality and human folly, and our laughter is warm and happy. Thersites, on the other hand, provides a cold and distanced type of mirth with which the audience will feel uncomfortable. Still Thersites, not Pandarus, is our stage clown. Pandarus's sphere is limited, and he never has a chance to extend his comments beyond the love intrigue between Troilus and Cressida. Thersites' comments, caustic and thorny as they are, succeed admirably in encompassing the whole world of the play. He is the one who opens our eyes and gives us an opportunity to form our own opinion about war and love.

In *Troilus and Cressida* we certainly see lovers, but not the happy union of the deserving couple after their difficulties have been amusingly overcome. The nature of the passion in this play is strangely unfamiliar. Paris's love of Helen, which launched the Greek army, has been reduced to something everyday and down-to-earth, but then the war has been going on for some time, and in Shakespeare's interpretation the relationship has definitely changed. Helen behaves like any popular socialite, flirting with her guests but secure in her relationship with Paris (III.i), and naturally the couple is gossiped about all over Troy. The relationship between Troilus and Cressida seems fated to fit the same pattern on a lower plane. Instead of Venus these two have their Pandarus to bring them together, and though they try to conceal their love, they too are much talked about. Through Cressida's fate, however, Shakespeare demonstrates how a woman, existing in a male dominated world on men's premises, has to shape herself and her feelings to circumstances in order to survive, and we may see that Helen has done this and been very successful. Cressida seeks to hide her true feelings from Troilus as long as possible, because

> Men prize the thing ungain'd more than it is.
> That she was never yet that ever knew
> Love got so sweet as when desire did sue.
> Therefore this maxim out of love I teach:
> 'Achievement is command; ungain'd, beseech.'
>
> (I.ii.294–298)

Her maxim is proved amply. Once Troilus has gained access to her bed, his passion changes from lover to possessor. It takes the threat of her removal from Troy to reawaken him, and her actual submission to Diomedes to bring back the flame of passion in him. Troilus is in love with the idea of love and actually happiest when sighing for fulfillment, while Cressida learns that true love cannot possibly exist under her social circumstances. Such a presentation of love and its relationship to other things in this world is most disillusioning.

The audience is never allowed to form an easy and happy attachment to any character in this play, which seems to be constantly working to create the greatest possible distance between stage and house. The choice of Thersites for the clown magnifies this effect. The style of the play invites analysis rather than involvement from the audience, and Thersites is ever ready to keep our feelings at a distance and invite our brains to action. Even before the play truly opens, we are presented with a distancing factor in the Prologue: the great events of the play are suspended with no true beginning or end in the midst of the Trojan War. Only knowledge of history or literature lets the audience know who won and who lost, and in the context of the play victory or defeat are utterly irrelevant, for everybody loses. War and love are set up as parallels and viewed as equally ridiculous. The only character to be taken seriously is Cressida herself, but the odds against women in general and her in particular jeopardize even her honesty, and she finally has to move with events to ensure her own survival.

Thersites unfailingly guides our eye to the ridiculous aspects of any given situation. Though it would not be traditional to do so, it would enhance the detached aspect of the play if the Prologue and Thersites were to double.[2] It is true that the expectations raised in the audience by seeing a famous clown are large and would lock the audience's perceptions from the very beginning of this play, but given its ironic distance that could be a result to be desired. On the other hand, Shakespeare's Prologue, starting *in medias res* as it does, is in itself a mockery of the whole heroic convention. Seeing a known clown actor in the Prologue's role would possibly hinder us from the full enjoyment of having our expectations of these conventions thwarted. Still, whether the clown is used for Prologue or not, the tone for the play is set immediately, and the audience should be prepared to laugh at rather than with the characters.

Thersites is certainly not the typical Elizabethan stage clown. He is a malcontent, happy only when biting, and not to be trusted. Even his clowning is satiricalsatire exposing everything to ridicule and never enlisting the audience on his side. His relationship with us is close indeed, but he appears to make use of us for his own reasons rather than to help our understanding along. We are not really prepared for Thersites before we meet him. Agamemnon does call him "rank Thersites" (I.iii.73) and contrasts him to Ulysses, but the reference is so short and so far removed from his first appearance that it will probably be forgotten by the time Thersites enters. When he does, he is rank indeed. He seems to be in a brown study, and he is very hard to reach:

> *Ajax.* Thersites—
> *Thersites.* Agamemnon—how if he had boils, full, all over, generally?
> *Ajax.* Thersites—
> *Thersites.* And those boils did run—say so—did not the general run then? Were not that a botchy core?
> *Ajax.* Dog!
> *Thersites.* Then would come some matter from him: I see none now.
> *Ajax.* Thou bitch-wolf's son, canst thou not hear?
> (II.i.1–10)

These poisonous remarks on Agamemnon must provoke laughter in the audience after the long-winded debate among the Greeks in I.iii, where little matter has come from Agamemnon. They also very summarily show Thersites' character; he is never at pains to hide it. During the ensuing argument with Ajax, later with Achilles present, we get Thersites' opinion of his own wit and intelligence:

> *Thersites.* . . . thou sodden-witted lord, thou hast no more brain
> than I have in mine elbows: an asinico may tutor thee . . .

>   . . .

> *Thersites.* You see him there, do you?
> *Achilles.* Ay: what's the matter?
> *Thersites.* Nay look upon him.
> *Achilles.* So I do: what's the matter?
> *Thersites.* Nay but regard him well.
> *Achilles.* Well?—why, so I do.
> *Thersites.* . . . whosomever you take him to be, he is Ajax.
> *Achilles.* I know that, fool.
> *Thersites.* Ay, but that fool knows not himself.
>
> (II.i.45–47, 59–68)

The altercation in which Ajax is called "fool" could have been found in many contexts, and the structure is used by many Shakespearean clowns. What makes Thersites' delivery different is his rank attitude combined with the context of war and physical violence. Ajax strikes him repeatedly, and Thersites comes back snapping like a mean-tempered cur. His "service" with Ajax is brought to stand for the whole Greek venture in the Trojan War:

> *Thersites.* I serve thee not.
> *Ajax .* Well, go to, go to.
> *Thersites.* I serve here voluntarily.
> *Achilles.* Your last service was suff'rance—'twas not
>   voluntary, no man is beaten voluntarily: Ajax was here the
>   voluntary, and you under an impress.
> *Thersites.* E'en so—a great deal of your wit too lies in your
>   sinews, or else there be liars. Hector shall have a great catch
>   and a knock out either of your brains: a were as good crack a
>   fusty nut with no kernel. . . . There's Ulysses, and Old
>   Nestor, whose wit was mouldy ere your grandsires had nails
>   on their toes, yoke you like draught-oxen and make you
>   plough up the wars.
>
> (II.i.94–109)

There is no glory, only glorified drudgery under bad leadership, and still the heroes imagine that they serve "voluntarily" for their own greater glory. Ajax and Achilles even regard Thersites as being in their service as their fool, whose function it is to provide laughter at their little courts.

Thersites, like most other clowns with a sizable part, is given a lengthy monologue (II.iii.1–35), but even here, in direct contact with the audience, his label of "rank" rings true. The clown's monologue usually follows a set pattern of complaints against unfairness or oppression. Thersites runs true to this formula, but he makes no attempt to engage the audience actively on his side. Where others employ comedy, Thersites employs satire and irony. His every comment has a sting to it, and his fundamental dissatisfaction never flags. Maybe this monologue more than anything else may explain the reserve many feel about calling Thersites a true clown; he is simply too bitter and indifferent to his effect on listeners to emerge as sympathetic at all:

> 'Sfoot, I'll learn to conjure and raise devils, but I'll see some issue of my spiteful execrations. . . . If Troy be not taken till these two [i.e., Ajax and Achilles] undermine it, the walls will stand till they fall of themselves. . . . I have said my prayers [for the whole camp to get venereal disease], and devil Envy say 'Amen'.
>
> (II.iii.5–22)

There is truth to his remarks about Ajax and Achilles, and the effect is humorous, but laughter could never have been achieved without the distanced attitude to events which Shakespeare employs in this play. Much of the humor is created by Thersites' constancy of character. He is unvaryingly the same whether he is among the Greeks or alone with the audience. Still for the most part the Greeks bear with him and even enjoy him. The better part of his raillery is nimble-witted and quick, and "he is a privileged man" as Achilles says; the other Greeks also label him as a sort of licensed jester (II.iii.60; 93–98).

When he is with his "patron," Thersites slips into the role of court fool. In II.iii, where he has changed allegiance, he employs these expectations as the wedge which splits Achilles from Patroclus, probably because he wants Patroclus's place for himself:

> *Achilles.* Why, my cheese, my digestion, why hast thou not served thyself in to my table so many meals? Come, what's Agamemnon?
>
> *Thersites.* Thy commander, Achilles; then tell me Patroclus, what's Achilles?
>
> *Patroclus.* Thy lord, Thersites: then tell me I pray thee, what's Thersites?
>
> *Thersites.* Thy knower, Patroclus: then tell me, Patroclus, what art thou?
>
> *Patroclus.* Thou mayst tell that knowest.
>
> *Achilles.* O tell, tell.
>
> *Thersites.* I'll decline the whole question. Agamemnon commands Achilles, Achilles is my lord, I am Patroclus' knower, and Patroclus is a fool.
>
> *Patroclus.* You rascal.
>
> *Thersites.* Peace, fool, I have not done.

> *Achilles.* He is a privileged man: proceed, Thersites.
> *Thersites.* Agamemnon is a fool, Achilles is a fool, Thersites
>   is a fool, and, as aforesaid, Patroclus is a fool.
> *Achilles.* Derive this: come.
> *Thersites.* Agamemnon is a fool to offer to command Achilles,
>   Achilles is a fool to be commanded of Agamemnon,
>   Thersites is a fool to serve such a fool, and this Patroclus is
>   a fool positive.
> *Patroclus.* Why am I a fool?
> *Thersites.* Make that demand of the Creator, it suffices me
>   thou art.
>
>   (II.iii.44–70)

Thersites is encouraged to enter into a traditional clown's routine and does so happily. While he reduces anybody and everybody, himself included, to "fools," Patroclus is the only fool whose status is not worth discussing, and yet the whole interchange has been thought up just to pin the label of "fool" on Patroclus.

It is also in this scene, intimately connected to this discussion of fools and folly, that Thersites begins the pattern of the parallel between sexuality and war on which this play depends. Such a parallel itself may be seen as trite and commonplace when it is employed by the lovers and Pandarus, but Thersites links war to much more than the amorous sparring between man and woman:

> Here [between the Greek commanders and Achilles] is such
> patchery, such juggling, and such knavery! All the argument is
> a whore and a cuckold: a good quarrel to draw emulous
> factions, and bleed to death upon. Now the dry serpigo on the
> subject, and war and lechery confound all!
>
>   (II.iii.73–77)

Not only the cause of the Trojan war is set in relief; the relationship between Troilus and Cressida is doomed, and everything is linked up with lechery and disease to boot. Patchery, juggling, and knavery is indeed what the circumstances, strongly aided by Pandarus, dish out for Troilus's courtship and Cressida's love. The connection between Troy and the Greek camp, however, is only made very late in the play, for not until then does Troy come to the camp, where Thersites roams exclusively.[3] Riddled as his speech is with images from sexuality and disease, his constant harping on the war and the fools that fight it cannot but make the audience connect the lovers and the war. Soon neither will have any romantic glow left.[4]

Thersites has strong opinions about the Greek heroes. Agamemnon is all boast and no matter, and Nestor is all withered age, but lowest of all he puts Menelaus:

> *Thersites.* To be a dog, a mule, a cat, a fitchook, a toad, a
> lizzard, an owl, a puttock, or a herring without a roe, I would
> not care; but to be Menelaus I would conspire against destiny.

> Ask me not what I would like to be, if I were not Thersites;
> for I care not to be the louse of a lazar, so I were not
> Menelaus.
>
> (V.i.60–66)

Ajax and Achilles, his patrons, have their share of invective as well, and
Thersites gives a delightful imitation of Ajax before the fight with Hector
(III.iii). The text is full of invitations to the actor to strut about and imitate and
overemphasize the characteristics of the Ajax we have come to know, as he
"stalks up and down like a peacock . . . ruminates like a hostess that has no
arithmetic . . . [and] bites his lip with a politic regard" (250–253). The
culmination is a miniature play put on for the benefit of Achilles, who is acting
as audience:

> *Thersites.* You shall see the pageant of Ajax.
> *Achilles.* To him, Patroclus. Tell him I humbly desire the
>   valiant Ajax to invite the valorous Hector to come unarmed
>   to my tent, and to procure safe conduct for his person, of the
>   magnanimous, and most illustrious, six or seven times
>   honoured captain-general of the Grecian army, Agamemnon,
>   et cetera. Do this.
> *Patroclus.* Jove bless great Ajax.
> *Thersites.* Hum!
> *Patroclus.* I come from the worthy Achilles—
> *Thersites.* Ha?
> *Patroclus.* Who most humbly desires you to invite Hector to
>   his tent—
> *Thersites.* Hum?
> *Patroclus.* And to procure safe-conduct from Agamemnon.
> *Thersites.* Agamemnon?
> *Patroclus.* Ay, my lord.
> *Thersites.* Ha!
> *Patroclus.* What say you to't?
> *Thersites.* God buy you, with all my heart!
> *Patroclus.* Your answer, sir?
> *Thersites.* If tomorrow be a fair day, by eleven of the clock it
>   will go one way or the other. Howsoever, he shall pay for
>   me ere he has me.
> *Patroclus.* Your answer, sir.
> *Thersites.* Fare ye well, with all my heart.
>
> (III.iii.270–297)

This whole interchange, like many of Thersites' other scenes, seems far removed
from the action of the play itself, interposed for pure enjoyment, but it serves to
alert the audience even further to the ridiculous aspects of war and heroism.
Again Thersites easily assumes the part of court fool. Achilles becomes a
delighted audience-and-director combined, and if the choice of director is made to
create homosexual connotations from the relationship between Patroclus and

Achilles, this is a good opportunity to have Achilles applaud his Patroclus. Thersites himself points an accusing finger at the Achilles-Patroclus liaison: "[B]e silent, boy, I profit not by thy talk; thou art said to be Achilles' male varlet . . . his masculine whore" (V.i.13–16), but then any close human relationship prompts spite from Thersites. In contradiction, much is made of Achilles' love of Priamus's daughter Polyxena.

While the relationship between Troy and the Greek camp is hostile, the war has been long enough for the parties to have relaxed their enmity enough for friendly interchanges. The Trojan lords are feasted at the Greek camp, and Achilles receives a letter from his love in the city (V.i). There is also a lively exchanging of prisoners, among them the Trojan hero Antenor, who is given back for Cressida. When Cressida is exchanged, we see an inverted parallel of the abduction of Helen.[5] A Greek hero goes to Troy, fetches the girl, and pays court to her, and despite her vows to Troilus she has to yield to him. Thersites proffers his opinion of this Diomedes, calling him "a false-hearted rogue, a most unjust knave" (V.i.87–88). In both cases blame is heaped upon the women. Cressida is used as a visible example. On her arrival she is kissed by the entire Greek camp, but she has the sense to make the best of it in the face of superior force (in IV.v), and both Thersites and Ulysses comment on her mercilessly during her tryst with Diomedes (V.ii). It is interesting to note that up to this point Thersites has remained detached from the action and has only commented mercilessly, but during the sparring between Cressida and Diomedes and witnessing the torments of Troilus, Thersites' excitement rises to such a pitch as to connote almost sexual excitement.

During V.ii, Cressida and Diomedes are usually far removed from the audience. We can then feel that we spy on them along with Ulysses and Troilus on one side of the stage and Thersites on the other. Thersites' function is mainly that of negative commentator and interpreter:

> *Diomedes.* How now, my charge.
> *Cressida.* Now, my sweet guardian. Hark, a word with you.
> *Troilus.* Yea, so familiar?
> *Ulysses.* She will sing any man at first sight.
> *Thersites.* And any man may sing her, if he can take her clef: she's noted.
>
> (V.ii.11)

Ulysses is irked by the whole business of the Trojan War and the lovers who caused it, and so he harps on the inconstancy of women, but Thersites immediately leaps to direct, sexually oriented comments. He may well be played as if strongly attracted to Cressida in spite of himself and disgusted by this. His line: "Now the pledge: now, now, now!" (65) invites an almost panting delivery. Troilus's intention to seek out Diomedes in battle for revenge also tickles Thersites mightily:

> Would I could meet that rogue Diomed!—I would croak like a
> raven: I would bode, I would bode. Patroclus will give me

> anything for the intelligence of this whore; the parrot will not
> do more for an almond than he for a commodious drab.
>
> (V.ii.188–193)

Thersites is a carrion crow and delights in it. His warped pleasures are always safely secondhand, and his knowledge of women only allows him to spite them. Still, both Cressida and Helen can be seen as displaying courage and resourcefulness in their impossible positions, making use of the only weapons they are allowed to ensure survival in this misogynistic man's world.[6] Thersites' closing comment to the miserable tryst between Diomedes and Cressida confirms the continuous parallel: "Lechery, lechery, still wars[7] and lechery! Nothing else holds fashion. A burning devil take them" (V.ii.193–195).

Thersites, more than any other clown, has been given a large number of monologues throughout the play. In fact, the major part of his role is delivered directly to the audience, either when he is alone on stage or behind the backs of his fellow characters. This may appear puzzling, given the lack of close and comfortable rapport between the audience and Thersites, but a reason can be found in the substance of his comments. No matter how malcontent and caustic his character, he is always the interpreter for the audience. Without him, the play's attitude to war and love would be much more difficult to see, for the Trojan War is controversially presented. Both heroism and grand passion is firmly put in its place thanks to Thersites, and no ulterior motive is missed, however well hidden. In the fifth act, when he is on stage numerous times, this function becomes apparent. Diomedes and Troilus are called "the sleeve and the other" (V.iv.18) when they engage in their duel over love; Menelaus and Paris, engaged in a parallel duel, are "the cuckold and the cuckold-maker" (V.vii.9). In both scenes Thersites has to worm his way out of fighting himself, but this presents no real problems as he does not recognize honor among his elements of character. To Hector, he claims to be a coward, "a rascal, a scurvy railing knave: a very filthy rogue" (V.iv.28–29), quite an insightful analysis; and to Margarelon, bastard, he claims to be "a bastard, too . . . a bastard begot, bastard instructed, bastard in mind, bastard in valor, in everything illegitimate" (V.vii.16–18). In both of these parallel scenes love and war meet, and Thersites gives perspective to the meeting.

Despite the remarks on his status within the play itself, it may be difficult to accept Thersites as a jester or the clown of the play, but it must be granted that his role as educator of the audience is the clown's role, and his wit, caustic and dry though it is, causes laughter. Also, Thersites exposes the structure of his society to examination and delivers its weak points to the audience to mull over, though we should not take all his comments at surface value. The difference between him and other clowns can be found in the specific nature of the play, which makes it so difficult to classify. Maybe the term "satire" suits it better than "comedy," especially because the audience is constantly distanced from characters with whom identification would be natural. Seen in this light, the role of the clown must be redefined to fit within the framework, and as always the Shakespearean clown molds himself to fit the play in which he operates.

NOTES

1. This may be why Lear's Fool has so often been played by an actress. Even to this day, *King Lear* may be seen with a woman cast in the part of the Fool.

2. Doubling the Prologue and Pandarus is apparently the more obvious choice for directors.

3. Thersites is given much less social and physical mobility than usually belongs with the clown's part.

4. Compare Chaucer's treatment of the heroine in his *Troilus and Criseyde,* and Robert Henryson's in his *Testament of Cresseid,* to which Thersites probably owes some of his attitudes to the female sex.

5. Pandarus has given much substance to such a parallel by constantly linking the two women, making comparisons between their looks and behavior.

6. Cressida herself gives a good basis for this interpretation in her monologue, I.ii.286–300.

7. The pun on "whores" should not be overlooked.

12

Lear's Fool in *King Lear*

In *Troilus and Cressida*, Thersites' continuous exertions to create and maintain distance between house and stage through caustic commentary shows us a clown whose lack of compassion and empathy makes the comedy work. The audience needs this distance not to become distracted from the main points of the play. In *King Lear*, the Fool's biting jests result from the very opposite. Lear's Fool is a creature whose whole being is founded on understanding of the human condition and pity for those who cannot cope with the harsh realities of Lear's world. Where Thersites willingly isolates himself from human contact and does his best to ensure that bonds are broken and illusions rent, Lear's Fool, though biting, is always loyal, caring, and compassionate.

Lear's Fool in is the only clown in a major part found in a tragedy, and this fact adds new dimensions to him. Apart from this instance, Shakespeare has employed clowns only in minor parts in tragedies, and mainly used them to illuminate a turning point in the action. Lear's Fool certainly helps focus our attention on crucial turning points, but he has a much more expanded function, if not easy to pinpoint. In the great comedies where we find the other court jester clowns, their function is straightforward and not far different from that of the minor clowns. The mere sight of the clown is a signal to the audience, and we are ready to laugh before we even know what the jest will be, or at whom it will be directed. The nimble tongues of these clowns never bring them trouble more serious than a remote threat of banishment. Their mobility is great and fascinating, and they are welcome and enjoyed anywhere.

Not so Lear's Fool. He is so glued to Lear that he becomes an added dimension of Lear himself, and both he and Lear seem aware that this is so, if only unconsciously. Nimble though the Fool may be in body and tongue, his is not an unproblematic existence, and he is repeatedly threatened with whipping.[1] On the background of these repeated threats and his worsening circumstances, our laughter becomes constricted and may even disappear. Indeed, the Fool more often than not has to labor to extract laughter even from his master. Yet there is no doubt of Lear's attachment to him and our need for his presence. Lear's Fool is a court jester, and his essential function is no different from that of the court jesters in the comedies; he too brings forth the aspect of human folly and holds it up to ridicule. In the comedies, however, the target is broad and includes general ideas, but in the tragedy of *King Lear* the King's folly is the main target, and our involvement with the King becomes so close that laughter at him will be perceived as directed at ourselves also. Growing old and being unable to sound the depths of our fellow human beings are both conditions common to us all. Our understanding of these plights, and our involvement in Lear's fate which stems from it, can easily make us incapable of objectivity. Though we may feel uncomfortable about the Fool, we need him to keep our perspective on King Lear. The Fool as mediator between stage and audience is not always welcome to us, and though he is loved, the Fool's comments are not always welcome to Lear either; but as the real world fades from Lear's view and his sight is directed inwards in madness we come to see the Fool in a different light.

It can be debated whether the Fool is present in the first scene of the play, where Lear divides his kingdom and banishes Cordelia. The Fool does have many periods of silent presence on stage throughout the play, and it may be argued that this whole scene is one of them; if so, the bond between Lear and his Fool can be forged from the very beginning. But the Fool can serve a better purpose as a voice of reason rather than as an outcropping of Lear only, and therefore should not come on stage until he is called for. In the first scene, Cordelia herself serves the purpose of distinguishing reasonable from unreasonable and truth from lies, a function the Fool will take over once she departs for France. The clown-as-truth-teller is no new thing with Shakespeare, but the genuinely and deeply sad clown is.

The Fool is mentioned before we meet him: "Did my father strike my gentleman for chiding of his Fool?" asks Goneril, and labels this as another "gross crime" of her father's (I.iii.1–2, 5). Again in I.iv the Fool is mentioned before he appears. He is called for no less than four times, and the link between him and Cordelia is strongly pointed out:

> *Lear*. But where's my Fool? I have not seen him this two days.
> *Knight*. Since my young Lady's going into France, Sir, the
>   Fool hath much pined away.
> *Lear*. No more of that; I have noted it well.
>
>   (I.iv.69–73)

Apparently the mention of dinner triggers Lear's wish to see his Fool, presumably to be entertained during the meal, but the skirmish between Kent and Oswald makes both him and us forget the Fool momentarily. Therefore the effect is one of great surprise once the Fool comes up and makes himself "visible." Lear praises Kent and makes a kingly gesture of bestowing his favors on him and hiring him, but the Fool puts things back in perspective:

> *Lear*. Now, my friendly knave, I thank thee: there's earnest of
>   thy service.
> *Fool*. Let me hire him too: here's my coxcomb.

> *Lear*. How now, my pretty knave! how dost thou?
> *Fool*. Sirrah, you were best take my coxcomb.
> *Kent*. Why, Fool?
> *Fool*. Why? for taking one's part that's out of favour.
>
> (I.iv.91–97)

The Fool glides up unnoticed and, ignoring Lear and his friendly question, proceeds to demonstrate the lie of the land for Kent. Only when this is accomplished does he do the same for Lear:

> How now, Nuncle! Would I had two coxcombs and two
> daughters!
> *Lear*. Why, my boy?
> *Fool*. If I gave them all my living, I'd keep my coxcombs
> myself. There's mine; beg another of thy daughters.
> *Lear*. Take heed, sirrah: the whip.
> *Fool*. Truth is a dog must to kennel.
>
> (I.iv.103–109)

The Fool implies, not untruthfully, that he has more to give away than Lear, if only his one coxcomb. Lear has decided to keep the outward show of kingship, but has given away the regal power to his daughters. The Fool offers to give away only the mark of his profession, his hood, and yet will keep his essence. The same sentiments are voiced later (189–191), when the Fool says: "[N]ow thou art an O without a figure. I am better than thou art now; I am a Fool, thou art nothing." He also keeps a firm grasp on the necessity to remain frugal in order to prosper, a piece of advice suited equally well to a pauper and a king:

> Have more than thou showest,
> Speak less than thou knowest,
> Lend less than thou owest,
> Ride more than thou goest,
> Learn more than thou trowest,
> Set less than thou throwest;
> Leave thy drink and thy whore,
> And keep in-a-door,
> And thou shalt have more
> Than two tens to a score.
> . . . Can you make no use of nothing, Nuncle?
> *Lear*. Why no, boy, nothing can be made out of nothing.
>
> (I.iv.116–130)

These three uses of "nothing" clearly recall the exchange between Cordelia and Lear in I.i (85–89). The echoes of Cordelia's speech in the Fool's lines serves to forge a bond of continuity between the two. The truly loving daughter is no longer with her father; his Fool, whose love is also great, has taken it upon himself to try to save Lear. The Fool's advice comes belatedly, however, as Lear has already sinned against all the commandments of rationality set up therein.

During this whole scene the Fool, in spite of threats of the whip, continues to press up to the fine line of Lear's tolerance. He calls Lear "Nuncle" and "my boy" (134), the same terms of endearment Lear uses for him, but in the same breath he also indirectly calls him a fool in one of the jingling rhymes he uses to get his points across (137–144). There is no doubt that of the two, Lear is the bitter fool.

The Fool also implies that Lear has entered into second childhood. He has "mad[e his] daughters [his] mothers" (168–169), and in the parallel of the egg and its two crowns (152–162) the Fool equates Lear with the meat of the egg, that which would become the chicken, but which is eaten here before its fulfillment. Lear's "bald crown" which used to bear the golden one, is the home of nothing; he has "pared [his] wit o'both sides and left nothing in the middle" (183–184). This continual prodding of Lear apparently pains the Fool: "I had rather be any kind o'thing than a fool; and yet I would not be thee, Nuncle" (181–183).

When Goneril enters, the Fool waxes daring and exploits her comments to further stress his point. Goneril is "the cuckoo" (213) which bit off the hedge-sparrow's head when there was no more need of food, and she is the one who blew out the light and left them "darkling" (215). She is also "the ass" (221), who sees the cart draw the horse. And to Lear's question: "Who is it that can tell me who I am?" the Fool replies: "Lear's shadow" (227–228). None of these parallels are flattering ones, and by his prodding the Fool fans the tempers of both father and daughter. Lear, insulted, leaves her house, and he forgets his Fool, both when he storms from the stage and finds half his knights gone and when he finally leaves in anger. Goneril sends him away:

> You, sir, more knave than fool, after your master.
> *Fool.* Nuncle Lear, Nuncle Lear! tarry, take the Fool with
> thee.
>> A fox, when one has caught her,
>> And such a daughter,
>> Should sure to the slaughter,
>> If my cap would buy a halter;
>> So the Fool follows after.
>
> (I.iv.312–320)

When present, the Fool easily dominates the business on stage, making himself the center of the audience's attention because of the truths he delivers, and certainly also because of his physical agility.[2] This is the only Shakespearean court fool who stays attached to one master, and it would be a mistake not to let him make use of the court fool's traditional acrobatics, at least while he is still at court. Many of his speeches, particularly the rhymed ones, can be underscored by nimble skipping and jumping, especially once Goneril comes on stage, when he can hide behind Lear or Kent and pop out for a quick verbal salvo. His power of repartee is strongly linked to this physical aspect of his stage presence. When Lear and Goneril have their thunderous confrontation, the Fool has a span of almost one hundred lines of silence before he is literally thrown out. He could make use of this time by gradually becoming immobile as the confrontation sharpens, finally to cower in real fear when Lear leaves him, and then regain his mobility when he exits.

The short doggerel he uses as his exit line is a theatrically interesting thing. The Fool makes the entire action freeze while he steps out of the play, but not of his role, and addresses the audience directly. He has a similar effect in III.ii, where he ends the scene alone with the audience and delivers Merlin's prophecy (81–96). In both instances he serves as a lull, an eye of the storm, and creates an instance of breathing space before the next onslaught. In the third act we are in the midst of the actual storm scenes, but the tempest of tempers in the first act is a necessary prelude, an end to the Fool's comfortable existence and the beginning of his efforts to keep together the tattered remnants of Lear's reason.

The Fool of the first act is still a court jester, but the storm Goneril and Lear create between them forges him so close to Lear as to make them almost one. William Willeford says of the court fool:

> The fool enriches the king as a symbol of the self by making a constant game of our tendency to take the symbol for granted. And when the king loses his power to symbolize an experience of the self, that experience is available by way of compensation through the fool and the dissolution of consciousness that he effects.[3]

Such is the expected relationship between king and jester, and that is what we encounter in *King Lear* when we first see the Fool in action. But after Lear's fortunes truly begin to slide, the change is obvious. This must be very clear from the Fool's bearing. His court jester nimbleness may surface from time to time, but the audience has to see the change between Lear the King and Lear the husk of the King, and one efficient way to make this come across is in the physical behavior of the Fool. The Fool will disappear from the play when the question of Lear's kingship is no longer as urgent as that of Lear's fundamental humanity, that is at the true turning point, the lowest point of Lear's fortunes, where he takes over from the Fool and begins to make fundamental discoveries about himself and his relationship to his world. Therefore the Fool may describe a downward curve like his master's, may dwindle before us like Lear's reason, and finally fade from the play when Lear's madness takes him over.

I.v is a short scene of transition. Lear is preoccupied and has begun to fear for his sanity. The Fool labors mightily to keep his attention fixed, but has so little success that he changes tactics, only to find Lear even less cooperative. At the beginning of the scene the daughters are still the focus of the Fool's jibes (14–24), and his first reference is directed at Goneril and Regan, but Lear does not rise to the bait; the second one is more subtle, but Lear does not even hear. It is as if his responses are triggered more by the Fool's tone of voice than his actual words. Lear should move about the stage in thought, and the Fool try to engage his attention by following close, sometimes even blocking his way only to be brushed absentmindedly aside. When he finally gets a true response from Lear, it is no credit to his fooling; the King steals the Fool's punch line from him:

> The reason why the seven stars are no mo than seven is a
> pretty reason.
> *Lear.* Because they are not eight?
> *Fool.* Yes, indeed; thou would'st make a good Fool.

(I.v.34–36)

The Fool exits on another of his little vignettes to the audience: "She that's a maid now, and laughs at my departure, /Shall not be a maid long, unless things be cut shorter" (48–49). He reminds the audience forcibly that though he is still trying to wring a smile from Lear by his jesting, he is cruelly aware of the seriousness of the situation, and the tragic implications of Lear's journey. The Fool has few of these moments completely devoted to the audience. Though he is our teacher and the clown of the play, his teaching is much less pleasant than that of the other court jesters. He teaches us much as he teaches Lear, and that can be caustic at times.

When Lear and the Fool come upon Kent in the stocks (II.iv), we see the same pattern. The Fool again attempts to catch Lear's attention, but now he gets even less response. We see a declining curve; Lear hears the Fool's words subconsciously, and reacts with a comment about his daughters, then about his impending madness, and finally not at all:

> *Fool.* Ha, ha! he wears cruel garters. Horses are tied by the
>   heads, dogs and bears by th'neck, monkeys by th'loins, and
>   man by th'legs: when a man's overlusty at legs then he
>   wears wooden nether-stocks.
> *Lear.* What's he that hath so much thy place mistook
>   To set thee here?
> *Kent.*   It is both he and she,
>   Your son and daughter.
> *Lear.* No.
>
>   . . .
>
> *Fool.*   Fathers that wear rags
>   Do make their children blind,
>   But fathers that bear bags
>   Shall see their children kind.
>   Fortune, that errant whore,
>   Ne'er turns the key to th'poor.
>   But for all this thou shalt have as many dolours for thy
>   daughters as thou canst tell in a year.
> *Lear.* O! how this mother swells up toward my heart;
>   *Hysterica passio!* down, thou climbing sorrow!
>   Thy element's below.
>
>   . . .
>
> *Lear.* O me! my heart, my rising heart! but, down!

> *Fool.* Cry to it, Nuncle, as the cockney did to the eels when
> she put 'em i'th'paste alive; she knapp'd 'em o'th'coxcombs
> with a stick, and cried 'Down, wantons, down!' 'Twas her
> brother that, in pure kindness to his horse, buttered his hay.
> (II.iv.8–14; 46–56; 118–123)

The Fool tries his best but never reaches his master, who probably does not even notice his presence. In all three cases the Fool makes use of traditional techniques: he equates man with animals; he delivers a bit of doggerel and puns; finally he ridicules human stupidity. But no matter how pointed the Fool's observations may be to the audience, Lear is oblivious to them. It should come as a relief to the Fool when Kent reacts to his joking in the expected manner and answers him in prose as a contrast to Lear's verse (61–83). But during Lear's absence and his bout with Kent, the Fool also manages to express his unswerving loyálty to Lear (79–82). It is to the Fool, all he has left, that Lear cries: "O Fool! I shall go mad" (284).

During Lear's confrontation first with Regan, then both daughters, we have another of the Fool's long periods of silent presence. He is given no *Exit* in the Folio, but Quarto Two gives him one with Lear between lines 284 and 285, leaving him on stage without speaking for about 160 lines. His behavior now should echo that of the first act, where he was in a similar situation. We have just seen him hard at work to reach Lear, and it has been a sad affair for the Fool. More than ever he is predisposed to shrink back behind the fighting giants and finally cower close to Lear, probably even cling to his robe, as the Folio's *Storm and Tempest* is heard at line 282. Shakespeare employs the traditional and moving image of the fool cowering under the mantle of the defiant king, which shows us, as it were, two aspects of the same thing simultaneously, but Lear and his Fool are no mere image. The mighty clashes between Lear and his daughters, and between Lear's inner and outer man, leave less and less room for the Fool as jester, even the Fool as critic. The Fool is becoming more a symbol than a clown; he always was a symbol of Lear's court that was, now he begins to signify Lear's dwindling powers of reasonable action and reaction.

There is little room for laughter in *King Lear*, and what there is, is different from our unrestrained response to the comedies. The nature of the tragic mode prevents us. In a comedy we are interested in the outcome, but we remain in a position from where we may regard the proceedings with some superiority. In tragedy, however, we easily lose such a perspective because of our great personal involvement in the target of the jokes, here Lear himself. The stage clown in the guise of the Fool does trigger some amused response in the audience periodically, but when he first comes on stage the tragedy has already advanced too far to allow him free play. Even his remarks directed to the audience alone are more moralistic than amusing. We have been prepared for such behavior in the Fool, who has "much pined away" and is not his true self even when we first meet him. From the beginning of our relationship with this clown, he comes to stand as a mirror for Lear's decline; but where Lear's outward show and just cause for anger may periodically divert us from the downward curve, the Fool's behavior helps refocus our attention. The mirroring becomes ever more significant as we move into the third act. While the storm is raging, we are prepared for our next encounter with Lear and his Fool. Lear is alone in the storm, striving "in his little world of man to out-storm/The to-and-fro-conflicting wind and rain," and with him is "None but the Fool, who labours to out-jest/His heart-strook injuries" (10–11, 16–17). The pattern we have become used to will continue.

Not until III.ii does the Fool truly begin harping on sexuality:

> The cod-piece that will house
>   Before the head has any,
> The head and he shall louse;
>   So beggars marry many.
> . . . For there was yet never fair woman but she made mouths
> in a glass.

> .   .   .

> *Kent.* Who's there?
> *Fool.* Marry, here's grace and a cod-piece, that's a wise man
> and a Fool.
>
> (III.ii.27–41)

Sexuality, indeed, becomes greatly important later in the play, when Lear in his madness confronts the blinded Gloucester:

> What was thy cause?
> Adultery?
> Thou shalt not die: die for adultery! No:
> The wren goes to't, and the small gilded fly
> Does lecher in my sight.
> Let copulation thrive;
>
> (IV.vi.109–114)

Sexuality and the resulting issue is the strongest link between Lear's and Gloucester's tragedies. Gloucester is first to draw attention to a sexual transgression. In I.i he presents his bastard son Edmund to Kent, and freely admits that he was begotten out of wedlock. Lear has committed no such violation, but his view of love is clearly warped; he accepts his daughters' professions that they love him above everything else, but Cordelia is aware that something is wrong: "Sure I shall never marry like my sisters, /To love my father all" (I.i.102–103). The Fool's sexual allusions are comparatively few; but like every remark the Fool makes, these comments reach out to encompass a large problem within the play and create echoes of things past and hints of things to come.

When Kent comes to offer Lear shelter in a hovel, Lear becomes truly aware of his Fool for the first time since I.iv, but as a fellow human being rather than his jester. The Fool answers with a song to fit them both:

> *Lear.*   My wits begin to turn.

> Come on, my boy. How dost, my boy? Art cold?
> I'm cold myself. . . .
> Poor Fool and knave, I have one part in my heart
> That's sorry yet for thee.
>
> *Fool.*   *He that has and a little tiny wit,*
>   *With hey, ho, the wind and the rain,*
>   *Must make content with his fortunes fit,*
>   *Though the rain it raineth every day.*
>
>   (III.ii.68–77)

Lear's anguish in combination with the storm has finally opened his eyes to the misery of the Fool, the one being more miserable than himself because he is more aware of Lear's decline. Lear's wits are slowly becoming extinguished, and when we meet him again after the storm is over, he must make do with what fortune has left him, nothing.

Merlin's prophecy, with which the Fool ends the scene, points in the same direction. When the world is turned upside-down, England shall "[c]ome to great confusion" (92). There is much truth to this prophecy. Lear's England, as well as Lear the microcosm, are both in great confusion, and the cause is to be found within Lear himself. Lear's idea that the essence and the show of kingship can be divided is as absurd as most elements in the prophecy "Merlin shall make" when his time comes. Only for Lear there is no hope of an Arthur to put things to rights. Though the Fool has this moment alone with the audience, he does not make use of it to solicit our laughter. Much of the prophecy can be seen as ridiculous and amusing when separated from its context of the storm scenes, especially the bits of social criticism and the fantastically Utopian ideas presented. But though the Fool steps out of the play and plot proper and creates an anachronism by drawing in Merlin, the prophecy is so well related to Lear's condition and its conclusion so apt to become true that the effect is one of sadness rather than mirth.[4] The Fool may not be a bitter fool, but he is a miserable one, and his handling of his misery does him credit.

The Fool as an extension of Lear is even more an object of our pity in III.iv. His court jester image has undergone a complete change. Though his jokes were unsuccessful, he constantly tried to amuse Lear in the past, but in this scene we hear no word from him till line 39. Lear is still concerned for him above himself: "In, boy, go first. You houseless poverty,—/Nay, get thee in" (26–27), and it is a measure of the Fool's misery that he does go in first. What he meets is not shelter, however, but Edgar disguised as Poor Tom. Edgar already has created a close intimacy with the audience, who has witnessed his transformation into Poor Tom. Our closeness with him allows him to put on and use several of the clown's characteristics, though he is no clown himself.[5] In certain ways his antics as Poor Tom are not unlike the Fool's efforts, but the underlying tragedy, which provokes most of the attempts at clowning, is an overwhelming presence and turns possible laughter into deep pity.

The Fool's first reaction to Edgar is fright: "Come not in here, Nuncle; here's a spirit. /Help me! help me! . . . A spirit, a spirit: he says his name's Poor Tom" (39–42). Lear's first reaction to this "spirit," however, is identification, not fright:

> Dids't give all to thy daughters?
> And art thou come to this?
>
> .   .   .
>
> What! has his daughters brought him to this pass?
> Couldst thou save nothing? Wouldst thou give them all?
>
> (III.iv.48–63)

In Edgar-as-Poor-Tom, Lear sees a mirror image of himself, a being reduced to nothing except what he was born with, and his identification will progress so far that he strips himself in order also to become "a poor, bare, forked animal" (105–106). But the Fool's courage and control rise for a moment as Lear's wane. When Lear sees Tom as another who has given his daughters "all," the Fool replies to Lear, but certainly more to the audience: "Nay, he reserv'd a blanket, else we had all been sham'd" (64–65), and shortly afterwards: "This cold night will turn us all to fools and madmen" (77). The first comment has an ironic distance, which the audience needs at this point not to become totally overwhelmed; we see a glimmer of the traditional stage clown in action. The second comment has great truth to it. The horror of the night has been created mainly by Lear's madness, which is pitifully real. Poor Tom's madness is an act put on to save life itself. Of the three, the Fool is the most rational-seeming creature, though he too has felt his world slipping away from under him. They are all three suspended in the storm with no well-known frame of reference; the storm itself has taken over the world as we know it, raging within Lear as well as outside of him. Neither Lear nor Edgar has anything left of what they formerly used to define themselves. The Fool, however, still has his coxcomb, though the rest of his old life is lost. The Fool's remnants of control surface again when Lear strips himself. The Fool gentles him as if he were a little child, a "fool": "Prithee, Nuncle, be contented; 'tis a naughty night to swim in. Now a little fire in a wild field were like an old lecher's heart; a small spark, all the rest on's body cold. Look! here comes a walking fire" (108–111). The Fool still does his best to help Lear and make his way smoother, but his misery is growing as can be seen from another of his long silences. His jester's function becomes suspended when Lear and he are not more or less alone together. When anything even remotely threatening occurs, he fades into the background and into his sorrow. When Lear walks off with Edgar he excludes the Fool, who feels it keenly. At this point in the action, where the Fool's role is almost played out, his physical action should be limited to an absolute minimum. There should be no sprightliness left; in its stead we should see the Fool shivering, hugging himself to regain a little of the warmth a house and friendship provides man with, except when he attempts to comfort Lear; then he should become almost protective. But by now he is his own greatest resource, and he is almost spent.

The Fool, however, does not represent the element of sanity the audience needs to cling to; Kent provides this point of stability and calm. All his attempts at comforting and calming Lear, however, come to nought. In III.vi, the Fool's last scene, Lear passes judgment on his daughters with the help of Tom and the

Fool. In this company the Fool resumes his joking, but he is still more the commentator than the court jester, and his subject is still Lear's problematic kingship:

> Prithee, Nuncle, tell me whether a madman be a gentleman
>   or a yeoman?
> *Lear.* A King, a King!
> *Fool.* No; he's a yeoman that has a gentleman to his son; for
>   he's a mad yeoman that sees his son a gentleman before
>   him. . . . He's mad that trusts in the tameness of a wolf, a
>   horse's health, a boy's love, or a whore's oath.
>
> (III.vi.9–19)

Even now, when the Fool gets Lear's full attention as he jokes, his jest goes awry. Lear, always afraid of madness, now readily sees it in himself. The true madman here is indeed a King, but that was not one of the original choices. Still the Fool, mostly to the benefit of the audience, goes through with first his joke, then his bit of moralizing. It seems as if the Fool gradually becomes separated from Lear after their meeting with Poor Tom; Lear in his present state identifies more readily with him. The Fool feels deeply that he is cut adrift. However, when the trial of Goneril and Regan is to commence, the Fool is probably the one Lear addresses as "most sapient sir" while Tom is the "most learned justicer" (22, 21). As the trial progresses, Tom is the one in close contact with the audience, and the one who diverts Lear when total breakdown threatens:

> [*Aside*] My tears begin to take his part so much,
>   They mar my counterfeiting.
> *Lear.* The little dogs and all,
>   Tray, Blanch, and Sweetheart, see, they bark at me.
> *Edgar.* Tom will throw his head at them. Avaunt, you curs!
>
> (III.vi.59–63)

During the whole trial Kent hovers in the background, but his attention is riveted on Lear, and he has none to spare for the audience. When Lear has reached a point of exhaustion he persuades him to rest, and Lear lies down:

> *Lear.* Make no noise, make no noise; draw the curtains: so, so.
>   We'll go to supper i'th'morning.
> *Fool.* And I'll go to bed at noon.
>
> (III.vi.81–83)

This is the Fool's last remark before he leaves with the party bearing Lear from the stage. Poor Tom is left to address the audience. Seven more or less credible meanings have been read into this one line,[6] but when we consider how the Fool's role has developed in relation to Lear, the meaning must be very simple. Lear, in need of sleep more than food, decides to sleep now and eat Gloucester's promised supper later. In the Fool this sparks one last remark about his topsy-turvy world: if Lear can eat supper at breakfast, the Fool can end his day at high noon and go to bed.

Of course there must be connotations of ending and death connected with the Fool's idea of going to bed, especially since the Fool has dwindled so drastically before our very eyes, but at this point there has been no warning that this is his last appearance. Lear himself disappears from our sight for a long time, and when he reappears his conditions are so changed and so many things have happened to shake us fundamentally that we most likely will have forgotten about the Fool. The triangle of Lear, Tom, and the Fool in the storm is appropriate for its place in the play, but the Fool would have made an awkward third at Dover Cliff, where none of the connotations he must carry with him *qua* his stage clown status would be appropriate. Moreover, his counterpart Cordelia will shortly reappear at Lear's side and take the Fool's place as truth-teller and healer of her father.

There may be one more reference to the Fool in the play. In V.iii.304 Lear says: "And my poor fool is hang'd! No, no, no life!" We know from line 273 that Cordelia was hanged. Lear is desperately and unsuccessfully trying to find the tiniest sign of life in her, so it seems most likely that the "fool" referred to is Cordelia, not the Fool, even though Lear's thoughts may also encompass the other person who truly loved him. This is very appropriate. The Fool, the court jester, is an intrinsic part of Lear-the-King, and his main focus concerns issues of kingship and Lear's wrongful idea that its outward show can be divided from its substance. In this connection the Fool becomes almost symbolic, the way the King's crown is. The crown stands for the totality of kingship, but the only one Lear has left is bald (I.iv.159), the "meat" itself is gone. The Fool comes to represent the idea of rationality, that which binds society together and gives meaning to existence, and his voice is always harping on the foolishness of deviating from the accepted patterns of human life and organization. His bauble and coxcomb are, after all, a mocking copy of the king's scepter and crown. Once Lear has left these patterns completely, he enters another dimension of existence and proceeds to examine his inner man, and there is no more need for the Fool's voice. The Fool as symbol disappears when his purpose is served.

Lear's Fool is a creature apart from the ordinary stage clown we encounter in Shakespeare's plays. He is bound to one other character, and therefore bereft of the volatility, freedom, and mobility lent the others of his kind. In Shakespeare's source play, *King Leir*, there is no court fool, and the conclusion of the play is happily romantic. Shakespeare changed his source into a tragedy, and the addition of the character of the Fool makes a great contribution toward this transformation. The Fool as an aspect of Lear's own tragedy makes many restrictions on his clown character, but the gain is immense in terms of the audience's understanding of events and characters. Where the stage clown usually remains personally aloof and unaffected by the other characters in the play, Lear's Fool is deeply touched by Lear's tragedy and shares in it himself. The stage clown will usually appear with a certain unexpectedness and say and do surprising and delightful things, but here we are prepared for the arrival of Lear's Fool as well as for his sadness. Still he is the audience's teacher and interpreter, possibly to a degree that surpasses any other stage clown, but his teachings are single-minded. He may be seen as more critic than clown, and the amusement he provides is always tinged with sorrow.[7] The Fool is the only major clown's part in a Shakespearean tragedy, and his function is eminently fitting to his role.

Thersites and the Fool share the role of the critic in a noncomedy, and they have much to say about the shortcomings of their respective worlds, but the way in which they use the critic's tools is widely different. Thersites is aggressive to the point of disgusting the audience, and this makes us doubt his value as truth teller. We tend to believe in likable people and go along with their ideas more readily. He is still our interpreter, though, only we have to interpret him as well as his comments, and our final views of the play may well be colored by our doubt of Thersites. Lear's Fool, on the other hand, is a lovable creature, and the failure of his efforts in his court jesterly role only endears him to us further. We soon recognize that his caustic comments spring from his deep love of Lear, and so his critical attitude serves to convince us of his value as commentator. He is a true guide and interpreter, whom we readily trust, and we feel for him all the more because his actions often go against his comments. He sees Lear's shortcomings and is critical of him, but his love prompts his every action.

Thersites and the Fool are both bitter fools, and their environments are hostile to human life and human feelings and therefore inviting of criticism, even satire; but where Thersites creates distance, the Fool invites closeness; where Thersites' bitterness is all-encompassing and inimical, the Fool's serves to deepen our understanding of Lear, indeed, he creates sympathy and even love from bitterness. Still, both clown characters are eminently well suited for the play in which we find them, and in both cases the audience stands well served by their commentary.

NOTES

1. Marvin Rosenberg, in *The Masks of King Lear* (Berkeley: University of California Press, 1972), makes much of these threats.

2. I am aware that the Fool has often been played by an old man. The effect desired is the creation of Lear's *Doppelgänger*, old and wise beyond Lear himself.

3. William Willeford, *The Fool and His Scepter* (Chicago: Northwestern University Press, 1969), 173.

4. "Albion" could well be used to mean Lear; in *Hamlet*, Claudius and the Elder Fortinbras are referred to as Denmark and Norway respectively.

5. It is interesting to see that, in the facsimile of the Quarto, the title page of King Lear (page 663) mentions "*the unfortunate life of Edgar, sonne and heire to the Earle of Gloster, and his sullen and assumed humor of Tom of Bedlam..*" The Fool is not mentioned.

6. See note to III.vi.83 in the Arden Edition of the play.

7. The combined Quarto edition of *King Lear* has fewer lines for the Fool than the Folio; the Quarto play reads as if the Fool is more of a clown and less of a critic, but he is certainly no fountain of laughter and merriment in the Quarto either.

Part V

Falstaff as Clown

13

The Henriad

Falstaff is the only Shakespearean clown character who has repeat performances. He appears in three of Shakespeare's plays and is mentioned in a fourth. Not everybody, however, will feel comfortable with the label of "clown" applied to him; indeed, Falstaff is often rather a genuine character than a clown, and at times the two aspects merge totally and almost confusingly. David Wiles argues that the role of Falstaff must have been written for Will Kemp, and therefore is the clown's.[1] He builds his argument on the assumption that while Will Kemp was working with the Chamberlain's Men, he would have a tailor-made part in every play of that period.

Another and perhaps better argument for Falstaff as the part for the clown is presented with varying degrees of directness by three critics: John Dover Wilson, David Grene, and James L. Calderwood. They all point to the theatricality inherent in his role. Dover Wilson constantly refers to Falstaff as a roleplayer and comments on his variety of tricks.[2] Grene sees Falstaff as "the spirit of the theatre itself in one of its aspects—that of the clown," so to him Falstaff incarnates this role.[3] Calderwood states it most clearly of the three:

> But Falstaff, whose origin is neither England's actual past nor Holinshed's pages, owes history nothing—not even if his name was once Oldcastle. . . Falstaff's origins are theatrical and literary: the Vice of morality tradition, the *miles gloriosus* and witty parasite of Plautine comedy, the clown-fool-butt-sponge-mocker-glutton of a thousand plays from Aristophanes to the anonymous author of *The Famous Victories of Henry the Fifth*. . . . Either divorced from the historical plot of usurpation and rebellion, or repudiating it with laughter, Falstaff is also divorced from the play as an illusion of historical life. His debts are not to the play as a mimesis of history but to the play as play.[4]

This is be the best possible argument for seeing the role of Falstaff as the clown's part, but whether Falstaff is constantly the pure clown is another matter.

Because of the size of his role, his repeat performances, and his general effect on the critic, spectator, and reader alike, it is difficult to see Falstaff as anything but a "real" human being with a personality, a sum of characteristics, a past, future, and present. Also, we want to see continuity in this "character," who bears the same name though he changes from play to play. Within any given play the Falstaff role is constant, but he undergoes marked changes between plays because the needs of the playwright are for a certain effect, not for Falstaff the character. The tendency to see a character aspect in Falstaff has made many speculate about Falstaff's fate after Hal rejects him, and critics have long argued over Falstaff's personality in the history plays,[5] first and foremost the question of courage or cowardice.[6] But Falstaff as a person is a stranger in history. The historical Prince Hal may have been wild, but there is no reference to a historical person like the Shakespearean Falstaff. Shakespeare creates him for *1 Henry IV* to fulfill a theatrical function, to give flesh and substance to the escapades of Prince Hal so Hal himself remains largely unblemished and may ascend the throne with unstained character. Both Shakespeare and Falstaff himself often draw attention to the element of theatricality surrounding Falstaff. There is no doubt that he most often is a function of the theatre rather than a human character, and his tasks call for so many different elements that one person, however large, would never be able to encompass them.

The two parts of *Henry IV* retell one aspect of the historical facts of the reign of the usurper. King Henry IV is a troubled human being, who is constantly thwarted by both external and internal circumstances; but though the two plays bear his name, they serve chiefly as an exploration of Prince Henry, now the profligate but soon to become the redeemer. Only Hal is always conscious of his obligations toward his future as king, and he is aware that his escapades are a temporary thing from which he may glean knowledge. The audience shares this awareness. In this connection Falstaff can be seen as a joker in Shakespeare's game of English history, serving in whichever capacity currently convenient for the playwright.

Because Hal and Hotspur will meet on the battlefield near the conclusion of *1 Henry IV*, Falstaff is a soldier. In this capacity he serves brilliantly to bring out several important aspects of the play. He draws our attention to the figurative tug-of-war going on over the prince, where he and Hotspur, both endowed with larger-than-life dimensions, stand at either end of the rope. Their two sides resemble a mediæval stage setting, Heaven at one side, Hell's Mouth on the other, and Prince Henry seemingly vacillating between the two. One important difference between Falstaff's and Hotspur's extremes is their patterns of movement. Hotspur knows little rest. He is always in motion, his mindset reflected in his speech patterns as well as his incessant walking about, his abrupt gestures, and his constant need to accomplish something. His personality is magnetic and infectious in its restlessness and in spite of all its blemishes. Whenever he is on stage, his every speech—as well as the comments he gets from others—suggests a stormy pattern of movement. He is so notorious for these traits that Prince Hal successfully parodies him and earns our laughter (*1 Henry IV*, II.iv.99–109). His magnetism reaches as far as King Henry IV, who wishes Hotspur were his son because of his kingly qualities (*1 Henry IV*, I.i.85–90).

In direct opposition we see Falstaff. Where Hotspur is lithe, Falstaff is enormous, and Hal lets no opportunity for telling us so escape him. Neither does Falstaff. Already at our first glimpse of him, he establishes himself as stationary. Falstaff does not act, he is acted upon, and he lends himself willingly as a butt for the young Prince's jokes. Where Hotspur is a creature of light, Falstaff is one of "Diana's foresters, gentlem[a]n of the shade, [minion] of the moon" (I.ii.25–26). Falstaff will not stand if he can sit, nor sit if he can recline. His preoccupation is not with glory and honor, but rather with avoiding the consequences of their opposites. He tries his best not to pay his tavern bills, because probably Hal will pay them, and as for the more serious aspects of his life, "[S]hall there be gallows standing in England when thou art king? . . . Do not thou when thou art king hang a thief" (I.ii.57–60). When it comes to courage and honor, he shows little understanding of the mettle of a true soldier:

> But tell me, Hal, art not thou horribly afeard? Thou being heir apparent, could the world pick thee out three such enemies again, as that fiend Douglas, that spirit Percy, and that devil Glendower? Art thou not horribly afraid? Doth not thy blood thrill at it?
>
> (*1 Henry IV*, II.iv.361–366)

Falstaff and Hotspur provide the two extremes, the two perfect backgrounds against which we see Hal's character develop, but the similarity between them is contrived. Shakespeare needs Falstaff's character to be a soldier in this play, so he makes him one and draws as much from this contrivance as he can. Certainly the clown speaks in IV.ii, when Falstaff's disreputable force is criticized (IV.ii.61–67). We never see these soldiers, who look as if Falstaff "had unloaded all the gibbets and pressed the dead bodies" (37–38). Their soldiering is a means to Falstaff's usual end, creature comforts, and after Falstaff has confided in the audience how he has made money on the King's press, we cannot believe that any real men will become cannon fodder. They are a joke of the clown's and cannot be taken seriously. Moreover this treatment of the soldiers serves to put the rebellion in perspective. Finally this is an example of the Elizabethan clown's traditional way of dealing with soldiers or other men in an organized group. Here we only hear about the situation, but we see it happen on stage between Falstaff and a different sampling of recruits in *2 Henry IV*, and we find another example in *Much Ado About Nothing*, where Dogberry lords it over the group of watchmen.

In *2 Henry IV*, Falstaff has apparently aged considerably, especially in outlook. He has been knighted and is consequently referred to as Sir John. His dress must undergo a change from the soldierly garb of *1 Henry IV*; as Dover Wilson points out.[7] He is probably afflicted with some fashionable illness, not wounded, and he is most definitely fashionably attired in yards and yards of flowing material. His age and size are accentuated even further by the tiny page, a sprightly fly attending an elephant. This change is caused by Shakespeare's present need to use Falstaff as one in a group of other old men. Hal, whose development is still the main concern, stands between his dying father and the Lord Chief Justice on the one side and his old companion Falstaff, who has found a friend in Justice Robert Shallow, on the other. The dying King and the Lord Chief Justice stand for duty and therefore constraints, but also for established values; Falstaff and Justice Shallow are all for the freedom of youth, only their advanced age has caught up with them pitifully. Falstaff never doubts that he will be preferred over the Lord Chief Justice once Hal becomes king, while the Lord Chief Justice himself is in severe doubt as to what his fate will be. By remaking Falstaff's role the way he does, Shakespeare prepares the ground—and the spectator's heart—for Falstaff's rejection at the end of the play.

Again the treatment of soldiers marks Falstaff (III.ii). The clown's happy confiding in the audience has disappeared in *2 Henry IV*. Not only do we see the men, we know their opinions and their names. This makes them real to us, and makes us interested in their fate. We also see Falstaff's trafficking with money and lives, and he addresses fellow characters on stage rather than his audience. We cannot but feel a hint of disgust. Of course the director's point of view will influence our perception of the situation and our feelings about Falstaff and his recruits. Still, even though Falstaff is allowed all the clowning imaginable, the men's presence on stage and the clown's lack of direct audience address will create a distance, and this invites the spectators to become less involved and more analytical.

The very versatility of Falstaff suggests the stage clown at work, but there has to be more consistency to Falstaff's character than to that of the other stage clowns, though the amount of debate among critics suggests that this character is difficult to pin down. First of all his part is large, and it would not do to have a main character, even a clown, change like a chameleon. Still, there is a clear change between the two parts of *Henry IV*, not only in Falstaff's apparent age but also in his effect on the audience. Though he remains our stage clown, and as such our ingress to interpretation, his attitude undergoes a marked change from a clown character of the festive mood into something like an unwilling Thersites. In *1 Henry IV* he is thoroughly lovable. It is impossible to resist his excessive good humor and his ability to turn every situation to his own advantage in the audience's eyes. In the second part this ability has become pinioned to a surprising degree. Falstaff is no longer the designated victim and therefore funny, now he victimizes others.[8] The change in Falstaff's behavior stems from a need to use the clown differently in the second part and can be seen clearly from a comparison of two situations of confrontation (Falstaff's first appearance in *1 Henry IV*, II.iv, and the meeting with The Lord Chief Justice in *2 Henry IV*, I.ii), and two situations of merrymaking (Falstaff's second appearance in *1 Henry IV*, II.iv, and the scene with Doll Tearsheet, *2 Henry IV*, II.iv). In all four cases we are taught something new and essential about the themes of the play, but the tone of the teachings varies widely, and so does Falstaff's message.

The confrontation between Hal and Falstaff after the unfortunate affair at Gad's Hill is a justly celebrated scene; it is exquisitely comic and opens possibilities for unending varieties of stage business and delightful twists. Falstaff knows that he is about to be made the butt of yet another of Hal's jokes, and he comes on stage prepared. His opening comments are those of the victim who has been most horribly abused. He speaks to the audience over the heads of whoever is on stage with him, yet well aware that he is heard if not completely understood by the other characters:

> A plague of all cowards, I say, and a vengeance too, marry and amen! Give me a cup of sack, boy. Ere I lead this life long, I'll sew nether-stocks, and mend them and foot them too. A plague of all cowards! Give me a cup of sack, rogue; is there no virtue extant? . . . You rogue, here's lime in this sack too: there is nothing but roguery to be found in villainous man, yet a coward is worse than a cup of sack with lime in it. A villainous coward! . . . there lives not three good men unhanged in England, and one of them is fat, and grows old, God help the while. A bad world I say.
>
> (*1 Henry IV*, II.iv.111–129)

Falstaff ignores everybody but the serving-boy and speaks directly to the audience. We have long been party to the plans laid by Poins and the Prince, and we have also seen Falstaff's ignominious departure from the scene of the robbery. Furthermore, Hal and Poins have fired our curiosity as to how Falstaff will react, and now, when Falstaff reenters, we are itching to see how he will extricate himself from this predicament in one large piece. His first line of counterattack is a beautiful piece of strategy. When Hal finally speaks directly to him, he whirls on him and charges:

> *Prince.* How now, wool-sack, what mutter you?
> *Falstaff.* A king's son! If I do not beat thee out of thy kingdom with a dagger of lath, and drive all thy subjects afore thee like a flock of wild geese, I'll never wear hair on my face more. You, Prince of Wales!
> *Prince.* Why, you whoreson round man, what's the matter?
> *Falstaff.* Are you not a coward? Answer me to that—and Poins there?
>
> (*1 Henry IV,* II.iv.132–140)

Before there has been any opening for the opponents, Falstaff, in wounded majesty, has established himself as the deserted hero. When the Prince goads him about the booty, Falstaff embarks on his heroic tale of Gad's Hill. Throughout this long narration the style is the same. Hal prods and Falstaff responds and everything develops just as Poins has foretold. First there is "a hundred upon poor four of us" (159–160), and the fight is so violent that Falstaff was "eight times thrust through the doublet, four through the hose, [his] buckler cut through and through, [his] sword hacked like a handsaw" (164–166). Then the numbers begin flying across the stage with the description of the new wave of attack. First it is impossible to establish how many travelers there were. Then begins the real sparring match over the fellows "in buckram." The number grows from two to eleven. Hal is convinced that he has the upper hand, and even finds time to snicker with Poins behind Falstaff's back. The speed of performance will leave the audience breathless and probably unable to remember the details, but it remains clear that Falstaff's professed prowess grows ever larger, and that he seems to have enmeshed himself in the Prince's net so tightly that he cannot well escape with dignity. The comedy is all the richer for both the conspirators and the audience because we have just witnessed the proceedings with our own eyes (II.ii). Then suddenly Falstaff changes tack and serves up "three misbegotten knaves in Kendal green," who attacked him from the back in darkness so dense "thou couldst not see thy hand" (216–217). This is too much for Hal, who stops feeding him lines and turns for an attack of his own: "Why, how couldst thou know these men in Kendal green when it was so dark thou couldst not see thy hand?" (226–228). Falstaff refuses to rise to the bait:

> *Prince.* Come, tell us your reason. What sayest thou to this?
> *Poins.* Come, your reason, Jack, your reason.
> *Falstaff.* What, upon compulsion? 'Zounds, and I were at the
> strappado, or all the racks in the world, I would not tell you
> on compulsion.
>
> (*1 Henry IV*, II.iv.228–233)

Hal finally gives a short, to-the-point account of the proceedings and accuses Falstaff, but contrary to all expectations Falstaff worms his way out from under:

> *Prince.* What a slave art thou to hack thy sword as thou hast
> done, and then say it was in fight! What trick, what device,
> what starting-hole canst thou now find out, to hide thee
> from this open and apparent shame?
> *Poins.* Come, let's hear, Jack, what trick hast thou now?
> *Falstaff.* By the Lord, I knew ye as well as he that made ye.
> Why, hear you, my masters, was it for me to kill the heir-
> apparent? should I turn upon the true prince? Why, thou
> knowest I am as valiant as Hercules: but beware instinct—
> the lion will not touch the true prince; instinct is a great
> matter.
>
> (*1 Henry IV*, II.iv.257–268)

It can be debated whether Falstaff emerges as the victor in this duel or not. Dover Wilson is certain that he does, and that he signals that he recognized the Prince once he brings up the men in buckram.[9] Even clearer proof is to be found in Shakespeare's preparation for the confrontation, and in the amount of pleasure we derive from Falstaff's exertions. Our sympathy is with Falstaff throughout. The scene opens with Hal and Poins waiting for Falstaff, and they spend the time playing a somewhat gratuitous trick on poor Francis the drawer. Though this is an amusing thing to watch, Shakespeare keeps the joke on the stage, in isolation from the audience. We are spectators here, not participants.The real comedy is reserved for Falstaff's entry.

Once he is on stage and the onslaught starts, Falstaff probably keeps his bulk stationary, but uses arms and head, rolling eyes, and feigned thrusts to illustrate his heroic struggle. He is allowed more time and audience control than Hal, is even allowed a long, monologuelike speech just at the time when Hal expects to have him cornered and ready for slaughter. Falstaff enlists the whole house as he responds. Busy as he is with his verbal fray, he is always in contact with the audience and never forgets to throw us a remark or wink, or to include us with the other guests in the tavern as he addresses Hal and Poins. He never admits to being bested, but succeeds in emerging as Hercules and the lion both, and when Hal attempts to goad him again, he only offers, "Ah, no more of that, Hal, if thou lovest me" (279), thus both closing the argument and brushing the whole thing aside as he makes ready for new mirth.

This totally happy scene is in glaring contrast to Act I scene ii of *2 Henry IV*, where Falstaff is confronted by the Lord Chief Justice. In *1 Henry IV*, Falstaff happily and readily throws himself into the battle, here he tries to avoid it (I.ii.55–59). In *1 Henry IV* the preparations for the confrontation were amusing, and the audience went into the confrontation scene well prepared and happily expectant. We are prepared here, too, but in a less fetching manner. Falstaff professes to be ill. This is no new thing with him. Throughout *1 Henry IV* he had been flirting with death and old age, but never seriously. Now, however, he really is afflicted: "A pox of this gout! or a gout of this pox! for one or the other plays the rogue with my great toe" (244–246). He enters in the company of the tiny page Hal has given him "to set me off" (12–13). The contrast, which could hardly be greater, certainly is comic, but it also serves to bring Falstaff's painful foot and advancing age into the foreground. The preparation for the actual confrontation, so happily expected in *1 Henry IV*, is short and potentially serious here. The Lord Chief Justice is "the nobleman that committed the Prince for striking him about Bardolph" (55–56), and Falstaff is "he that was in question for robbery" (60). The Gad's Hill robbery of *1 Henry IV* is a phenomenon of the stage, and the incompetence of the robbers is so great that no one in the audience can believe that harm could come to Falstaff. So much is made of it that the outcome must be happy. Here the threats are indirect, but the reference is to a realistic world where crimes are punished, even if the perpetrator is the Prince of Wales.

In spite of all this, Falstaff is still our clown. His attempts to avoid the confrontation are hilarious. He tries to hide his bulk on Shakespeare's open stage; he plays deaf; he repeats "your lordship" so often that the address becomes meaningless. The Lord Chief Justice is his direct opposite. He is calm, urbane, the symbol of tradition and morality, and he has immense dignity. Moreover he dislikes Falstaff and does not hesitate to say so. But the Lord Chief Justice does one more important thing: he holds up Falstaff's age for our inspection. The audience knows that he has been "old John" throughout, is wrinkled, and still flirts with crime, sex, youth, age, and death; but here the truth of the matter is brought home to us by somebody who cares very little about Falstaff and his age but all the more about his effect on the young Prince. Therefore his testimony carries great weight. We will not take to the Lord Chief Justice the way we did to Falstaff, but we are impressed with him because he is a symbol of the immutable and necessary to society's function:

> *Falstaff.* You that are old consider not the capacities of us that
> are young; you do measure the heat of our livers with the

> bitterness of your galls; and we that are in the vaward of our
> youth, I must confess, are wags too.
> *Lord Chief Justice.* Do you set down your name in the scroll
> of youth, that are written down old with all the characters of
> age? Have you not a moist eye, a dry hand, a yellow cheek,
> a white beard, a decreasing leg, an increasing belly? Is not
> your voice broken, your wind short, your chin double, your
> wit single, and every part of you blasted with antiquity? And
> will you yet call yourself young? Fie, fie, fie, Sir John!
>   (*2 Henry IV*, I.ii.172–185)

The Lord Chief Justice holds up a mirror to Falstaff, but the spectators look into
it as well. We seem not really to have seen Falstaff before, certainly not in this
light, and here this new character cuts him down to size from top to bottom and
is not even interrupted. And moreover it is difficult not to smile, or perhaps even
laugh, with him. He makes no overt attempt at comedy, but his list includes all
the ingredients we know from *1 Henry IV*. There these words were put into the
mouth of Hal or Falstaff, their weight was light, and their potential seriousness
not recognized because the context was so utterly humorous. We are still amused
by the inventory of Falstaff's parts, but now we laugh or even snicker at him,
and he has not prompted our laughter as he promised: "The brain of this foolish-
compounded clay, man, is not able to invent anything that intends to laughter
more than I invent, or is invented on me" (8–9). Dover Wilson's theory is that
Shakespeare wrote this confrontation to "disturb, if not exactly to destroy, our
pleasure in Falstaff's company,"[10] and whether we are consciously aware of this
or not, we are more reserved towards Falstaff and more ready to judge and
condemn him.

Should we be in doubt about the outcome of this miniature battle, the Lord
Chief Justice delivers the final blow just as he leaves, and with a joke at that.
Falstaff, who is flat broke as usual, attempts the impossible:

> *Falstaff.* Will your lordship lend me a thousand pounds to
> furnish me forth?
> *Lord Chief Justice.* Not a penny, not a penny; you are too
> impatient to bear crosses. Fare you well: commend me to
> my cousin in Westmoreland.
>   (*2 Henry IV*, I.ii.224–228)

The scene is almost at its end, and little is done to restore Falstaff's position
with the audience. He exits fully intending to make the best of things as usual,
but also to attempt a deceit of a new kind with him:

> Go, bear this letter to my Lord of Lancaster; this to the Prince;
> this to the Earl of Westmoreland;—and this to old mistress
> Ursula, whom I have weekly sworn to marry since I perceived
> the first white hair of my chin. About it .... 'Tis no matter if I
> do halt; I have the wars for my colour; and my pension shall

seem the more reasonable. A good wit will make use of
anything; I will turn diseases to commodity.
                                                    (*2 Henry IV*, i.II.239–250)

Falstaff's effect on the audience has changed radically from the first to the
second part of *Henry IV*. The most probable explanation for this could be that in
the first part Shakespeare is in need of a traditional clown with some character
elements, because this clown is given a major part and has more direct
interaction with his fellow characters than usual for a clown. In the second part,
the clown is given more character traits than clown traits, and the issue of his
clown status may sometimes be in doubt because of this. Already in his first
scene of *2 Henry IV*, he does not make use of his time on stage to make an
alliance with the audience. His character-side may not really be aware that a
struggle is forthcoming, and even the Lord Chief Justice may not have persuaded
him of this. His joking is with the Page rather than with the house, and where
there is a question of our sympathy he tends to take us for granted to such a
degree that it may jar on us. The character and function of the Lord Chief Justice
brings this home to us. We begin to pull away from Falstaff and may even
begin to be slightly disappointed in our expectations. Still, all the clown
trappings are there to be enjoyed. The excessive halting, the contrast between the
mountainous Falstaff and his mouse of a page, his clothes which, with a solid
basis in the text, can be made ridiculously overfashionable for one so huge, all
of this points to the clown character; but somehow we are not totally satisfied
with what we get.

The contrast becomes more obvious after a comparison of the two tavern
scenes. In *1 Henry IV*, when Falstaff reenters after having seen the King's
messenger (II.iv.322), he is suddenly very knowledgeable about politics and the
characters of the leaders of the rebellion. Shakespeare uses this short political
discussion to remind us of Hotspur, and have us compare them both with Hal,
but soon Falstaff turns the potential dangers to theatricality. He stage-manages
the "play extempore" promised in line 276. Hal has to "practise an answer"
(369–370) before he is actually rebuked by the King, his father, and Falstaff as
King Henry quickly provides everything necessary:

This chair shall be my state, this dagger my sceptre, and this
cushion my crown. . . . Give me a cup of sack to make my
eyes look red, that it may be thought I have wept, for I must
speak in passion, and I will do it in King Cambyses' vein. . .
[*to the Hostess, who has not been given a part before*] Weep
not, sweet Queen, for trickling tears are vain.
                                            (*1 Henry IV*, II.iv.373–386 [my stage directions])

The stage props already in use are turned into something else, and Falstaff thinks
of make-up as well as more characters, all in one breath. Here he is the clown in
his element, that of sheer artificiality and theatricality. He even speaks a line of
verse for good measure. His speech becomes loaded with metaphors, and he holds
up the royal household to our inspection so we realize that its problems and
worries often are no different from our own; fathers will have trouble with sons.

He makes use of his new exalted position to put in many good words for himself. He is

> a virtuous man . . . [a] good portly man, i'faith, and a
> corpulent; of a cheerful look, a pleasing eye, and a most noble
> carriage; and, as I think, his age some fifty, or by'r lady,
> inclining to three score. . . . If that man should be lewdly
> given, he deceiveth me; for Harry, I see virtue in his looks.
>
> (*1 Henry IV*, II.iv.413–422)

The "King," on the other hand, recognizes himself in Hal; they have the same "villainous trick of [the] eye, and a foolish hanging of [the] nether lip" (399–400). This self-glorification of Falstaff's becomes too much for Hal, who demands that they exchange parts. Falstaff takes it all in his stride, and asks both the on-stage audience and us in the house to be the judge of who makes the better king as well as the better prince (433). Hal wants the king's part to get back at Falstaff, but he is immediately bested. After he has given a lengthy catalogue of Falstaff's imperfections and abominations, but without mentioning his name, Falstaff delivers the answer that will enable him to continue his self-eulogy:

> I would your Grace would take me with you: whom means
> your Grace?
> *Prince.* That villainous abominable misleader of youth,
> Falstaff, that old white-bearded Satan.
> *Falstaff.* My lord, the man I know.
>
> (*1 Henry IV*, II.iv.454–458)

He then proceeds to number all the negative qualities Falstaff has succeeded in making endearing to us, because we know that he is no realistic person, he is our stage clown. We are so taken with this Falstaff, who is given adjectives such as "sweet," "kind," "true," and "valiant," that the threat of banishment with which Hal closes the play extempore may easily escape us (475). Falstaff the clown certainly chooses to ignore it, though the remark is addressed to him. With this line, Hal steps out of both his roles, and he addresses the audience self-consciously in anticipation of the future.

Hal's "I do [banish Falstaff], I will," though simultaneously spoken in the character of the King his father, signals a new development: Falstaff is being tracked down by the Sheriff's men and is almost found. But the on-stage play and the sweet sound of all these wonderful adjectives have made Falstaff totally oblivious to the grim realities of being caught. First he wants to continue with the "play extempore" to further flesh out this wonderful Falstaff of his own making, but as there is no denying the Sheriff, he takes the new Falstaff upon himself and becomes true, kind, and valiant:

> Never call a true piece of gold a counterfeit: thou art
> essentially made without seeming so.
> *Prince.* And thou a natural coward without instinct.

> *Falstaff.* I deny your major. If you will deny the sheriff, so; if
> not, let him enter. If I become not a cart as well as another
> man, a plague on my bringing up.
>
> (*1 Henry IV*, II.iv.485–491)

Falstaff does hide, but once the crisis is over and he can come forth freely, he is
discovered snoring behind an arras. When Hal searches him, he finds a tavern bill
listing food and drink, all the delicacies of which the clown is so fond, but spiced
with "an intolerable deal af sack" (534). He is presumably semicarried or dragged
off stage, providing as much comedy sleeping as he did awake, and again veiling
with his bulk the seriousness of the rebellion. Hal's threat to "procure this fat
rogue a charge of foot, and I know his death will be a march of twelve score"
(538–539) is so much within the comical and theatrical pattern created by
Falstaff that we only see the promise of yet another joke played on him.

The mood of this tavern scene is as light and happy as anyone could desire,
and it stands forth brilliantly against the serious background of the King's
worries over the succession and the looming rebellion and civil war. Nothing
serious is allowed a firm foothold, and should anything threaten this almost
magical sphere, it is soon averted or turned to mirth. This is all Falstaff's doing.
His fertile brain and nimble tongue, his ability to sustain long monologues, and
his apparent control over his entire environment make comedy sparkle and shine.
Falstaff is firmly established with the spectators as a clown extraordinary, whose
every appearance later will be greeted with delight and high expectations. The
Boar's Head scene stands forth so sharply because of Falstaff's ability to distance
himself and this night of merrymaking from reality, and to create theatre-within-
theatre twice over. For what is the recital of great deeds at Gad's Hill but a long-
sustained comic show carried by one man? The clown provides us with comic
fiction within the fictitious history play. But there is something missing from
this scene, and this may well be what makes the airy comedy possible. We do
see revellers and are reminded of food and drink and much else that takes place in
a tavern, but the true female element is missing. Though Mistress Quickly
appears, it certainly is not for her sexual potential. Her presence as stage
audience during the theatricals adds to the comedy, but she never becomes a
sexual being.

In *2 Henry IV*, II.iv, on the other hand, there is no such lack of female
companionship. The hostess herself provides Doll's services, and the mere idea
of leaving Falstaff the clown seemingly alone with a lady of ill repute while the
Prince and Poins watch in the guise of drawers is a promise of great comedy. We
catch the pair after a supper which has left them slightly the worse for wear, but
Falstaff does not succeed in lightening the mood:

> *Falstaff.* How now, Mistress Doll?
> *Hostess.* Sick of a calm, yea, in good faith.
> *Falstaff.* So is all her sect; and they be once in a calm, they are
> sick.
> *Doll.* A pox damn you, you muddy rascal, is that all the
> comfort you give me?
> *Falstaff.* You make fat rascals, Mistress Doll.

> *Doll*. I make them? Gluttony and diseases make them, I make
> them not.
> *Falstaff*. If the cook help to make the gluttony, you help to
> make the diseases, Doll; we catch of you, Doll, we catch of
> you; grant that, my poor virtue, grant that.
> *Doll*. Yea, joy, our chains and our jewels.
>
> > (*2 Henry IV*, II.iv.34–47)

There is comedy here, and the audience is amused, but the comedy is of the dark variety, and the jokes remain on stage. The bickering between Falstaff and Doll can be made more or less serious, but the possibility to involve the audience's participation is very slight. First of all the Hostess is there as a third party already. Interested as she is, she generates comedy by her use of malapropisms and by general misunderstandings. Doll herself is no representative of the straight man who can feed lines to Falstaff after the pattern of Hal in the former tavern scene. Rather than relying on Falstaff's bond with the audience, the comedy depends on Doll's ability to get back at Falstaff and give as good as she gets. The sparkle of the first tavern scene never emerges.

As the scene proceeds, the Hostess and Doll between them provide most of the comedy. The Hostess's wordiness and Doll's wildcat temper and spicy language disable Falstaff to a large extent. The women are left to fight the battle with Pistol almost to the bitter end with no help, and though it is conceivable that Falstaff could sit back and enjoy the proceedings as if he had staged them, his remarks to Pistol and Bardolph and the final drawing of swords seem to indicate otherwise.[11] Falstaff's temper is not what it was, and there is no more happy turning black to white and threats to mirth. Falstaff is old, grumpy, and tired.

The sexually loaded part of the comedy is also provided by the women. The Hostess is worried about Falstaff's ability: "Are you hurt in the groin? Methought he made a shrewd thrust at your belly" (207–208), and the fight and sight of blood has excited Doll: "Ah, you whoreson little valiant villain, you" (206); "Ah, rogue, i'faith I love thee" (215–216). However, the fight has left Falstaff melancholy and tired, with more thoughts about old age and death than sexual prowess:

> *Doll* [*on his lap*]. . . . when wilt thou leave fighting a-days
> and foining a-nights, and begin to patch up thine old body
> for heaven?
> *Falstaff*. Peace, good Doll, do not speak like a death's-head, do
> not bid me remember mine end.
>
> > (*2 Henry IV* , II.iv.228–232)

And later:

> *Falstaff*. Thou dost give me flattering busses.
> *Doll*. By my troth, I kiss thee with a most constant heart.
> *Falstaff*. I am old, I am old.
> *Doll*. I love thee better than I love e'er a scurvy young boy of
> them all.
> *Falstaff*. . . . Thou't forget me when I am gone.

Doll. By my troth, thou't see me a-weeping . . .
                                        (*2 Henry IV*, II.iv.266–275)

Since we met him Falstaff has been harping on his age whenever it suited him, but here he seems genuinely old and frightened by the thought of death on this eve of his departure for the field. The comedy follows a well-known pattern: the old man in his cups complaining to the younger woman of the unfairness of the world.

Doll tries to cheer Falstaff by turning the conversation to the Prince and Poins, but to no avail. Only their actual arrival perks Falstaff up somewhat, but we never reach any level of comedy even close to the former tavern scene. Falstaff rises to the occasion because it is expected of him, but he remains defensive and does not attempt to enlist the audience on his side:

Falstaff. Didst thou hear me?
Prince. Yea, and you knew me as you did when you ran away
    by Gad's Hill; you knew I was at your back and spoke it on
    purpose to try my patience.
Falstaff. No, no, no, not so; I did not think thou wast within
    hearing.
Prince. I shall drive you to confess the willful abuse, and then
    I know how to handle you.
Falstaff. No abuse, Hal, o' mine honour, no abuse.
Prince. Not?—to dispraise me, and call me pantler, and bread-
    chipper, and I know not what?
Falstaff. No abuse, Hal.
Poins. No abuse?
Falstaff. No abuse, Ned, i'th'world, honest Ned, none. I
    dispraised him before the wicked that the wicked might not
    fall in love with thee: in which doing, I have done the part
    of a careful friend and a true subject, and thy father is to give
    me thanks for it. No abuse, Hal; none, Ned, none; no, faith,
    boys, none.
                                        (*2 Henry IV*, II.iv.302–321)

The Prince and Poins are as disappointed in Falstaff as we are. He does not truly make any of his well-beloved and well-known attempts to wiggle out from under the charges and come forth victorious, rather he makes weak excuses for no real offense. Even his attempt to put the blame on Doll's seductive powers falls flat, for both the audience and the listening Prince have heard Falstaff's real and believable jealousy of Poins underlying the "dispraise."

The need for Falstaff to be less of a clown and more of a character in *2 Henry IV* may stem from a necessity to create a chasm between Falstaff and the Prince; that of age versus youth is an excellent choice. Falstaff is no longer of the same group as the young Prince; he is among those waning from the center of things. Among the old men only the Lord Chief Justice emerges from *2 Henry IV* unchanged, for without him at his side the new King would not be able to demonstrate the depth of his good intentions. Justices Shallow and Silence cling to youth along with Falstaff, but their attempt to recover lost wonders is a miserable one. We do not need Falstaff's often caustic asides to see that their memories are tinged with sadness, for their era is long dead. Falstaff himself loses much of his appeal as we watch his interaction with his fellow players. He uses and abuses them only to gain advantages for himself, not to provide easy laughter for the spectators. His moments alone with the audience are mainly spent in demonstrating this trait, not to sweep us over to his point of view. As a matter of fact we have many opportunities to see a very unpleasant side to Falstaff, but he is still our teacher to a large extent. He becomes the incorporation of everything Hal must shed to become Henry V.

Still, seeing Falstaff as a character does not work well in *2 Henry IV*. He has more interaction with his fellow characters and less with his audience, and so his function as interpreter and teacher is somewhat more difficult, but if we attempt to look at him as a person in his own right the picture emerging is sketchy. Falstaff is still to a large extent a conglomerate of clown traits, and he relies heavily on clown staples to create his effect. The clown character of *2 Henry IV* is a much darker and more complex one, who delivers a critical view of many of the functions of society and shows how to exploit them for personal gain. The happy clown with whom the audience feels comfortable because we know what to expect is gone from *2 Henry IV*.

Because of the sheer size of Falstaff's combined roles, he becomes more confusing to the audience than any other clown. The consistency of a genuine character such as Hal is total. The audience is never deceived about his inherent goodness and his determination to become a distinguished ruler, though his fellow characters on stage may be. Such a consistency is lacking in Falstaff. We meet a true stage clown, but gradually his composition changes; he becomes alienated from the audience. From the commentator and outside controller with a function within the play as well as between play and audience, he becomes an entity which can be affected by the chronological progress of the play; he becomes absorbed by the plot.

Falstaff's most interesting clown performance in the history plays can be found in the fifth act of *1 Henry IV*. Here he is all clown, and uses all the tricks of his trade. His first appearance is in the first scene, in preparation for the battle of Shrewsbury. We find him in the company of his betters and he is mostly silent, but his one remark indicates that the Prince has a difficult time trying to keep him quietly in his place:

> *Worcester.*   For I protest
>   I have not sought the day of this dislike.
> *King.* You have not sought it? How comes it, then?
> *Falstaff.* Rebellion lay in his way, and he found it.
> *Prince.* Peace, chewet, peace!
>
>   (*1 Henry IV*, V.i.25–29)

Falstaff's remark, thrown to the audience and overheard by the Prince, gives us a humorous angle on the making of rebels. But Hal, firmly within the frame of the fiction, sees the possibility for offense to Worcester and silences Falstaff. He remains quiet throughout the parlay, and because he is not the most popular member of the King's inner circle, he can probably be found away from the center of the talks in close contact with the audience. The more valiant and honorable the proceedings, the more signals Falstaff will send to the audience about his own distrust in all this lofty stuff. After the formal talks end and Hal refuses to "bestride [him]" (121) should he stumble during the coming battle, a fear emerges with which we can sympathize: "I would t'were bedtime, Hal, and all well" (125). When Hal brushes him off and leaves him alone with us, Falstaff first works on his courage, then gives it up and delivers his honest opinion about honor:

> Well, 'tis no matter, honour pricks me on. Yea, but how if honor prick me off when I come on, how then? Can honour set a leg? No. Or an arm? No. Or take away the grief of a wound? No. Honour hath no skill in surgery then? No. What is honour? A word. What is in that word Honour? What is honour? Air. A trim reckoning! Who hath it? He that died a-Wednesday. Doth he feel it? No. Doth he hear it? No. 'Tis insensible, then? Yea, to the dead. But will it not live with the living? No. Why? Detraction will not suffer it. Therefore I'll none of it. Honour is a mere scutcheon—and so ends my catechism.
>
> (*1 Henry IV*, V.i.129–141)

Like Feste and Launcelot Gobbo in their discussions with themselves, Falstaff has to make himself into two persons for this speech. On the one hand he presents a youthful, innocent aspect, on the other an old man's disillusioned one, but the issue is never truly in doubt. Worldly experience wins the day; death is grim, and if death is the price, Falstaff wants nothing to do with honor. On the background of Hotspur's fire and the Prince of Wales' newly demonstrated valor the comedy of this monologue is wonderful.

When we next meet him battle rages on all sides, but Falstaff himself has succeeded in remaining in a little pocket of safety. With him we see only Blunt's corpse, but Falstaff makes a mockery of his valiant death. He tells us that his "ragamuffins" have all been killed or maimed, seemingly to no avail. In reality a dead body is only a dead body, no matter how valiant or cowardly the man once was. For Falstaff true virtue lies in staying alive and gaining as much as possible, be it worldly possessions or undeserved honor. When the Prince comes to ask for his sword, Falstaff refuses to give it to him, for he holds life dearer than his duty towards the heir. His resolution made during the honor-speech has borne strange fruit: there is a bottle of sack in the holster where his pistol should be, a great source of courage! When the Prince leaves him in disgust, Falstaff again sums up the most important things to keep in mind:

> Well, if Percy be alive, I'll pierce him. If he do come in my way, so: if he do not, if I come in his willingly, let him make a carbonado of me. I like not such grinning honour as Sir Walter hath. Give me life, which if I can save, so: if not, honour comes unlooked for, and there's an end.
>
> (*1 Henry IV*, V.iii.56–61)

The most important person on the field is one's self, and if damage can be avoided so much the better.

The audience is now more than familiar with Falstaff's attitude towards battle, honor, and glory. With this firmly fixed in our minds nothing could be more beautifully timed than his entry in V.iv in the midst of the duel between the two most honorable and glory-seeking characters, Hotspur and Hal: "Well said, Hal! To it, Hal! Nay, you shall find no boy's play here, I can tell you" (74–75). James L. Calderwood says of this entry:

> For a disconcerting moment or two we may realize that "boy's play" is precisely what we shall find, *are* finding, here—mock combat, bated swords, the carefully rehearsed thrust and riposte, with Hotspur maneuvering surreptitiously to let Hal stab him in the vest pocket where a small bladder of pig's blood is concealed to make the groundlings grunt and the ladies squeal. Boy's play is as prominent here as it is a bit later when Douglas rushes on stage to pursue that great bladder of blood and sherris, the squealing Falstaff, who saws the air with his sword while hunting a comfortable place to collapse in mortal agony.[12]

Indeed, this is a spot where theatre and history meet and clash, and the clash will become louder still. Hal and Hotspur have uplifted our patriotic souls more than once, and never higher that in their precombat courtesies towards each other. But how can even such glory stand against a Falstaff on the sidelines, shouting encouragements and reminding the audience that this is after all only historical fiction. We see the well-known clown pattern in full flower here. Part of the clown's function is taking care that the audience does not become too deeply involved emotionally, and so he provides us with the possibility of a cooler and more analytical outside view. Falstaff can jump about at a safe distance from the sword points, but possibly a more effective playing style would be to copy the audience, sit down, and enjoy. This would make Douglas's entry and attack so much more ridiculous, because Falstaff has to maneuver his bulk off the ground and get himself running with the point of Douglas's sword very close behind him, only to "die" gratefully as soon as possible. Whatever playing style is chosen for Falstaff, he has to jump back and forth across the fine line that separates the play's fictional world from the everyday world of the audience, and Falstaff the clown does this exceptionally well. Whether the audience realizes consciously that what we see is in reality "boy's play" is of no matter; subconsciously we cannot help grasping this.

The mock-combat between Falstaff and Douglas runs parallel with the deadly serious one between Hal and Hotspur. Falstaff and Hotspur fall at about the same moment during the battle and on the same stage, but worlds apart. Hotspur dies firmly fixed within the fiction, maintaining his character to the very last.

The director has two wonderfully comic opportunities for staging Falstaff's "death." He can keep the audience in the dark, so they believe that Falstaff is truly a closed chapter, or he can let Falstaff inform the spectators that he is far from dead and only biding his time and saving his hide. The two possibilities naturally create two very different clown performances. Should the director choose to leave the audience in the dark, we will feel some grief for our Falstaff and much regret that he should come to such an end, only to be doubly delighted at his comic resurrection. This method of staging will leave Falstaff less opportunity for clowning than the second option, where he would send us constant signals about his state of mind and body until the moment he can begin speaking to us again. Hal's speech over the "dead" Falstaff becomes completely comic if we are allowed to see Falstaff's mounting fear of being "embowelled" as he strives to stay "dead" until the Prince leaves. Given Falstaff's urge to remain in constant contact with the audience and his habit of communicating more closely with us than with most of his fellow characters, the second option seems the more obvious choice.

Falstaff can easily make it clear to us that he is keeping an eye on the goings on from his state of feigned death, partly to make sure that Hotspur is safely dead, and partly in order that the audience shall not become too absorbed in the proceedings. Once he gets back on his feet, he first lectures the audience on "counterfeiting," but then remembers that Hotspur is lying close by, and his fear returns:

> 'Zounds, I am afraid of this gunpowder Percy, though he be dead; how if he should counterfeit too and rise? By my faith, I am afraid he would prove the better counterfeit; therefore I'll make him sure, yea, and I'll swear I killed him. Why may not he rise as well as I? Nothing confutes me but eyes, and nobody sees me: therefore sirrah, with a new wound in your thigh, come you along with me.
>
> (*1 Henry IV*, V.iv.120–128)

His plan clearly is formed as he speaks. First he winces away from Hotspur in fear, but gradually Hotspur becomes less of the hero and more a mere corpse to Falstaff. He approaches him slowly, and finally addresses him familiarly and stabs him in the thigh. So much for glory and honor. But the truly interesting clown observations are on "counterfeiting." Falstaff reminds us that after this scene is over, the actor playing Hotspur will indeed rise just as Falstaff did, but out of our sight, for Hotspur belongs in the fiction. This whole speech is addressed to the audience, for there is nobody else to hear; still, the audience is also made a fiction of, for "nobody sees me." Falstaff juggles the world of the fiction and the world of the audience back and forth with great speed and dexterity and succeeds in making a mockery of everything heroic. The mere thought of what the explosive Hotspur would have said and done had he known of this is enough to set one laughing.

As Falstaff is getting a good grip on Hotspur's dead body, the two Princes enter, and our mirth rises as Hal says, "[T]hou art not what thou seem'st," and Falstaff replies, "No, that's certain" (136–137). This is true on more levels than one. Falstaff is in reality an actor in a play, as he has just reminded us, but he also had been declared dead, which is obviously not the case, and now he claims to have killed Hotspur. Nothing is what it seems. And on this background Shakespeare uses Falstaff to mock the avidity with which his audience swallows stories about kings and princes: "I look to be either earl or duke, I can assure you," says Falstaff (141–142); so much for the nobility.

Hal knows well that he killed Hotspur, but he pretends to believe in Falstaff's yarn; he even promises that "if a lie may do thee grace, /I'll gild it with the happiest terms I have" (156–157). He then exits with his brother to celebrate the victory, leaving us alone with Falstaff one last time. Falstaff is at a high point, he believes. The Prince has promised to lie for him and give him the honor of killing Hotspur, so now the sky is the limit. In a realistic modern production, this lie of Falstaff's may conceivably be seen as dishonorable and repulsive, but though the presentation may seek to convey such a feeling, the audience is too deeply in love with this bundle of energy to change their feelings. Falstaff can get away with such a trick because he is a clown and not a genuine character. He even promises to "purge, and leave sack, and live cleanly as a nobleman should do" (163–164), but the audience fears no such thing. He has taught us too well about fiction within fiction. Honor has indeed come "unlooked for" to our stage clown, but not by his own death as he feared in V.iii. Falstaff has had the luck to cheat not only Hal but the entire history book also, and we have been made party to his deceit.

When both *Henry IV* plays are seen together, Falstaff serves as an excellent example of how difficult it is to create a clown's part of such large proportions. Falstaff must be given some character traits to be able to function well in such a lengthy part, and the need to use him as a character seems to gain the upper hand in *2 Henry IV*, but in *1 Henry IV* he is one of Shakespeare's most brilliant clown figures. He has the space and the scope to shine forth in all manner of functions and to create laughter from the most incredible situations. Still he serves as an aspect of Hal's character formation, and he is never allowed to transcend that role. He is never given the close intimacy of Poins, he remains temptation refused, and he never succeeds in undermining Hal's credibility as the rightful heir. If anything, he lends to the future King Henry a depth of humanity on which he depends in *Henry V*. Moreover, Falstaff acts as a counterweight to Hotspur, and Shakespeare often puts them in parallel situations. In each of these, Falstaff's mockery provides the audience with a more detached view of the proceedings, a distance of which we are much in need. Hotspur without Falstaff would be a compelling character and much too serious competition for the Prince. So again we see the stage clown as our teacher and guide as well as the provider of mirth and enjoyment. If any one character opens our eyes and makes us see clearer, he is Falstaff.

NOTES

1. David Wiles, *Shakespeare's Clown* (Cambridge and New York: Cambridge University Press, 1987), 118–119.

2. J. Dover Wilson, *The Fortunes of Falstaff* (Cambridge and New York: Cambridge University Press, 1943), 32–33.

3. David Grene, *The Actor in History: A Study in Shakespearean Stage Poetry* (Pennsylvania State University Press, 1988), 76–77.

4. James L. Calderwood, *Metadrama in Shakespeare's Henriad: "Richard II" to "Henry V "* (Berkeley and Los Angeles: University of California Press, 1979), 73.

5. Due to the very different nature of Falstaff's three plays, I shall consider *The Merry Wives of Windsor* after the two parts of *Henry IV*, and avoid speculations about where in the historic sequence the comedy belongs.

6. The controversy began with Maurice Morgann, *An Essay on the Dramatic Character of Sir John Falstaff* (1777), and seems still to be going on.

7. Dover Wilson 91.

8. See Calderwood, 95, for a good analysis of this point.

9. Dover Wilson 50.

10. Dover Wilson 99.

11. See the Hostess' "put up your naked weapons" (line 203).

12. Calderwood 69–70.

14

The Merry Wives of Windsor

Falstaff in *The Merry Wives of Windsor* is Falstaff in a comedy, and though this makes for differences there are numerous similarities as well. In the *Henry IV* plays we see a wealth of comic characters, but Falstaff is never truly part of a comic group. Where he makes use of Hal and the audience for effect, the others are a source of comedy because of their names or some such trait as Bardolph's nose and the Hostess's malapropisms. The comic characters all belong to the group of London low-lifes surrounding Falstaff. In *The Merry Wives of Windsor* this aspect has changed, and Falstaff becomes the intruder into an established world. Similarly to *1 Henry IV*, Falstaff is again maneuvered into difficult situations, and we watch him trying to struggle out. The great difference is that while he formerly always succeeded, here Falstaff cannot predictably exercise the control commonly associated with the stage clown in a major part. Most of the comedy depends on Falstaff's inflated belief in his own superiority, primarily as a seducer.

In *The Merry Wives of Windsor* Falstaff has a great number of appearances, most of them short, and more often than not his entry has been well prepared for; before his first appearance (I.i.100), for example, he has been the subject of discussion since the play began. Falstaff's entries are set up by groups and individuals, by indignant, expectant, and angry people, and always the audience is aware of the direction the scene is to take. Soon we learn in what combinations Falstaff comes out the victor and when he is bested. These fixed patterns may be why many critics find this play less interesting than most of Shakespeare's other comedies.

In *The Merry Wives of Windsor* an attempt is made to include the well-known, attention-consuming Falstaff in the plot, where he would traditionally be relegated to the subplot. Without his angle, there would still be a traditional plotline of love's intricacies, and in any other comedy Anne Page's winding way to the altar would be the main focus of our interest, while the stage clown would be our guide along the path. But Falstaff has no interest in the plot surrounding

Anne Page. He creates his own "love interest" plot, which would traditionally be a mirroring subplot, but which here is given such weight that it almost submerges the plot of the young lovers. Shakespeare makes Falstaff so preoccupied with his own plotting and scheming that his status as stage clown is jeopardized from time to time. His involvement with his fellow characters becomes so deep that he periodically forgets to cultivate his rapport with the audience. We are laughing at him as often as with him. These may well be two more reasons why *The Merry Wives* is not regarded among Shakespeare's most successful comedies. The patterns we expect are not forthcoming, and the plots are interwoven to such an extent that any possibility for mirroring is lost. Many comic characters, who would traditionally be quite minor, are given greater weight than they would merit in a traditionally structured comedy. It becomes difficult or impossible to divide the characters into convenient groups because everybody belongs in more than one place. Slender, Doctor Caius, and Sir Hugh Evans, for example, are comic characters, but they are also social equals to the Pages. Still, Falstaff has the opportunity for much delightful clowning, and when he remembers the audience he has much to give. But he is further removed from close audience contact than a true clown would be, and even his long monologues could well be something we overhear rather than receive. He does not make use of his time alone with the audience to teach or inform, he merely enlarges comically and from a completely personal angle upon things we know well from other characters, from our own observations, and from himself. It may be said that in this play Falstaff the clown has become Falstaff the character.

When a foreign element of Falstaff's magnitude is let loose upon an established society there are many possibilities for reception. He can be rejected altogether; permitted to stay, but in isolation; accepted on a trial basis; or immediately assimilated. In *The Merry Wives of Windsor* the measure of Falstaff's lacking closeness with the audience can be judged from these patterns. We know much more about the other characters' true feelings than Falstaff does, and where he believes himself to be in one position, we know that he is in another. Falstaff is ignorant about numerous goings on which concern the heart of the comedy. Such lack of awareness is not customary in a stage clown, who would usually be the one to set up the situation or present it for our inspection and guide us in our interpretation. Here we come to rely on other characters for setting up the comic situation, and on the judgment of a variety of characters, but mostly our own, when it comes to digesting what we saw. Falstaff has been reduced in stature, for where we expect the clown we are presented with a stock comic figure, the gullible old man. The comedy tries to accomplish more than the medium will comfortably hold with less than we expect, and Falstaff and the audience are losers in this bargain.

The situations where Falstaff and the audience are most comfortable together are those in the Garter Inn, where Falstaff sets up quarters and hatches the plot to seduce the two wives. When the plot of seduction is set in motion and the women take control, Falstaff's awareness wanes considerably. The first of these scenes is I.iii, where Falstaff, in debt as always, wrings his brains to find ready money. His first solution is "getting rid of some of [his] followers" (4–5), Bardolph, Nym, Pistol, and Robin. Bardolph is easily provided for:

> *Host.* I will entertain Bardolph; he shall draw, he shall tap.
> Said I well, bully Hector?
> *Falstaff.* Do so, good mine host. . . . Bardolph, follow him. A
> tapster is a good trade; an old cloak makes a new jerkin; a
> withered serving-man a fresh tapster. Go; adieu.
>
> (I.iii.11–17)

Thus Bardolph is no longer Falstaff's financial responsibility but still conveniently at hand to serve him. Nym and Pistol are equally readily got rid of, but less pleasantly. When Falstaff tells them that he must "cony-catch", must "shift" (31–32), and presents them with his plan to seduce Ford's wife, for "she has all the rule of her husband's purse" (49–50), they both approve of the plan. When he reveals that he intends to attempt to seduce Page's wife as well, for "she bears the purse too" (64), things go wrong:

> *Falstaff.* I will be cheaters to them both, and they shall be
> exchequers to me; they shall be my East and West Indies,
> and I will trade to them both. Go bear thou this letter to
> Mistress Page; and thou this to Mistress Ford: we will
> thrive, lads, we will thrive.
> *Pistol.* Shall I Sir Pandarus of Troy become,
> And by my side wear steel? Then Lucifer take all!
> *Nym.* I will run no base humour. Here, take the humourletter;
> I will keep the haviour of reputation.
> *Falstaff* [*to Robin*]. Hold, sirrah, bear you these letters tightly;
> Sail like my pinnace to these golden shores.
> Rogues, hence, avaunt, vanish like hailstones; go;
> Trudge; plod away i'th'hoof; seek shelter, pack!
> Falstaff will learn the honour of the age;
> French thrift, you rogues—myself and skirted page.
>
> (I.iii.65–80)

The audience is certain to enjoy this example of honor among thieves. Seducing one wife for gain and not for love is perfectly acceptable, but seducing two simultaneously is totally unpalatable to Pistol and Nym. Under cover of indignation Falstaff succeeds in ridding himself of two more mouths to feed, and he does so impressively. His wrath is apparent in the change of style from his customary prose to verse worthy of Pistol himself. The change in Falstaff's behavior is delightfully comic. He moves from plotting on a level with his intimates, reveling in the anticipation of success, to drawing himself to his full height and bulk and storming at them; but he never forgets how practical this is.[1] Without any remark from him, the audience is well aware that Falstaff seizes this chance to reduce his expenses, and his playacting in verse will delight the house. What Falstaff has not reckoned with is the equally great indignation kindled in the breasts of his dismissed servants. The scene ends with the audience's anticipation sharpened by their plans to reveal the whole thing to the respective husbands.

The placing of the second of Falstaff's scenes at the Garter Inn is perfect. The audience has just met with the two wives marked for Falstaffian seduction, and their ready wit and resolute measures have made a favorable impression on us. Now their plans for trapping Falstaff are fresh in our minds, and so are Pistol's revelations and Ford's fear of cuckoldom. II.ii opens with an argument between this same traitorous Pistol and Falstaff himself over money and honor. As could be expected, Falstaff's opinion on the subject is somewhat questionable:

> I have been content, sir, you should lay my countenance to pawn; I have grated upon my good friends for three reprieves for you and your coach-fellow Nym—or else you had looked through the grate, like a geminy of baboons; I am damned in hell for swearing to gentlemen my friends you were good soldiers and tall fellows; and when Mistress Bridget lost the handle of her fan, I took't upon mine honour thou hadst it not.
>
> *Pistol.* Didst not thou share? Hadst thou not fifteen pence?
>
> *Falstaff.* Reason, you rogue, reason: think'st thou I'll endanger my soul gratis? . . .You'll bear no letter for me, you rogue? You stand upon your honour? Why, thou unconfinable baseness, it is as much as I can do to keep the terms of my honour precise.
>
> (II.ii.3–21)

Falstaff argues that doing the dishonest thing may be justified by certain circumstances, but in Pistol's case these were not present. In the end Pistol understands and agrees.

When the Page announces Mistress Quickly, the audience knows what message she is carrying but not how it will be delivered. We have witnessed her skills as a go-between earlier and are familiar with her ingratiating manner, and again we are given a wonderful performance. She begins by playing Falstaff like a fish, getting him ever closer to her, and throwing a little attempt to lure him to herself into the bargain. She is not a "goodwife" (32), he finds out, but a "maid" (34), and most unattached into the bargain. Quickly delivers her message in her own time, making Falstaff desperate to have it, but once she gets moving there is no stopping her. She creates Mistress Ford's history from whole cloth with a surprisingly well developed talent for narrative, and soon we know that Mistress Ford is a virtuous wife though all manner of sieges have been laid to her. Moreover, Master Ford is jealous and does not trust her. The point of her story is that Master Ford will be absent "between ten and eleven" (80), when Falstaff may come and "see the picture . . . that you wot of" (82–83).

In Mistress Quickly, Falstaff has a great rival for both the position at center stage and for our sympathy and laughter. Quickly can be as voluminous as Falstaff himself, but where he remains relatively stationary, she can circle him like a busy moon. Her verbal virtuosity, the skill with which she leads Falstaff on, and his willingness to be led, all make her the focus of our attention for the moment, and she is a wonderful, comic dynamo to watch. She skilfully cultivates Falstaff's inflated belief in his own irresistibility, and as could be expected he falls right into her trap and lets her soothe him into belief that all is well. She does after all see him as "a wanton" with "charms" (53; 98). In addition to making him ludicrous in the eyes of the audience, she lures his page and his purse from him. Even Pistol is impressed: "[S]he is my prize, or ocean whelm them all!" (132).

Quickly's function reaches beyond her exit. She has had a prodigious effect on Falstaff's ego, and has left him grateful to his marvellous body:

> Say'st thou so, old Jack? Go thy ways; I'll make more of thy
> old body than I have done. Will they yet look after thee? Wilt
> thou, after the expense of so much money, be now a gainer?
> Good body, I thank thee. Let them say 'tis grossly done; so it
> be fairly done, no matter.
>
> (II.ii.133–138)

This little speech demands a mirror to preen to. Falstaff can use an actual mirror, or he can see his glorious reflection in the audience, but he has to pirouette and try to catch a glimpse of all his alluring parts. Immensely satisfied with the interview with Quickly and with himself, he is now ready to be generous with his next visitor.

Ford-as-Brook knows Falstaff's weak points, his love of wine, his love of money, and his love of self, and he plays on all. He introduces himself with a draught of sack sent to Falstaff's room. Next he presents himself in just the right way to catch Falstaff's undivided attention:

> *Ford.* Sir, I am a gentleman that have spent much; my name is
> Brook.
> *Falstaff.* Good Master Brook, I desire more acquaintance of
> you.
> *Ford.* Good Sir John, I sue for yours; not to charge you, for I
> must let you understand that I think myself in better plight
> for a lender than you are—the which hath something
> emboldened me to this unseasoned intrusion; for they say, if
> money go before, all ways do lie open.
> *Falstaff.* Money is a good soldier, sir, and will on.
> *Ford.* Troth, and I have a bag of money here troubles me; if
> you will help to bear it, Sir John, take all, or half, for
> easing me of the carriage.
>
> (II.ii.155–168)

The bag produced should be a sizable one with a lusty jingle to it. Falstaff grows very interested, and listens with apparent sympathy, well seasoned with self-satisfaction, to Ford's tale of woe. If anything could further swell Falstaff's ego, this is the thing. Here is a rich man, a big spender, who has been repeatedly scorned by the very lady at Falstaff's feet. Quickly has sown the seed; Ford is to reap the harvest.

The contrast between Falstaff and Ford must delight any audience. We know more about the lady in question than either of them, and we are free to take delight in Ford's tortured squirming as he confronts the very man he believes is about to give him the dreaded horns. Simultaneously we laugh at Falstaff because we know that unexpected things are in store for him at the hands of his lady love. As the interview progresses, Ford's self-torture and Falstaff's self-satisfaction grow. Ford finds himself voicing his fears about his wife (213–216), and Falstaff revels in the compliments paid to him. Still, he is bewildered that a man would employ another to seduce his love, but when Ford has explained this predicament, Falstaff allows himself free rein:

> I will first make bold with your money; next, give me your
> hand; and last, as I am a gentleman, you shall, if you will,
> enjoy Ford's wife. . . . I shall be with her, I may tell you, by
> her own appointment; . . . I shall be with her between ten and
> eleven; for at that time the jealous rascally knave her husband
> will be forth. . . . I will use her as the key of the cuckoldly
> rogues coffer, and there's my harvest home.
>
> (II.ii.243–264)

Ford's attempts to solicit some respect for the husband are bowled over as the triumphant Falstaff, bursting with vitality, denies any danger from that direction. To him Ford is despicable, a jealous husband and a cuckold-to-be, and Ford could hardly agree more heartily.

The comedy lies in the gradual inflation of Falstaff's ego. To get the most out of it, Falstaff's actor has to play his part carefully. We must laugh at his conceitedness, but also with his irresistible energy and good spirits. Ford's case is just, but his jealousy makes him the target of our laughter as does the elaborate plan he is carrying out to his own torment. Moreover, Falstaff has enough contact with the audience to ensure support. We laugh at his antics but are still charmed by the performer, and therefore we are able to love the clown unreservedly. Neither of the three actors in this scene is in control, however; the absent wives are pulling all the strings.

Act III, scene v, is a repetition Act II, scene ii. Again we see Falstaff at a low point, this time from his terrible experiences in the Ford household, but again Quickly—aided by sack—imbues him with new vigor, and Ford-as-Brook is first given the account of the assignation, then new promises of success. The main source of comedy in this scene is Falstaff's account of the horrible things he went through, for they are not viewed from the perspective of a thwarted lover. Falstaff is concentrating on what his body was subjected to, a typical clown reaction:

> I quaked with fear lest the lunatic knave would have searched
> [the basket]; . . . I suffered the pangs of three several deaths.
> First an intolerable fright, . . . and then to be stopped in like a
> strong distillation with stinking clothes that fretted in their
> own grease—think of that—a man of my kidney—think of
> that—that am as subject to heat as butter; a man of continual
> dissolution and thaw: it was a miracle to 'scape suffocation.
> And in the height of this bath, when I was more than half

> stewed in grease, like a Dutch dish, to be thrown into the
> Thames and cooled, glowing hot, in that surge, like a horse-
> shoe—think of that—hissing hot—think of that, Master
> Brook!
>
> (III.v.94–113)

The promised prowess of the invincible lover has been turned into a fantastic narrative with imagery drawn mostly from ordinary household affairs. While this narrative is delivered, at least as much to the house as to Ford, Falstaff the clown has his audience totally under control. We know what happened and also what Falstaff's ego must have endured, but still we cannot wait for the next simile.

Ford expects Falstaff to have had enough, but no. Falstaff is ready to "be thrown into Etna" (117) as he was into the Thames, and refuses to give up. Again his impetuous delight in himself and his own prowess carries the scene and brings us laughter and joy. His vitality is in direct opposition to Ford's miserly love of his wife, and we delight in witnessing the torture Falstaff unknowingly subjects him to.

Falstaff's last appearance as Herne the Hunter in the last act shows a clown's typical ability to be in two positions at the same time. On one level, he is perfectly well aware of the ridiculousness of his situation, but on another he cannot help himself, driven as he is by love of money and inflated ego. But he also displays the clown's reservations when confronted with the female:

> Now, the hot-blooded gods assist me! Jove, thou wast a bull
> for thy Europa; love set on thy horns. O powerful love, that in
> some respects makes a beast a man; in some other, a man a
> beast. You were also, Jupiter, a swan for the love of Leda. O
> omnipotent love, how near the god drew to the complexion of
> a goose! A fault done first in the form of a beast: O Jove, a
> beastly fault! And then another in the semblance of a fowl:
> think on't, Jove, a foul fault! When gods have hot backs, what
> shall poor men do? For me, I am here a Windsor stag, and the
> fattest, I think, i'th' forest. Send me a cool rut-time, Jove, or
> who can blame me to piss my tallow.
>
> (V.v.2–15)

When Mistress Ford arrives, she is "[m]y doe with the black scut" (18). This speech displays humor on many levels. The mere idea of likening Falstaff's pursuit of Mistress Ford to Jupiter's lust for mortal women is ridiculous. Falstaff the clown, of course, sees this, and latches on to the two most appropriate of the god's disguises: the bull and his horns, which suggest cuckoldom; and the swan, so close to the goose and its professed stupidity. Falstaff himself is the fattest stag in Windsor Forest, and therefore a prize for a hunter. He will indeed be hunted, and will be caught and exposed.

While the fairies attack him, Falstaff again shows double awareness. In the midst of his fright, he still has time to make an observation to the audience: "Heavens defend me from that Welsh fairy, lest he transform me to a piece of cheese" (82–83), which lends credence to his self-justification after the fairies show themselves for what they are: "I was three or four times in the thought they were not fairies" (122–123). When he is ridiculed for his failure and credulity, he admits defeat: "I am your theme: you have the start of me. I am dejected. . . . use me as you will" (162–165). But when it turns out that the Pages have been cheated, he happily bounces back: "When night-dogs run, all sorts of deer are chas'd" (235), and he is included in the festivities.

The Garter Inn scenes and the last scene in Windsor Forest are true clown scenes. No other character type could fill the part so well. Any comedian could be funny when stuffed into the basket in III.iii or dressed in woman's clothes in IV.ii. Apart from the actual verbal exchange between the "lovers," the comedy of these scenes depends on Falstaff being manhandled by others according to plan. The audience is allowed to side with the other characters against the clown, and Falstaff only saves himself by his own wonderful accounts of the proceedings. It goes against the very design of the clown's part to be made into a principal character as Falstaff is in *The Merry Wives of Windsor*, and under these circumstances his clown characteristics often have to be eclipsed by character traits.

Still, Falstaff must be regarded as a stage clown, but one of a different breed from his colleagues. His freedom is severely restricted by the constant need for him to relate to other characters in a believable way, and his ability to comment and expose wanes as his character aspects take over. He is always a great source of comedy, but he is our victim as often as our dear guide. He is lovable because of his ability to rebound from every fall, his unquenchable spirits, and his fascination with himself, his accomplishments, and his physical advantages. Only rarely does he lose his vitality. Unlike many other clowns, Falstaff is a product and creature of the world of the play, though with a certain license to transcend both time and place. The size of his part and the historical context restrict him and make it very difficult to develop the clown's part to its full potential.

The character elements in Falstaff's role enable Shakespeare to write him out of *Henry V* with apparent ease. The audience has been promised a continuation of "the story, with Sir John Falstaff in it" (*2 Henry IV*, Epilogue, 28), but in that play he is present only in the spectators' memory. His old associates relate to us the circumstances of his last illness and death, but we never see him again. Despite the promise that Falstaff will reappear, we never miss him in the last Henriad play. It may be that Shakespeare originally wrote him into *Henry V* as some critics claim after a close analysis of Pistol's role with its Falstaffian elements and references. But with the fate Falstaff's associates are to meet in France, and the shining example of true kingship presented by King Henry, a clown would have a difficult existence at best. Falstaff belongs with King Henry's youthful pranks and is a closed chapter once Henry reaches the throne.

Falstaff, like many fellow clowns, disappears from view and is not truly missed. But Falstaff disappears into the world of the characters of the Henriad rather than out of it. His first demise is that of the clown developed into comic character, and this opens the way for his final illness and death.

NOTE

1. The notes to the Arden Edition suggest that "French thrift" may equal modern "Scottish thrift"; this suggestion is both amusing and within character for Falstaff, who begins this scene intending to reduce his staff considerably.

Part VI

Clown Characteristics in Nonclown Characters

15

Philip the Bastard in *King John*

Many of the characteristics that combine to form the clown personality can be seen in a wealth of other Shakespearean characters. Direct address to the audience, for example, is employed by almost all protagonists, male or female. A few of these knowingly assume certain clown characteristics in order to achieve certain effects. This does not make clowns of them, but the conscious use of clown traits adds dimensions and possibilities to their characters, which allow them greater freedom and more power in the manipulation of their fellow characters and the audience.

One result can be the fluidity of personality associated with the clown; this may well be intended to confuse the audience and make it difficult to form a fixed opinion about characters or proceedings when employed by Philip Faulconbridge in *King John*. And Hamlet employs the idiot-as-clown as well as the court jester disguise to fool his on-stage audience while he employs the entire house as his confidants with a result surprising to both us and himself.

A director has the choice whether or not to stress the clown elements in these characters when the plays are produced. It may well be profitable, for because of the clown's popularity and great effect on even our modern-day audience, an exciting and sometimes eye-opening effect can be achieved when a nonclown actor is allowed the freedom his part has room for.

Philip the Bastard of *King John* has the unique and clownlike position of being outside looking in.[1] Philip does not even have a fixed identity at the outset, something strange in the world of the histories, where everything depends on relations between families and position within them. When we first see him at John's court where he and his brother have come about their inheritance, he is interested in physical appearance rather than legitimacy:

> But whe'r I be as true begot [as my brother] or no,
> That still I lay upon my mother's head;
> But that I am as well begot, my liege—

> Fair fall the bones that took the pains for me!—
> Compare our faces and be judge yourself.
> If old Sir Robert did beget us both
> And were our father, and this son like him,
> O old Sir Robert, father, on my knee
> I give heaven thanks I was not like to thee!
>
> (I.i.75–83)

The Bastard pays no respect to such customs of social intercourse as protecting the family name and showing awe in the presence of the King. He is as unrespecting as any clown, and delights in embarrassing his fellow characters. King John is amused by him and calls him "madcap" (84), but Queen Eleanor, who is at first repelled by his lack of concern for his mother's reputation, soon sees a family resemblance to her son: "He hath the trick of Cœur-de-lion's face" (85), and takes a liking to him. The Bastard is quick to latch on to this new possibility:

> *Robert.* My gracious liege, when that my father liv'd,
>   Your brother did employ my father much—
> *Bastard.* Well sir, by this you cannot get my land:
>   Your tale must be how he employ'd my mother.
>
> (I.i.95–98)

The Bastard is finally recognized and knighted and contentedly gives his brother the land. When left alone with the audience, he shows clownlike pleasure in his new status, at the same time managing a few nicely aimed remarks at the nobility:

> Well, now I can make any Joan a lady.
> "Good den, Sir Richard!"—"God-a-mercy, fellow!"—
> And if his name be George, I'll call him Peter;
> For new-made honour doth forget men's names:
> 'Tis too respective and too sociable
> For your conversion. . . .
> For he is but a bastard of the time
> That doth not smack of observation;
> And so am I, whether I smoke or no.
> And not alone in habit and device,
> Exterior form, outward accoutrement,
> But from the inward motion to deliver
> Sweet, sweet, sweet poison for the age's tooth:
> Which, though I will not practise to deceive,
> Yet, to avoid deceit I mean to learn;
> For it shall strew the footsteps of my rising.
>
> (I.i.184–216)

The Bastard certainly means to make the most of his newfound glory but laughs at himself the while. He will now join the targets of his barbs. His assessment of life in the higher circles resembles Touchstone's equally unrespecting remarks on the same subject. When his mother arrives at court and admits to his newfound parentage, he is made even happier:

> Madam I would not wish a better father.
> Some sins do bear the privilege on earth,
> And so doth yours: your fault was not your folly . . .
> With all my heart I thank thee for my father!
>
> (I.i.260–270)

The Bastard has succeeded in establishing himself with the audience immediately. His lack of respect for social convention, his lighthearted approach to life in general, his childlike happiness, and his direct address to us have all contributed to make him a commentator worth our while to pay attention to. He will have a different approach to show us.

The second act opens in France, where the English are embroiled in a dispute over land. The Archduke of Austria is soon established as the direct opposite of the Bastard, and the moment the Bastard enters he latches on to Austria, ironically resembling a yapping terrier worrying a lion:

> *Austria.* Peace!
> *Bastard.*   Hear the crier!
> *Austria.*   What the devil art thou?
> *Bastard.* One that will play the devil, sir, with you,
>   And a may catch your hide and you alone:
>   You are the hare of whom the proverb goes,
>   Whose valour plucks dead lions by the beard.
>   I'll smoke your skin-coat, and I catch you right;
>   Sirrah, look to't; i'faith I will, i'faith.
> *Blanche.* O well did he become that lion's robe
>   That did disrobe the lion of that robe!
> *Bastard.* It lies as sightly on the back of him
>   As great Alcides' shoes upon an ass:
>   But, ass, I'll take that burthen from your back,
>   Or lay on that shall make your shoulders crack.
> *Austria.* What cracker is this same that deafs our ears
>   With this abundance of superfluous breath?
>
> (II.i.134–148)

This short interchange can be made comic indeed, and the fun does not have to stop with the dialogue. The Bastard has ample time during the various disputes when both he and Austria are silent to keep on worrying the great man, nudging him and generally bothering him in his attempts to support Arthur's claim. The text lends some support for this way of acting, for their conversation picks up even more heatedly later:

> *Bastard.*   . . . Sirrah, were I at home,
>   At your den, sirrah, with your lioness,

> I would set an ox-head to your lion's hide,
>   And make a monster of you.
> *Austria.*   Peace! no more.
> *Bastard.* O tremble: for you hear the lion roar!
>
> (II.i.290–294)

At this point the Bastard is still unproven, and there is no reason for the audience not to enjoy him as he struts about, searching out the chinks in the proven warrior and courtier's armor. Austria has had quite enough at the end of their first interchange.

The untried boy is all for action, and with his newfound close relationship to King John he has the opportunity to display some cunning. He suggests that both armies attack the troublesome town of Angiers before they settle their own dispute. His sense of strategy is not unlike that of Richard of Gloucester, and he is quite put out when a peaceful marriage is suggested as a substitute for battle. Again, in the midst of battle plans and other serious business, the impetuous youth comes across as amusing because he loses no opportunity to inform the audience in his every feeling. Lines 455–467 and 504–509 can hardly be addressed to anyone but the audience:

> Here's a stay
> That shakes the rotten carcass of old death
> Out of his rags! . . .
> Zounds! I was never so bethump'd with words
> Since I first called my brother's father dad.
>
> Drawn in the flattering table of her eye!
>   Hang'd in the frowning wrinkle of her brow!
> And quarter'd in her heart! he doth espy
>   Himself love's traitor: this is pity now,
> That, hang'd and drawn and quartered, there should be
> In such a love so vile a lout as he!

He amply displays the clownlike trait of direct honesty. He never attempts to veil any feeling, and by the same token he manages to show us the lack of wisdom in King John, who leans to the side that last won a hearing. The two kings' approach to the lands under dispute also angers the Bastard:

> Mad world! mad kings! mad composition!
> John, to stop Arthur's title in the whole,
> Hath willingly departed with a part:
> And France . . .
> Hath drawn him from his own determin'd aid,
> From a resolv'd and honourable war,
> To a most base and vile-concluded peace.
>
> (II.i.561–586)

We need these remarks from Philip, who, like the clown, puts things into a larger perspective for us. We could easily have lost sight of this point in proceedings which promise us the pomp of a royal wedding, and where talk of war and blood is easily changed into talk of love and marriage. But with the clown's honesty the Bastard proceeds to inform us why he cares so deeply, and what his approach now will be:

> And why rail I on this commodity?
> But for because he hath not woo'd me yet:
> Not that I have the power to clutch my hand,
> When his fair angels would salute my palm;
> But for my hand, as unattempted yet,
> Like a poor beggar, raileth on the rich.
> Well, whiles I am a beggar I will rail
> And say there is no sin but to be rich;
> And being rich, my virtue then shall be
> To say there is no vice but beggary.
> Since kings break faith upon commodity,
> Gain, be my lord, for I will worship thee!
>
> (II.i.587–598)

Like the clown, the Bastard is the outsider looking in and interpreting proceedings. For the position he has, he has had relatively little interaction with the other characters on stage and much with the audience. Shakespeare uses this means to bring out his status as the "other," which is the status of the clown. As the play proceeds, the Bastard becomes more involved with his fellow characters and less with the audience, but we do not feel rejected by him. He is just swallowed by the action, much in the way the clown fades from view.

He does give us one more laugh, though, again during rivalry with Austria, but this time the outcome will be serious and certainly no laughing matter. According to the stage direction of Folio I, the Bastard enters with Austria's head at the opening of the next scene. Now Constance still urges war on account of her son's claim and will not let Austria calm her:

> *Constance* . Thou wear a lion's hide! doff it for shame,
>   And hang a calve's-skin[2] on those recreant limbs.
> *Austria* . O, that a man should speak those words to me!
> *Bastard* . And hang a calve's-skin on those recreant limbs.
> *Austria* . Thou dar'st not say so, villain, for thy life.
> *Bastard* . And hang a calve's-skin on those recreant limbs.
>
> (III.i.54–59)

Austria gets his wish, a man gives him exactly the same insult, but he does not pursue his hot words and challenge the Bastard. The repetition of the same line cannot fail to get laughter from the house, and we have another three reminders of the calf's-skin to come (125, 146, and 225), each one more taunting than its predecessor. But when the rivalry between the Bastard and Austria ends in Austria's death, Philip leaves the ranks of the untried and goes in search of gain as he promised. We do not lose sight of him or his career, but his close contact with us is at an end; now he becomes merely another character as the drama unfolds.

Philip Faulconbridge is not a stage clown, naturally, but he is well suited to borrow from the clown's stock-in-trade. The outsider carries with him something of the clown's status upon entering, and he knows how to make the best use of what he has. The result is an expanded view and a broader experience for the audience, as well as some much-needed laughter in the midst of the serious business of war.

NOTES

1. There are many similarities between this and another bastard, Edmund in *King Lear*, but where the *King John* Bastard has clown traits, Edmund's humor is always sardonic and bitter.

2. The calf's-skin coat is the well-known mark of the fool.

16

Hamlet in *Hamlet*

The Bastard's role is similar to the later and much more developed role of Hamlet. Though Hamlet's melancholy seems greatly removed from the Bastard's devil-may-care attitude to life, the structure of the two roles has much in common. Shakespeare builds on the experience from the Bastard's character in the creation of Hamlet and even employs structural similarities between the two plays. Philip and Hamlet both stand opposite a king who is more a politician than a hero, and who does not hesitate to employ methods distasteful to the young men. Both are given the opportunity to show their worth opposite rivals, Austria and Laertes, and both finally complete a rite of passage and grow into maturity. Shakespeare places them both outside the social interaction of the play, Hamlet because of his sorrow, Philip because of his birth, and both are given close and intimate contact with the audience, which they strengthen by employing clown elements. But where Philip is a comparatively uninterested party, to whom manipulation is largely a game, Hamlet is deadly serious and deeply involved, and therefore he is much more interesting to the audience.

Hamlet is a play rich in clowns and fools. The Danish court does not sport a court jester. Yorick is long dead and buried, and nobody has formally taken his place, but Polonius and Osric periodically and unconsciously contend for the title, and Prince Hamlet himself makes his own contribution. Moreover, Elsinore holds a gravedigging clown whose function is like the skeleton's in the Dance of Death, and who brings home to Hamlet that whatever we were in life, kings or jesters, we shall all be reduced to bare bones in the end.

Hamlet himself is a unique protagonist. Within his person he represents the totality of human experience with both its tragic and comic elements. He is the one mediator between stage and audience, and he even to some extent mediates between the gravedigging clown and the spectators. Many if not all of his fellow characters serve to bring to the fore yet another side to Hamlet, while Hamlet himself contains innumerable angles on life to expose and examine.

When Hamlet decides to "put an antic disposition on" (I.v.180), he is in a state of emotional turmoil after the encounter with his father's ghost. He feels the responsibility of revenge weigh heavy on his shoulders, and at the same time he wonders whether this was an honest ghost. His scholar's mind makes him doubt from the first, while his grieving heart simultaneously prompts him to belief. Hamlet has the gift of ironic repartee as well as considerable intellectual nimbleness, and decides to make use of both in his quest for the truth, which soon becomes his quest for true adulthood. Hamlet chooses to make himself into a combination of the "natural fool" and the court jester clown, and to draw on this figure's license in order to expose the truth he needs. The audience has been subtly prepared for such a role before Hamlet announces his decision. His first on-stage audience, the common soldiers and Horatio, amply demonstrate that Hamlet knows how to make men of all walks of life like him if not love him. They all willingly take part in the formal oath on his sword, which both Hamlet and the Ghost demand, but which with all the moving about, and Hamlet's running commentary, becomes something of a charade:

> *Hamlet.* Upon my sword.
> *Marcellus.* We have sworn already.
> *Hamlet.* Indeed, upon my sword, indeed.
> *Ghost.* Swear.
> *Hamlet.* Ah ha, boy, say'st thou so? Art thou there,
>   truepenny?
>   Come on, you hear this fellow in the cellerage.
>   Consent to swear.
> *Horatio.*   Propose the oath, my lord.
> *Hamlet.* Never to speak of this that you have seen.
>   Swear by my sword.
> *Ghost.* Swear.
> *Hamlet. Hic et ubique?* Then we'll shift our ground.
>   Come hither, gentlemen,
>   And lay your hands again upon my sword . . .
> *Ghost.* Swear by his sword.
> *Hamlet.* Well said, old mole. Canst work i'th'earth so fast?
>   A worthy pioneer! Once more remove, good friends.
> *Horatio.* O day and night, but this is wondrous strange.
>   I.v.154–172)

Horatio's comment is indeed aimed at the Ghost and the strange proceedings of the night, but it is also valid for Hamlet's performance. The Ghost, formerly treated so reverently and called "Hamlet,/King, father, royal Dane" (I.iv.44–45), is now "boy," "truepenny," "old mole," and "pioneer." Hamlets behavior has undergone a strange change. His words are "wild and whirling" (I.v.139), and his pattern of movement should reflect this. He dances about like a court jester clown, and by the repetition makes a joke out of this solemn occasion. The reference to "the cellerage" is one of numerous reminders within this play that we are in a theatre and watching a play. The clown most often makes such remarks to remind the spectators that the play is there for their analysis; but in

Hamlet there are numerous instances when Hamlet-as-clown uses a play and acting to draw a parallel to his own reality within the play, and so opens up to us the possibility to do something similar ourselves.

With Horatio, his chronicler and partial confidant, Hamlet shows his gift of wit:

> *Horatio.* My lord, I came to see your father's funeral.
> *Hamlet.* I prithee do not mock me, fellow-student.
>   I think it was to see my mother's wedding.
> *Horatio.* Indeed, my lord, it followed hard upon.
> *Hamlet.* Thrift, thrift, Horatio. The funeral bak'd meats
>   Did coldly furnish forth the marriage tables.
>
> (I.ii.176–181)

This is the type of jest a court jester clown would come up with, and which Hamlet will later employ while he plays the clown. It has a distinct sting to it, and is directed as much at Hamlet's own breast as at Horatio's. Indeed, all of Hamlet's jesting is doubly or triply aimed, and one of the recipients of the prod is usually himself. Only after his voyage to England do his jokes change into a more mellow pattern.

The court jester's license is already Hamlet's. As Gertrude's son and close to the throne, he can get away with more than any jester before repercussions hit. Finally Hamlet positions himself as the one person in whom the audience can place trust. He is insecure, but this only conveys honesty and openness to us. He utilizes every moment alone with the audience to share his thoughts and feelings and to expand on the situations he has created or finds himself in. Soon we become familiar with Hamlet's patterns of behavior and have no trouble following his sudden leaps from one role to another. We can now sit back and enjoy. Hamlet's intimacy with the audience is greater than any clown's, because Hamlet has a much broader spectrum to share with us, but it is an intimacy like the one we share with a clown. Hamlet too is our guide and teacher, albeit a less objective one than a clown, and he also gives us new and different ways to interpret situations and characters. Hamlet, however, has a distinct effect on the plot of the play, and this is made possible because of his chosen role as court jester.

Though playing the clown himself, Hamlet sees fit to comment on others in a similar position. We are all familiar with his address to the players (III.ii.38–45), but this piece of advice most probably shows us the Prince and the young man of the world sporting his superior judgment and learning. We need to be reminded of this side of Hamlet repeatedly. His deprecatory remarks on the way clowns play their parts may also indirectly be aimed at Polonius, who often in his wordiness and bumbling reminds one of the pedantic philosophizing of many clowns (for example II.ii.86–103). Polonius often speaks much more than the situation sets down for him, but he is not the clown to everybody. King Claudius sees in him a good and true advisor, and his children both love him. Hamlet, however, sees his clownish side and enjoys his sparring matches with him:

> *Polonius.* Do you know me, my lord?
> *Hamlet.* Excellent well. You are a fishmonger.
> *Polonius.* Not I, my lord.
> *Hamlet.* Then I would you were so honest a man.
> *Polonius.* Honest, my lord.
> *Hamlet.* Ay sir. To be honest, as this world goes, is to be one
>   man picked out of ten thousand.
> *Polonius.* That's very true, my lord.
>
>   (II.ii.173–180)

Polonius, who ought to feel the barbs of these reminders, tries his best to get through to Hamlet, who only makes an exposition of his clownish qualities. The same pattern is repeated wonderfully in the scene of cloudwatching (III.ii). Hamlet makes both Polonius and the Globe audience look into the sky and see the shapes change from a camel to a weasel to a whale, and presumably ultimately into the Queen, whose constancy is much like that of a cloud. We seem all to be clowns together. Here Polonius is bewildered as always, but the audience can follow Hamlet's train of thought.

There is a parallel between Polonius and Osric, but Hamlet's encounters with Osric are quite different from those with Polonius. Osric, the man whom "'tis a vise to know" (V.ii.85–86), only appears on stage after Hamlet's journey to England, when Hamlet has matured and has come to terms with his own position as a mortal among mortals in the ever-changing patterns of the world. But he has also turned into something of a Machiavellian manipulator if yet only in thought. Hamlet mocks Osric by using his very patterns of speech and movement as he joins in pleasantries, bowing, and scraping:

> *Osric.* Sir, here is newly come to court Laertes—believe me,
>   he is an absolute gentleman, full of most excellent
>   differences, of very soft society and great showing. Indeed, to
>   speak feelingly of him, he is the card or calendar of gentry;
>   for you shall find in him the continent of what part a
>   gentleman would see.
> *Hamlet.* Sir, his definement suffer no perdition in you, though
>   I know to divide him inventorially would dozy th'arithmetic
>   of memory, and yet but yaw neither, in respect of his quick
>   sail. But, in the verity of extolment, I take him to be a soul
>   of great article and his infusion of such dearth and rareness
>   as, to make true diction of him, his semblable is his mirror
>   and who else would trace him his umbrage, nothing more.
> *Osric.* Your lordship speaks most infallibly of him.
> *Hamlet.* The concernancy, sir? Why do we wrap the gentleman
>   in our more rawer breath?
> *Osric.* Sir?
> *Horatio.* Is't not possible to understand in another tongue? You
>   will to't, sir, really.
> *Hamlet.* What imports the nomination of this gentleman?
> *Osric.* Of Laertes?

Horatio. His purse is empty already, all's golden words are
    spent.

(V.ii.106–130)

In contrast to Polonius's bustling innocence, Osric, the modern courtier, becomes aware of Hamlet's treatment of him, and finally leaves somewhat befuddled. Osric is a symbol of the hollowness of the court under Claudius, a contrast to the honesty and straightforwardness Hamlet earlier professed to stand for. Now, at a more mature point, he has learned to play with the weapons of the enemy and beat him at his own game. While Hamlet lets us see the foolishness of this "lapwing" who "runs away with the shell on his head" (183), and has us laugh along with Horatio and himself, he also demonstrates a deviousness we have not been aware of before. This is also evident in his address to Laertes later:

> If Hamlet from himself be ta'en away,
> And when he's not himself does wrong Laertes,
> Then Hamlet does it not, Hamlet denies it.
> Who does it then? His madness. If't be so,
> Hamlet is of the faction that is wrong'd;
> His madness is poor Hamlet's enemy.

(V.ii.230–235)

Both we and Hamlet know that this "madness," with which he excuses his rash behavior at Ophelia's graveside, was put on for a purpose and therefore is no true excuse. In this act Hamlet has reached the point where he can believe that "[a] man's life's no more than to say 'one'" (74). Hamlet has changed, and so has his relationship to the audience. We are party to a plan, into which Hamlet will walk relatively unprepared. Though he voices some apprehension to Horatio, the plot to poison him comes as a surprise to him, and it is his anger, not his own planning, which finally completes his revenge.

Hamlet's clown behavior is richer in variety and detail than any true clown's. He utilizes every aspect available and creates out of himself a wide spectrum of clown types, easily assuming the mental disguise that will serve his purpose. He draws most often on the court jester's role, but sometimes plays the natural fool and the madman and freely combines all of these when it suits his purpose. Often within the same scene he has to change behavior drastically, and does so with skill and dexterity. The most difficult tests of his "antic disposition" are, of course, at the beginning. When Rosencrantz and Guildenstern announce the players (II.ii), and Polonius arrives with the same information shortly afterwards, Hamlet must suit himself to two different expectations of his "madness." When the players themselves arrive, he returns to the role of the well-informed young man of the world. The players, "the abstract and brief chronicles of the time" (520), will become his tool in the coming plot to disclose the King's guilt, but they also become a model to Hamlet; he too must attempt to transform himself into what he is not.

With Rosencrantz and Guildenstern he faces a difficult task. Like Horatio, these two are old friends, and Hamlet greets them as such when they meet in II.ii, but he soon suspects them. When Guildenstern finally admits that the King and Queen have sent for them, Hamlet prepares them subtly for the strange behavior he is beginning to put on. He has "lost all his mirth" (296), and now "[m]an delights me not—nor woman neither, though by your smiling you seem to say so" (309–310). His description of his state of mind resembles a beginning depression, and he manages an almost peevish tone. He also warns them that "I am but mad north-north-west. When the wind is southerly, I know a hawk from a handsaw" (374–375). When questioned by the King and Queen about this first encounter (III.i), Rosencrantz and Guildenstern's impression is that Hamlet has drawn back from them rather than demonstrated madness.

Their next encounter is just after the "mousetrap" play. Hamlet continues his "wild" behavior, but in the manner of a clown he finds double and triple meanings in whatever is said to him and makes a joke out of the most serious matters. Rosencrantz and Guildenstern catch only his strangeness, while the audience understands the breadth of his implications:

> *Guildenstern.* The King, sir —
> *Hamlet.* Ay, sir, what of him?
> *Guildenstern.* Is in his retirement marvellous distempered.
> *Hamlet.* With drink, sir?
> *Guildenstern.* No, my lord, with choler.
> *Hamlet.* Your wisdom should show itself more richer to
>   signify this to the doctor, for for me to put him to his
>   purgation would perhaps plunge him into more choler.
>   (III.ii.291–299)

When the two make yet another attempt to sound Hamlet out, they are rebuffed soundly: "'Sblood, do you think I am easier to be played on than a pipe?" (360–361). The same pattern of rebuffs is repeated and strengthened in IV.ii, when Rosencrantz and Guildenstern are sent to find Polonius's body. Rosencrantz is now "a sponge"; with his description of how a sponge absorbs only to be squeezed dry again, Hamlet may be warning them that the life of a spy is tenuous, and that the King and Hamlet both may prove a danger to them. With each encounter Hamlet withdraws further from Rosencrantz and Guildenstern, and his double and triple meanings become more difficult for them to understand. After Polonius's murder they have had enough and openly declare themselves the King's creatures as they drag Hamlet along to Claudius. We last see them leaving the stage at a run in hot pursuit of Hamlet, who is on his way to England (IV.iv).

Hamlet is disappointed in Rosencrantz and Guildenstern. Their deceitful behavior becomes one lesson of many in the fundamental principle of the mutability of the world. Hamlet's manner of clowning with them is playing hard to get verbally and psychologically. There is a hint of revenge in his interaction with them, and they are killed in England on Hamlet's instigation. Through his relationship with Rosencrantz and Guildenstern Hamlet himself demonstrates his ability to change; he turns from friend to foe, and the innocent young Hamlet of the opening of the play becomes quite a Machiavel.

Hamlet has few opportunities to play the jester with the King and Queen to expose them to ridicule. He is alone with Claudius only once, but then the King is unaware of his presence (III.iii). And it is important for his purpose to undeceive his mother, so he comes to her in his own person in III.iv, though the Ghost, seen by Hamlet but unperceived by Gertrude, almost thwarts his intentions. Apart from the "mousetrap" scene, the royal couple receive only few sexually loaded hints, and these carry as much pain for Hamlet as they do for them. Only after he has instructed his mother how to tackle the King does Hamlet give his clowning free rein in the face of Claudius:

> *King.* Now, Hamlet, where's Polonius?
> *Hamlet.* At supper.
> *King.* At supper? Where?
> *Hamlet.* Not where he eats, but where he is eaten. A certain convocation of political worms are e'en at him. Your worm is your only emperor for diet: we fat all creatures else to fat us, and we fat ourselves for maggots. . . . A man may fish with the worm that hath eat of a king, and eat of the fish that hath fed of that worm.
> *King.* What dost thou mean by this?
> *Hamlet.* Nothing but to show you how a king may go a progress through the guts of a beggar.
> *King.* Where is Polonius?
> *Hamlet.* In heaven. Send thither to see. If your messenger find him not there, seek him i'th'other place yourself. . . . Farewell, dear mother.
> *King.* Thy loving father, Hamlet.
> *Hamlet.* My mother. Father and mother is man and wife, man and wife is one flesh; so my mother. Come, for England.
>   (IV.iii.16–56)

Hamlet plays with the King like a true court jester. Now when he no longer needs to feel the barbs of his own sexually loaded jesting so keenly, he can both threaten the King with murder through the example of Polonius and emasculate him verbally. Hamlet is as disrespecting as any court jester and draws heavily on his license as both the Queen's son and a madman. He employs the clown's well-known mock logic and also his manner of telling the truth in riddles which the audience can see through effortlessly, but which the recipient may or may not decode.

The most difficult of Hamlet's clowning tasks is opposite Ophelia. He has been paying court to her quite openly, for Laertes sees fit to warn her not to respond too warmly (I.iii.5–44), and Gertrude hopes for a marriage (V.i.237). Ophelia is a loving, obedient daughter, deeply attached to her family, and when Polonius adds his warnings she can only obey and withdraw from Hamlet. Hamlet feels this as yet another in the series of betrayals which began with his mother's remarriage, and he signals early on that he blames Polonius and his morals more than Ophelia:

> For if the sun breed maggots in a dead dog, being a good
> kissing carrion—Have you a daughter?

> *Polonius.* I have, my lord.
> *Hamlet.* Let her not walk i'th'sun. Conception is a blessing,
>   but as your daughter may conceive—friend, look to't.
>   (II.ii.181–186)

Hamlet's associations are as free as any clown's, and though Polonius chooses to think that Hamlet has not recognized him, "he knew me not at first; a said I was a fishmonger" (188–189), it is clear to the audience that Hamlet blames the father's motives.

When Polonius stages his own little charade in III.i and hides with the King to see how Hamlet reacts to the well-instructed Ophelia, Hamlet soon has clues that they are not alone. His first address to her, "Nymph, in thy orisons/be all my sins remember'd" (89–90), has been spoken in numerous ways, and indeed the critical debate about whether Hamlet sees the spies or not has been lengthy. But why cannot Hamlet, taken by surprise at her presence as he is, address her in his wonted manner, continuing the courtship? Then possibly she looks towards the hiding place for a clue, for how can she respond to this? Or her general behavior seems put on and false to him, and he deduces that they are watched and proceeds accordingly. His vicious attacks, which in some productions have been made physical as well as verbal to draw out the listeners, can be explained by a deep and fresh feeling of betrayal from a beloved person, in a way a repetition of his mother's betrayal and therefore doubly painful.

Hamlet's numerous sexual allusions and attacks, which will culminate in the "mousetrap" scene, are a continuation of his conversation with Polonius. Again he harps on honesty in all its connotations, and on how trust may be abused:

> *Hamlet.* Are you honest?
> *Ophelia.* My lord?
> *Hamlet.* Are you fair?
> *Ophelia.* What means your lordship?
> *Hamlet.* That if you be honest and fair, your honesty should
>   admit no discourse with your beauty.
> *Ophelia.* Could beauty, my lord, have better commerce than
>   with honesty?
> *Hamlet.* Ay, truly, for the power of beauty will sooner
>   transform honesty from what it is to a bawd than the force
>   of honesty can translate beauty into his likeness. This was
>   sometime a paradox, but now the time gives it proof.
>   (III.i.103–115)

Like a court jester clown addressing more than one audience, Hamlet goes on to attack the vulnerable Ophelia, but his manner is strained as well as overly vicious. Unlike the clown he is an interested party, and he wounds himself as he wounds his target. After the attack on her honesty, he begins on the hopes and dreams of marriage, happiness, and children common to most young girls, and finally he criticizes her innocent attempts to make herself attractive, all of which has presumably delighted him before. Ophelia is unaware that his barbs are directed at the listeners also and is deeply wounded by Hamlet's treatment; but the audience sees the remarks on honesty as aimed at Polonius, the abolition of marriage at the King, and jibes at make-up and fancy manners could well be directed at Gertrude, for Hamlet cannot know whether she is among the listeners. In another context much of this clowning could be pure comedy, but the audience is emotionally involved with Hamlet in a way never permitted with a stage clown, and Ophelia too has our sympathy, so the potential comedy produces a deep sadness which a mere confrontation never could have created. The attempted clowning only serves to underscore Hamlet's emotional turmoil.

The most complex clowning scene in *Hamlet* is the "mousetrap" scene. His task in this scene is extremely complicated, because he has to suit his behavior to both the situation and the various members of the court, whom he has treated in different ways in his assumed madness. He begins and ends the scene with Horatio, who is "not a pipe for Fortune's finger" and "not passion's slave" (III.ii.70, 72), but the only person with whom Hamlet feels free to talk openly. He gives Horatio, and the audience along with him, the duty of watching the King and determining his guilt because he correctly anticipates that his own job will be complex and distracting. Horatio will later be an objective judge. Hamlet himself is too interested a party to serve in this capacity.

Even as the on-stage audience enters, Hamlet has a loaded remark for each of them as he busily arranges them about his stage area to best advantage:

> *King.* How fares our cousin Hamlet?
> *Hamlet.* Excellent i'faith, of the chameleon's dish. I eat the air, promise crammed. You cannot feed capons so.
>
> . . .
>
> *Hamlet.* What did you enact?
> *Polonius.* I did enact Julius Caesar. I was killed i'th'Capitol. Brutus killed me.
> *Hamlet.* It was a brute part of him to kill so capital a calf there.
>
> . . .
>
> *Gertrude.* Come hither, my dear Hamlet, sit by me.
> *Hamlet.* No, good mother, here's metal more attractive.
>
> . . .
>
> *Hamlet.* Lady, shall I lie in your lap?
> *Ophelia.* No, my lord.
> *Hamlet.* I mean, my head upon your lap.
> *Ophelia.* Ay, my lord.
> *Hamlet.* Do you think I meant country matters?
>
> (III.ii.92–115)

With all the airy manner of a court jester Hamlet informs the King that he feels surpassed. To the delight of the audience he makes Polonius talk about acting, and they step out of the play for a moment and discuss *Julius Caesar*, a play in which the same two actors of Shakespeare's company might well have met earlier. Gertrude and Ophelia are set up as rivals and Ophelia is preferred only to be confused by Hamlet's loud, sexual innuendo. When everybody is seated to Hamlet's satisfaction, the King and Queen are far back in state, while he and Ophelia are very close to the audience in order to let Hamlet mediate for both the on-stage audience and the house comfortably. Moreover his conversation with Ophelia is relevant for us, because it recalls Hamlet's purpose and reflects on the play-within-the-play to come:

> *Hamlet.* For look you how cheerfully my mother looks and
>   my father died within's two hours.
> *Ophelia.* Nay, 'tis twice two months, my lord.
> *Hamlet.* So long? Nay then, let the devil wear black, for I'll
>   have a suit of sable. O Heavens, die two months ago and not
>   forgotten yet! Then there's hope a great man's memory may
>   outlive his life half a year.
>
>   (III.ii.124–130)

Physically, on stage, Hamlet has put himself in the most advantageous position to play the jester. When the players enter and begin, Hamlet jumps into the clown's position of interpreter and mediator. Whenever there is a possibility for a loaded remark, Hamlet pounces on it. He ridicules contemporary playing style as well as his own position as commentator and actor when the Prologue enters, and at the same time manages to keep up his siege of Ophelia and the royal couple:

> *Ophelia.* Belike this [dumb-]show imports the argument of the
>   play.
> *Hamlet.* We shall know by this fellow. The players cannot
>   keep counsel: they'll tell all.
> *Ophelia.* Will a tell us what this show meant?
> *Hamlet.* Ay, or any show that you will show him. Be not you
>   ashamed to show, he'll not shame to tell you what it means.
> *Ophelia.* You are naught, you are naught. I'll mark the play.
>   (III.ii.136–143)

Hamlet has several opportunities to send forth his little darts. Lying or half sitting with Ophelia between the audience and the players, he is in a wonderful position to keep up his contact with the audience, and his remarks can easily reach across the playing area to the listening King and Queen. During the first part of the play-within-the-play all Hamlet's remarks, even those ostensibly addressed to Ophelia, are meant for the Queen's ears. Hamlet juggles both the house and the on-stage audience expertly. His anticipation of success generates an excitement which lends even more energy and vitality to his acting. The clown's part is an excellent disguise for Hamlet to assume, for boundless energy was never part of his behavior when in his own person.

Goaded by Hamlet's hints, The King and Queen become apprehensive:

> *Hamlet.* Madam, how like you this play?
> *Gertrude.* The lady doth protest too much, methinks.
> *Hamlet.* O, but she'll keep her word.
> *King.* Have you heard the argument? Is there no offence in't?
>
> *Hamlet.* No, no, they do but jest—poison in jest. No offence
> i'th' world. . . . Your Majesty, and we that have free souls,
> it touches us not. Let the galled jade wince, our withers are
> unwrung.
>
> (III.ii.224–238)

Hamlet's remarks sting sorely, though on the surface they seem intended to put the royal couple at their ease. Gertrude smarts from the parallel with the Player Queen, and Claudius, whose soul is far from "free," is apprehensive. Ophelia is the only one who still keeps her surface calm intact and even reproaches Hamlet for his behavior to herself and others, but again Hamlet the jester gets the last word.

> *Ophelia.* You are as good as a chorus, my lord.
> *Hamlet.* I could interpret between you and your love if I could
> see the puppets dallying.
> *Ophelia.* You are keen, my lord, you are keen.
> *Hamlet.* It would cost you a groaning to take off my edge.
> *Ophelia.* Still better, and worse.
> *Hamlet.* So you mis-take your husbands.
>
> (III.ii.240–246)

Finally the excitement grows too large for Hamlet to contain, and again he makes use of his position as jester and chorus to speed things along rather more quickly than in the original plan. He sums up the action to come, and Claudius rushes from the room followed by everyone but Hamlet and Horatio. Hamlet is still so immersed in his jesterly role that his success sweeps him on still within it. He continues clowning, and now sings a typical clown song, half nonsense, half truth:

> Why, let the strucken deer go weep,
> The hart ungalled play;
> For some must watch while some must sleep,
> Thus runs the world away.
> Would not this, sir, and a forest of feathers, if the rest of my
> fortunes turn Turk with me, with Provincial roses on my razed
> shoes, get me a fellowship in a cry of players?
>
> (III.ii.265–272)

Here for the first time, Hamlet refers to himself as the stage clown in all his regalia, so the rhyme is probably accompanied by a wild dance, which would also be the natural outlet for his pent-up excitement.[1] It seems that Hamlet-the-clown is in total control here, but it is debatable whether Hamlet-the-Prince is served by this or possibly is deceived. Hamlet's actions have exposed the King, but the costs are probably greater than a sober Hamlet would want to pay. Horatio, equally swept along by Hamlet's success, joins in the fun, and further fuels Hamlet's mood:

> Half a share.
> *Hamlet.* A whole one, I.
>   For thou dost know, O Damon dear,
>   This realm dismantled was
>   Of Jove himself, and now reigns here
>   A very, very—pajock.
> *Horatio.* You might have rhymed.
>
>   (III.ii.273–279)

This second jingle is probably delivered mock-seriously with all the gestures and manners of grand acting, only to end in giggles at the "ass," which we all know is the suitable rhyme. Hamlet closes off the incident with a call for music and another clown jingle: "For if the King like not the comedy,/Why then, belike he likes it not, perdie" (286–287). The laughter and closeness with Horatio gives Hamlet the needed breathing space and release, which makes it possible for him to jump back into his watchful clowning with Rosencrantz and Guildenstern immediately afterwards.

Hamlet's farewell to the jesterly role takes place at Ophelia's graveside towards the end of his conversation with the gravedigging clown. The Gravedigger must be placed by or in the stage trapdoor so he can lug up bones by the spadeful from below, while Hamlet is further forward on stage with Horatio in his usual position to mediate to the audience. At the end of their conversation, the Gravedigger throws up the skull of Yorick, King Hamlet's jester:

> Here's a skull now hath lien you i'th'earth three and twenty
> years.
> *Hamlet.* Whose was it?
> *Gravedigger.* A whoreson mad fellow's it was. Whose do you
>   think it was?
> *Hamlet.* Nay, I know not.
> *Gravedigger.* A pestilence on him for a mad rogue! A poured a
>   flagon of Rhenish on my head once. This same skull, sir,
>   was Yorick's skull, the King's jester.
> *Hamlet.* This?
> *Gravedigger.* E'en that.
> *Hamlet.* . . . Where be your gibes now, your gambols, your
>   songs, your flashes of merriment, that were wont to set the
>   table on a roar? Not one now to mock your own grinning?
>   Quite chop-fallen? Now get you to my lady's chamber and

tell her, let her paint an inch thick, to this favour she must
come. Make her laugh at that.

(V.i.166–189)

The Gravedigger and Hamlet both remember Yorick fondly for his mad pranks. There has been no such jesting since Yorick died, and though Hamlet apparently has taken him as his example, he certainly never set any company "on a roar" with merriment. During King Hamlet's reign, Denmark had room for true jesting as represented by Yorick, but now everything is a mockery. The King is a "pajock," the Queen's marriage not valid, and Hamlet neither a true jester nor a true prince. Yorick's skull is a better jester than Hamlet ever was. It can get laughter from the Gravedigger when it prompts fond memories, and from Hamlet it prompts more wholehearted jesting than we have seen before.

The confrontation with the gravedigging clown, which helps Hamlet realize the finality and inevitability of death, and with Yorick's skull, which shows him the power memory has to keep the dead with us in the shape we prefer, both show the audience how Hamlet has matured. The clown in his grave with all his jesting bears the message that everybody will need such a grave sooner or later, and Hamlet's acceptance of this fact and invitation to Yorick to continue his jesting mark the end of Hamlet's career as mock clown. Hamlet's choice of the clown's role was made in order to become as different from himself as possible, but also because of the freedom such a role would give him. Now, at a more mature stage, he does not need to put on a show.

The combination of Hamlet and the clown's part is ingenious. Hamlet is on stage frequently in his various capacities, and when absent he is the chosen topic of conversation, so our strengthened intimacy with him gives us an excellent position to gather information. The audience profits immensely from the close contact with Hamlet and from participating in his playacting with more knowledge than anybody on stage. Hamlet becomes the key to his own interpretation and opens up such a rich and varied view into human nature that nobody can avoid finding himself therein. Whatever reason the melancholy Prince of Denmark may give to legitimate his surprising behavior, it gives the audience a wonderful new experience. Hamlet obviously comes to need the release his clowning brings, and the audience readily identifies, simultaneously reveling in the new and broadened perspective.

Without ever entering into the clown's role completely, the Bastard of *King John* and Hamlet employ a variety of clown traits to enrich and deepen the audience's experience. The clown's ability to relate freely to the spectators as a matter of course, and his accepted and time-honored way of delivering information, mediating, and interpreting, make us smile as we learn and absorb our lesson all the better. When clown traits are used by a nonclown protagonist, a greater intimacy is created, and we are allowed insights not otherwise accessible to us. The Bastard's clowning helps us gain perspective in *King John*'s world of turmoil, and Hamlet becomes even more complex as well as more open to us through his clowning. We are invited to participate in the whole painful processes of maturing and coming to terms with the hitherto unacceptable. Hamlet's lashing out at everybody as well as at himself gives him an opportunity to voice things that would not otherwise have come out, and we can suffer through the whole process with him, knowing that his pain and his feeling of betrayal make him inflict pain and betray, and we still understand and love. The ability of these protagonists to assume elements of the clown's part enriches the plays for the audience and gives us a broader basis for our interpretation. The clown characteristics, even without an actual clown present, are easily recognized, and we adjust to their new use with a minimum of confusion only to gain from the experience.

NOTE

1. David Wiles sees this as a jig. David Wiles, *Shakespeare's Clown* (Cambridge and New York: Cambridge University Press, 1987) 57.

Conclusion

Shakespeare's clowns exist within a rich and long-reaching dramatic tradition. There has always been room for the character who prompts our laughter, and presumably there always will be. Human nature craves periodic release from everyday humdrum existence, and a wonderful escape is provided by the freedom of laughter. The more structured our day-to-day existence is, the more enjoyable and necessary is the freedom found in the holiday or carnival ritual, which allows us the possibility of becoming somebody else by dressing in borrowed robes; or we can enjoy somebody else's performance. Comedy provides an organized and socially acceptable outlet to channel potentially riotous feelings into collective laughter, and the vicarious experience liberates us. When an audience shares laughter, there is almost always an element of recognition of foolish aspects of ourselves and our world involved, and the collective experience strengthens the effect. The clown figure presents an antisocial element which we recognize and enjoy, and which we may also both accept and reject. Often we will see our neighbor, not ourselves, in this character.

On the Shakespearean stage, the clown became an institution. The combination of the clown's role and the well-known actor filling it was a delight in itself, and his disrespect and total lack of inhibition was a large element of his appeal. The combination of the well-known actor in the equally well-known pattern of the clown's role is especially suited to exercise control over the audience's perception of and response to the play. The clown actor, then as well as now, is in a unique position, simultaneously inside and outside the proceedings, and therefore able to make us feel like active participants in the experience of the drama. His direct address and appeal helps us see more and gain deeper insights.

Comedy is the clown's natural element, and in every Shakespearean comedy we see the clown at work, but he has a function reaching beyond the power to amuse. For the most part Shakespeare resists the temptation to allow his clown to become a character within the play, and even a clown in a large part will keep his distance from his fellow characters. Because of his position as an outsider, who stands between the play and the audience in a unique position to mediate, the clown is able to enlarge and expand the comic effect. He constantly reminds the audience that they are watching a play, and constantly sees to it that potential identification and involvement with the characters is turned into laughter. The clown himself remains elusive, an amusing conglomerate who can shape himself to every social situation and any environment at will.

Shakespeare's contemporaries often relegated their comic figures and clowns to the subplot of the play, even in comedies, but we never see Shakespeare doing this. There is always a clear connection between every level the play presents. The clown's appearance in a comedy serves the play as a whole, not a segment only; and because he is a collection of traits rather then an actual person he is free to move about at will and create his effect whenever and wherever he is needed, a functional element indeed. Shakespeare never allows his clown a gratuitous appearance, there is always a purpose and a reason behind the clowning.

In the tragedies and history plays the clown's appearance is often a surprise. We have seen how he alerts the audience to thematic elements such as turning points, but his presence may have a psychologically important function as well, making the clown of the comedies, tragedies, and history plays intimately connected. When Shakespeare has Hamlet play the clown in the midst of his personal tragedy, the Prince experiences an unexpected personal release. He finds clowning to be a much-needed safety valve, a means to express what decorum and social position make inexpressible, and he conveys the same feelings of release to the audience. On top of this we learn more about Hamlet the man and the traits we share with him, and we recognize the need of any human being to relieve extreme pressure in an explosion of destruction or laughter. The same dichotomy is apparent in Lear and his Fool.

Even a minor clown figure in a tragedy may be said to serve a related purpose. The clown carries with him his established effect on the audience regardless of circumstances. In a tragedy, unexpected as he may be, his very presence alters the audience's perspective on the scene. We are suddenly allowed to step back from the intensity of our involvement, and maybe we are even allowed a small explosion into laughter. The clown becomes our safety valve. He allows us a short breathing space to collect ourselves and prepare our minds for the next peak of intensity, which can be all the more painful as a result.

The clown in the history plays has much the same function. The history play presents the past in order to alert us to circumstances in the present, and the appearance of a clown like Falstaff at Hal's side serves to make the Prince's escapades endearing and ultimately leave him blameless. Moreover the spectator's journey through time is made both richer and more enjoyable because of the presence of the clown, which puts the issues of kingship in the play into brilliant perspective.

Whenever he uses him, Shakespeare's clown is valuable to the audience. He unites us because of our need for the release laughter provides, but his main function is that of audience teacher, guide, and mediator, a function he fulfills in the smallest as well as the largest part. This happens even when he is present only vicariously, when a main character has borrowed certain traits from him.

For the audience, Shakespeare's clown becomes an significant tool for interpretation, and his teachings are important. The lesson we learn through laughter is always remembered.

Appendix: The Elizabethan Clown

In the Elizabethan theatre specifically we find a rich variety of clown figures. They all share inherent artificiality, often underscored by articles of dress. They move freely up and down the social scale, using their own individual language wherever they may find themselves, and they are always in contact with the audience.

The Elizabethan stage clown has ancestors as far back in time as Greek and Roman theatre, where Menander explores the comic servant, and Plautus the swaggering soldier. The comic characters of the *Commedia dell'Arte*, the Zanni, may be seen as a continuation of these early "clowns." Other roots can be found in the mediœval theatre, where the devil as well as the villain or Vice are given many comic traits, often playing the audience for laughter. We find a clown ancestor in yet another professional capacity as a court fool or jester, the "artificial fool," who made a living clowning at the local court. Finally, there is the comedy of the simpleton, who has always been the butt of jokes.

The plays acted and printed[1] in the period leading up to Shakespeare's mature plays show a wealth of clown parts, but still it will not be possible to find a Touchstone or a Feste among the crowd. It even seems that a printer changed the texts of at least one play. Marlowe's *Tamburlaine* has a note from the printer, saying that he left out unwanted lines for the clown. On the other hand, in *A Pilgrimage to Parnassus* (about 1598), a clown emerges from nowhere, pulled onto the stage with a rope.[2] He is totally disconnected from the play's plot, and he is given only a short time to captivate the audience before he is thrown off stage not to be seen again. These two instances demonstrate the volatility of the clown's part, but also indicate its popularity. *Tamburlaine* did have a clown or clowns at the time of performance, and the clown of *Parnassus* says that "a playe cannot be without a clowne[.] Clownes have been thrust into playes by head and shoulders, ever since Kempe could make a scurvey face." The figure may not have been equally pleasing to everybody, but he is in high demand with the paying public.

By far the greater majority of clowns we find before 1595 are servants in some capacity.[3] This is not difficult to understand, as several of the clown's ancestors were servants,[4] but there are also clowns belonging to other categories such as "the rustic." In Elizabethan times, the word clown was often used as a term for a country bumpkin, a clod, or a person lacking in mental capacity, all these often found in one and the same person. In *Cambises* (1569) we find the word clown used with just this meaning about Hob and Lob, two "clownish countrymen." The character who could be called a stage clown in the making in *Cambises* would be Ambidexter, the Vice, whereas Hob and Lob could be labeled comic characters. These two have many of the characteristics of the stage rustic. They speak dialect, they admit their own stupidity, they show no diligence in the use of language, they come off badly when they leave their tiny sphere of market and produce, and they are far from valiant; Hob's wife is a better fighter than both of them put together. Their fight with Ambidexter will probably require some tumbling skills, but Ambidexter's part requires much more physical dexterity.

Ambidexter has a successor in Diccon the Bedlam of *Gammer Gurton's Needle* (1575).[5] He, too, is a master planner and double-dealer, but his intent is much more benign and harmless than Ambidexter's, and he is in nobody's service. He does, however, display numerous clown traits. He has songs to sing, and much of his conversation is taken up with food and drink and how to get them easily and cheaply. He moves freely within the section of society presented in the play, even equals himself with the curate, Dr. Rat. At the same time he is in constant league with the audience, explaining to them what he is going to do next and what effect he is aiming for. Hodge, the comic servant to Gammer Gurton, addresses the audience too, but establishes no give-and-take. He only succeeds in making himself ridiculous in the spectators' eyes, especially in matters concerning his love affair and his fear at Diccon's conjuring up of the devil. Diccon, on the other hand, makes the audience his accomplices in the comic plot. Therefore we find his punishment at the end sufficient, though it turns out to be no punishment at all, and we have no trouble laughing at the pain inflicted on Hodge when he finds himself pierced by the missing needle. Diccon does not speak dialect, while Hodge and most of the other characters in the play do. His language and his status as the mastermind behind the comic plot set him above the proceedings; without him there would be no comedy.

In George Peele's *The Old Wives' Tale* (1595)[6] we find three comic characters, Antic, Frolic, and Fantastic, who are almost as separated from the proceedings as is the *Parnassus* clown. These three become part of a frame for the "old wives' tale" told at night by Madge, the wife of the smith in whose house they find lodging. The listeners have no influence on the plot of the unfolding fairy tale, their only contribution is a comment thrown in here and there, in fact, they are in a totally different world from the storyline. Madge knows the end of the tale, it cannot be altered, only commented on by its audience. The audience of the play itself is in much the same position, isolated from the frame as well as the tale. Antic, Frolic, and Fantastic seem to change when the telling begins. Their punning banter at the beginning of the play gives way to very straightforward comments, and not even at the end of the play are they allowed to return to their former language. Within the framework of the unfolding story there are comic characters, notably Huanebango[7], but none of these is a clown, and the position of Antic, Frolic, and Fantastic themselves is debatable.

The figure of Robin in Christopher Marlowe's *Doctor Faustus* (1588?/1604) seems to stand between the Vice-like clown and the totally detached clown.[8] Robin makes his presence count several times in the play, but he has no power over the chain of events, and his main function seems to be illuminating the actions and choices of other characters. We see three types of service in this play: Wagner, who is a servant/pupil of Faustus; Faustus himself, who becomes a servant of evil without fully realizing it before it is too late; and finally Robin, who is pressed into service by Wagner, who emulates his master as much as he possibly can, even conjuring up the devil to force Robin to be his servant. Marlowe uses Robin repeatedly to cast a revealing light upon the actions of Faustus himself. In I.iv (page 36), Robin's first scene, he is "so hungry that [Wagner] know[s] he would give his soul to the devil for a shoulder of mutton, though it were blood-raw." He is then threatened into service by Wagner, but soon learns to appreciate the opportunities his new position allows. Wagner promises to teach him how to transform himself into "a dog or a cat or a mouse or a rat or anything," and Robin exclaims "Brave Wagner!" In the very next scene Faustus signs his pact with the devil. What the audience laughed at a short while ago becomes grave reality. In his very first scene, short as it is, Robin demonstrates several of the traits of the stage clown. He shows an interest in food, does not understand scholarly language and makes fun of it, and is capable of some repartee and much adjustment. When we next see him in II.iii (page 52), he demonstrates laziness and bawdy language. His attempts at magic are sorry at best, and again we are reminded of Faustus's impossible position. In III.ii (page 61) we see Faustus waste his devilgiven powers, stealing wine and dishes from dignitaries of the church. To further emphasize the futility of Faustus's undertaking, Robin and his friend Dick steal a cup in III.iii (page 65), and they, too, find it necessary to have a devil's assistance. They call up Mephistophilis himself "in jest," which of course makes him threaten punishment. In IV.vi (page 82), we see how Faustus has again wasted time and power by playing jests, this time on the lowest segment of society. Robin and his associates go off to punish him in IV.vii (page 85), mistaking a Duke's palace for an inn. When the clown and Faustus finally meet, Faustus strikes the clown dumb, thus silencing the only voice expressing the futility of a pact with the devil. Ironically enough this "banishment" of the clown happens just as Faustus's own soul is about to be banished to hell for all eternity. We never see Robin again, but we do not miss him; he has no place in the serious business at the conclusion of the play, when no salvation is possible. Though Robin is a "servant" to Wagner, he is not in any way hampered or subdued by his position. He is a servant in name only, moving about freely without remembering his master. He is there to let Marlowe demonstrate to the audience how puny is the human being who ridiculously imagines himself to have control over the powers of evil.

In Robert Greene's *The Honourable History of Friar Bacon and Friar Bungay* (1594) we see another instance of failure coming from meddling with the devil.[9] The aspect often mentioned by Chambers of the natural idiot having superhuman contacts apparently fascinated several playwrights, who used it in a more sophisticated form for their clowns. Miles, the servant/pupil to Friar Bacon, does not have a role as significant for the understanding of the play's main theme as does Robin. For the most part, Miles is relegated to the subplot, and only a few times is he allowed contact with the main plot. Greene does not need him there, and needs no free mobility among all groups of society; his master serves that purpose, and he is also the main link between plot and subplot. Miles is allowed to disclose certain important facts about characters' true identity in doggerel, and delightfully botches up his job of serving a meal to the great people of the play, but his most memorable scenes are his two last ones, the watch with the Brazen Head (pages 206–209), and the ride to hell at the end of the play (pages 218–219). The comedy of the scene with the Head is enhanced by the figure of Friar Bacon, asleep through the repeated "great noise," the Head's speeches, and the thunder and lightning as the Head is demolished. Miles again demonstrates his inability to understand and obey commands. When Friar Bacon is finally called and sees that all is lost, he curses Miles, who answers, "'Tis no matter, . . . The more the fox is cursed, the better he fares." Miles appears again close to the end of the play, now used to being haunted by devils and not respectful of them either. Friar Bacon's curse

> Some fiend or ghost haunt on thy weary steps,
> Until they do transport thee quick to hell:
> For Bacon shall have never merry day,
> To lose the fame and honour of his head.[10]

is fulfilled. Miles is indeed carried "quick" to hell, but in the spectators' eyes he may well come out the victor, for not only does he ask go there himself, he rides the devil's back, tormenting him with spurs all the way. Miles does have a significant part to play in the subplot, but his doings have no real effect on the romantic main plot; the two are indeed so far from each other in content that any real connection seems improbable.[11] The figure of Miles is amusing indeed, but it carries much less weight than that of Robin, though it may be claimed that Miles contributes to the "tragic" elements of his plot and is probably the more memorable of the two clowns.

Robin and Miles, small though their parts may be, still make themselves noted throughout the plays in which we find them. So does Mouse in *Mucedorus* (1598),[12] whose part is considerably larger, and who is more integrated in the structure of the play. *Mucedorus* is a comedy which makes use of all the ingredients available to the genre. There is, among a wealth of other things, a love interest and more than one conflict to go with it; there is mistaken identity and disguise, and friends almost killing each other, but united at last; and there is a clown, Mouse, son of Rat. This character shows all the traits attributable to the Elizabethan stage clown. He is lazy, gluttonous, boastful, has no courage in the face of danger, real or imaginary, banters about sex, mistakes words unknown to him, equals himself with his betters, provides comic mirrors for the main characters, moves freely among all social groups of the play, all the while amusing the audience and often addressing the spectators. Indeed, the play proper closes with his pun on the King's and courtiers' lofty speech (page 257). Mouse is a servant to a powerful man, but he begins his career as a rustic and carries his humble origins with him through thick and thin. He does not speak dialect exactly, and he is able to mimic the speech he hears, but his preferences remain the same throughout the play, and he never masters the language of the court. Part of his comic effect is based on just this discrepancy between humble origins and a position he imagines to be lofty.[13] Characteristically he ends by unashamedly begging fine clothes from the king himself, for "should lords go so beggarly as I do?" (page 257). Mouse is one clown the spectators will remember fondly after the play is done.

There is also a court jester to be found among the comic characters of the non-Shakespearean Elizabethan playwrights, Babulo of Dekker's *Patient Grissil* (1603).[14] What distinguishes this figure from Shakespeare's jester clowns is his gradual involvement in and identification with the action of the play. Where Shakespeare's jesters stand apart from true involvement, Babulo's interest in the intrigue mounts to the point where the comic character seems to end and the compassionate human being emerges. When he loses distance from the fate of Grissil, Babulo loses his ability to comment on the proceedings. His jokes become exhortations; he becomes much like a fond uncle in Grissil's period of distress.

Shakespeare's plays were written into a rich tradition of clowning with deep and varied roots. His wonderful clowns probably owe their lasting success and effect to the fact that Shakespeare had the possibility of writing for a company he knew intimately,[15] and the great good luck to have as clowns actors as gifted in their various ways as Kemp and Armin to write for. Another reason is the care with which Shakespeare's plays have been preserved for us in the First Folio and in the many editions in quarto available for study.[16] Other playwrights were not always treated as seriously, as we know from the printer's note in *Tamburlaine* about the comic characters deliberately left out. On the other hand, so much of the clown's part depends on improvisation that no printed edition, no matter how scrupulously it tries to report actual performed text, can hope to capture a kind of performance that is not the same two days running.

NOTES

1. The date of the first performance, or performance in general, is hard or impossible to establish for many of these plays, and often printing seemed to come late. An instance in point is Marlowe's *Doctor Faustus*, printed eleven years after its creator's death, but probably acted as early as 1588.

2. In the fifth act of the play. For one analysis, see Edward Berry, *Shakespeare's Comic Rites* (Cambridge and New York: Cambridge University Press, 1984), 109. Berry reminds his reader of the entertainer-status of Kemp and his colleagues, who are said to have had "less need of the stage than the stage had of them." Sandra Billington, in *A Social History of the Fool* (New York: St. Martin's Press, 1984) sees Tarlton, Kemp, and Armin as the first "respectable fools," because they were accepted by the church, and also because they were able to move with ease from theatre to court to ordinary society, a trait which I find they share with many of Shakespeare's clowns. Billington 29; 42.

3. A few examples would be Nimble in *Thomas of Woodstock*, the clown in *Mother Bombie*, and Trotter in *Fair Em* . See Alfred Harbage, *Annals of English Drama, 975-*

1700: An Analytical Record of All Plays, Extant or Lost, Chronologically Arranged and Indexed by Authors, Titles, Dramatic Companies, &c. revised by S.Schoenbaum (London: Methuen, 1964) for the dates of these plays.

4. The influence from Roman comedy gives us a comic servant, the Vice is a servant of the devil, and the *Commedia dell'Arte zanni* is a servant too.

5. In IV.ii.49; *Five Pre-Shakespearean Comedies, [Early Tudor Period]*, ed. Frederick S.Boas (London: Oxford University Press, 1934), 249.

6. Found in *The Minor Elizabethan Drama (II); Pre-Shakespearean Comedies*, ed. Ashley Thorndyke (London: Everyman's Library).

7. This character seems to be closely related to Shakespeare's Don Adriano de Armado, the "fantastical Spaniard" of *Love's Labour's Lost*.

8. This play was not printed until 1604, but it seems to have been acted as early as 1588. I quote from the Signet Classic edited by Sylvan Barnet, New York, 1969.

9. Found in The *Minor Elizabethan Drama (II)*. The year 1594 is the year of printing.

10. *Friar Bacon* 209.

11. Indeed, it is difficult to say which plot is the main one. The title of the play points to the friars and the problems of the Brazen Head, but the weight of the text points to the romantic love interest as most important.

12. An anonymous play, found in *A Select Collection of Old English Plays*, revised and enlarged by W.Carew Hazlitt (originally published 1874-1876, reissued London and New York, 1964).

13. Notably page 251, where he joins the group of suitors for the hand of Amadine and bids her choose.

14. The date of this play is quite late, and the character of Babulo may well have been influenced by figures like Touchstone and Feste.

15. See Thomas W. Baldwin, *The Organization and Personnel of the Shakespearean Company* (New York: Russell and Russell, 1961).

16. See the address to the readers by Hemminge and Condell which begins the Folio.

Bibliography

Baldwin, Thomas W. *The Organization and Personnel of the Shakespearean Company.* New York: Russell and Russell, 1961.

Barber, C. L. *Shakespeare's Festive Comedy: A Study of Dramatic Form and Its Relation to Social Custom.* Princeton: Princeton University Press, 1959.

Barish, Jonas. *The Antitheatrical Prejudice.* Berkeley: University of California Press, 1981.

Barton, John. *Playing Shakespeare.* London and New York: Methuen, 1984.

Baskervill, Charles Read.*The Elizabethan Jig and Related Song Drama.* 1929. New York: Dover Publications, 1965.

Beaumont, Cyril W. *The History of Harlequin.* 1926. New York: B. Blom, 1967.

Beckerman, Bernard. *Shakespeare at the Globe: 1599–1609.* New York: Macmillan, 1962.

Berger, Thomas L., and William C. Bradford Jr. *An Index of Characters in English Printed Drama to the Restoration.* Englewood, Colorado: Microcard Ed. Books, 1975.

Berry, Edward. *Shakespeare's Comic Rites.* Cambridge and New York: Cambridge University Press, 1984.

Billington, Sandra. *A Social History of the Fool.* New York: St. Martin's Press, 1984.

Boaden, Ann, and Karin Youngberg. "Kemp's Nine Daies Wonder." *British Heritage* April/May (1983): 38–43.

Brandes, Georg. *"Det uendelig Smaa" og "Det uendelig Store" i Poesien.* Copenhagen, 1870.

Brown, John Russell. *Discovering Shakespeare: A New Guide to the Plays.* London and Basingstoke: Macmillan, 1981.

———. *Free Shakespeare.* London: E. Arnold, 1974.

———. *Shakespeare's Plays in Performance.* London: E. Arnold, 1966.

Brownlow, F. W. *Two Shakespearean Sequences: Henry IV to Richard II and Pericles to Timon of Athens*. Pittsburgh: University of Pittsburgh Press, 1977.

Bucknell, Peter A. *Entertainment and Ritual, 600–1600*. London: Stainer and Bell, 1979.

Burns, Elizabeth. *Theatricality: A Study of Convention in the Theatre and in Social Life*. London: Longman, 1972.

Busby, Olive Mary. *Studies in the Development of the Fool in the Elizabethan Drama*. London: H. Milford, 1923.

Butler, Guy. "Shakespeare and Two Jesters." *Hebrew University Studies in Literature and the Arts* 11, no. 2 (1983): 161–204.

Calderwood, James L. *Metadrama in Shakespeare's Henriad: Richard II to Henry V*. Berkeley and Los Angeles: University of California Press, 1979.

Chambers, E. K. *The Elizabethan Stage*. Vol. 1–4. Oxford: Clarendon Press, 1923.

————. *The Medieval Stage*. Vol 1–2. Oxford: Clarendon Press, 1903.

Conell, Charles. *They Gave Us Shakespeare*. Portland, Oregon: Oriel Press, 1982.

Davison, Peter. *Popular Appeal in English Drama to 1850*. Totowa, New Jersey: Barnes & Noble, 1982.

Farnham, Willard. *Shakespeare's Grotesque: Its Genesis and Transformation*. Oxford: Clarendon Press, 1971.

Fenton, Doris. *The Extra-Dramatic Moment in Elizabethan Plays Before 1616*. 1930. Folcroft, Pennsylvania: Folcroft Press, 1970.

"Gammer Gurton's Needle." *Five Pre-Shakespearean Comedies [Early Tudor Period]*. Edited by Frederick S. Boas. London: Oxford University Press, 1934.

Gill, William Arthur, ed. *Morgann's Essay on the Dramatic Character of Falstaff*. London, 1912.

Goldsmith, R. H. *Wise Fools in Shakespeare*. East Lansing: Michigan State University Press, 1955.

Granville-Barker, Harley. *Prefaces to Shakespeare: Othello and Love's Labour's Lost*. Vol. 4. 1930. London: Batsford, 1969.

Greene, Robert. "Friar Bacon and Friar Bungay." *The Minor Elizabethan Drama*. Ed. Ashley Thorndyke. London: Everyman's Library [no date in book].

Grene, David. *The Actor in History: A Study in Shakespearean Stage Poetry*. University Park: Pennsylvania State University Press, 1988.

Harbage, Alfred. *As They Liked It: An Essay on Shakespeare and Morality*. New York: Macmillan, 1947.

————, Editor. Revised by S. Schoenbaum. *Annals of English Drama 975–1700: An Analytical Record of All Plays Extant or Lost, Chronologically Arranged and Indexed by Authors, Titles, Dramatic Companies, &c*. London: Methuen, 1964.

Hartwig, Joan. "Feste's 'Whirligig' and the Comic Providence of *Twelfth Night*." *ELH* 40.4 (1973): 501–513.

Holmes, Martin. *Shakespeare and Burbage*. London and Chichester: Philmore, 1978.

Hotson, Leslie. *Shakespeare's Motley*. London: Rupert Hart-Davis, 1952.

Isaacs, J. "Shakespeare as Man of the Theatre." *Shakespeare Criticism 1919–1935*. Ed. Anne Ridler. Oxford University Press: World Classics 436, 1936.

Kökeritz, Helge. *Shakespeare's Pronunciation*. New Haven: Yale University Press, 1953.

Kyd, Thomas. *The Spanish Tragedy* . Edited by Charles T. Prouty. Arlington Heights, Illinois: Croft Classics, 1951.

Langer, Susanne K. *Feeling and Form: A Theory of Art*. New York: Scribner, 1953.

Lawrence, W. J. *Speeding Up Shakespeare*. London: Argonaut Press, 1937.

Lea, K. M. *Italian Popular Comedy: A Study in the Commedia dell'Arte, 1560–1620 with Special Reference to the English Stage*. Vol. 1–2. 1934. New York: Russell and Russell, 1962.

Marlowe, Cristopher. *Doctor Faustus*. Edited by Sylvan Barnet. New York and Scarborough, Ontario: Signet Classics, 1969.

Melchiori, Giorgio. "Peter, Balthasar, and Shakespeare's Art of Doubling." *Modern Language Review* 78.4 (1983): 777–792.

Mellamphy, Ninian. "Pantaloons and Zanies: Shakespeare's 'Apprenticeship' to Italian Professional Comedy Troupes." *Shakespearean Comedy*. Edited by Maurice Charney. New York: Literary Forum, 1980. 141–151.

"Mucedorus." *A Select Collection of Old English Plays*. Revised and enlarged by W. Carew Hazlitt. 1847–1876. London and New York, 1964.

Mullini, Roberta. *Coruttore di Parole; Il Fool nel Teatro del Shakespeare*. Bologna: Clueb, 1983.

———. "Playing the Fool: the Pragmatic Status of Shakespeare's Clowns." *NTQ* 1.1 (1985): 98–104.

Nagler, A. M. *Shakespeare's Stage*. 1917. New Haven and London: Yale University Press, 1981.

Nuttall, A. D. *A New Mimesis: Shakespeare and the Representation of Reality*. London and New York: Methuen, 1983.

Parker, Patricia, and Geoffrey Hartman, ed. *Shakespeare and the Question of Theory*. New York: Methuen, 1985.

Partridge, Eric. *Shakespeare's Bawdy*. New York: Dutton, 1955.

Peele, George. "The Old Wives Tale."*The Minor Elizabethan Drama*. Edited by Ashley Thorndyke. London: Everyman's Library [no date in book].

Plautus. "The Brothers Menaechmus [Menaechmi]." *The Pot of Gold and Other Plays*. Harmondsworth: Penguin Books, 1965.

Preston, Thomas. "A Lamentable Tragedie, Mixed Full of Pleasant Mirth, Containing the Life of Cambises, King of Persia." *Chief Pre-Shakespearean Drama: A Selection of Plays Illustrating the History of the English Drama from Its Origin down to Shakespeare*. Eited by John Quincy Adams. Boston: Houghton Mifflin, 1924.

Purdom, C. B. *Producing Shakespeare*. London: J. Baker, 1950.

Quincey, Thomas De. "On the Knocking at the Gate in *Macbeth*." *The London Magazine*. October 1823.

Rosenberg, Marvin. *The Masks of King Lear*. Berkeley: University of California Press, 1972.

———. *The Masks of Macbeth*. Berkeley: University of California Press, 1978.

————. *The Masks of Othello: The Search for the Identity of Othello, Iago, and Desdemona by Three Centuries of Actors and Critics.* Berkeley, Los Angeles, and London: University of California Press, 1971.

Salingar, Leo. *Shakespeare and the Traditions of Comedy.* London and New York: Cambridge University Press, 1974.

————· "Falstaff and the Life of Shadows." *Shakespearean Comedy.* Edited by Maurice Charney. New York: New York Literary Forum, 1980. "

Shakespeare, William. *The Arden Edition of the Works of William Shakespeare.* London and New York: Methuen [revision ongoing].

————.*The First Folio of Shakespeare* (The Norton Facsimile). Prepared by Charlton Hinman. New York: W. W. Norton, 1968.

————. *Shakesperare's Plays in Quarto: A Facsimile Edition of Copies Primarily from the Henry Huntington Library.* Edited, with Introduction and Notes, by Michael J. B. Allen and Kenneth Muir. Berkeley, New York, and London: University of California Press, 1981.

Slater, Ann Pasternak. *Shakespeare the Director.* Totowa, New Jersey: Barnes & Noble, 1982.

Sløk, Johannes. *Shakespeare: Renaissancen som drama.* Copenhagen: Centrum, 1990.

Smith, Winifred. *The Commedia dell'Arte.* New York: Columbia University Press, 1912.

Spivack, Bernard. *Shakespeare and the Allegory of Evil: The History of a Metafor in Relation to His Major Villains.* New York: Columbia University Press, 1958.

Sprague, Arthur Colby. *Shakespeare and the Actors: The Stage Business in His Plays (1660–1905).* Cambridge, Massachusetts: Harvard University Press, 1944.

————. *Shakespeare and the Audience: A Study in Technique of Exposition.* Cambridge, Massachusetts: Harvard University Press, 1935.

Styan, J. L. *Drama, Stage, and Audience.* Cambridge and New York: Cambridge University Press, 1975.

————. *Shakespeare's Stagecraft.* Cambridge and New York: Cambridge University Press, 1967.

————. *The Shakespeare Revolution.* Cambridge and New York: Cambridge University Press, 1977.

Swain, Barbara. *Fools and Folly during the Middle Ages and the Rennaissance.* New York: Columbia University Press, 1932.

Taylor, Gary. "*Measure for Measure* IV.ii.41–46." *Shakespeare Quarterly* 29.3 (1978): 418–419.

Tillyard, E. M. W. *The Elizabethan World Picture.* London: Pelican Books, 1943.

Weimann, Robert. "Laughing with the Audience: *The Two Gentlemen of Verona* and the Popular Tradition of Comedy." *Shakespeare Survey: An Annual Survey of Shakespearean Study & Production* 22 (1969): 35–42.

————. *Shakespeare and the Popular Tradition in the Theatre: Studies in the Social Dimension of Dramatic Form and Function.* Edited and translated by Robert Schwartz. Baltimore and London: Johns Hopkins University Press, 1978.

Welsford, Enid. *The Fool, His Social and Literary History*. London: Faber and Faber, 1935.

Wickham, Glynne. *The Medieval Theatre*. Cambridge and New York: Cambridge University Press, 1974.

———. *Shakespeare's Dramatic Heritage: Collected Studies in Mediaeval, Tudor, and Shakespearean Drama*. New York: Barnes & Noble, 1969.

Wiles, David. *Shakespeare's Clown: Actor and Text in the Elizabethan Playhouse*. Cambridge and New York: Cambridge University Press, 1987.

Willeford, William. *The Fool and His Scepter*. Chicago: Northwestern University Press, 1969.

Williams, V. A., ed. *The Fool and the Trickster: Studies in Honour of Enid Welsford*. Cambridge and New Jersey: Cambridge University Press, 1979.

Wilson, J. Dover. *The Fortunes of Falstaff*. Cambridge and New York: Cambridge University Press, 1943.

———. *Life in Shakespeare's England: A Book of Elizabethan Prose*. Cambridge: Cambridge University Press, 1926.

Youngberg, Karin. "Comedy as Celebration." *The Masks of Comedy: Papers Delivered at the Humanities Festival, 1978, Augustana College*. Edited by Ann Boaden. Rock Island, Illinois, 1980.

Index

Index of Acts and Scenes

Plays listed in approximate order of writing.

About the Author

BENTE A. VIDEBÆK is an Adjunct Professor of English at Suffolk County Community College. Born in Denmark, she holds degrees in English and Danish/Scandinavian from the University of Copenhagen. After moving to the United States, she obtained a doctoral degree in English literature from Northwestern University.

ISBN 0-313-29872-6

9 780313 298721

HARDCOVER BAR CODE